مــن حــولهــم

Echoing the Land

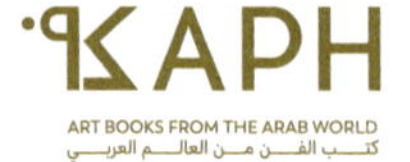

KAPH
ART BOOKS FROM THE ARAB WORLD
كتـــب الفـــن مـــن العالـــم العربـــي

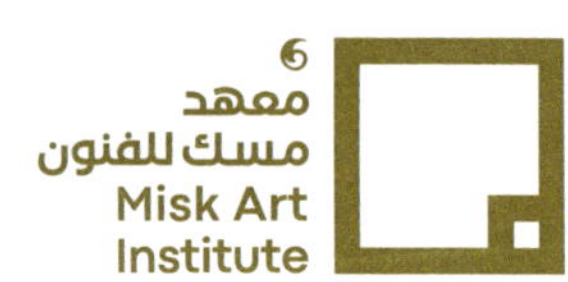

معهد
مسك للفنون
Misk Art
Institute

من حولهم
Echoing the Land

كتيّب المعرض

Exhibition Catalog

مقدمــة
Introduction

بسمة الشثري
Basma Alshathry

Before the proliferation of cameras in the public realm and the influx of photographic documentation we take for granted today, the historical milestones of Saudi Arabia were recorded through the works of artists, their vision and perspective.

The chronicled chapters in the narrative of the Saudi arts landscape began in 1953 when the Makkah Institute of Sciences showcased a group of talented young artists in what was the first art exhibition in the history of primary public education. Since then, the story has continued to unfold in a myriad of ways, bringing us to the present-day arts scene that is set on a course of growth and discovery in response to the keen interest and support we are witnessing in the culture and arts sector.

A Timeline of Historic Milestones

Dr. Mohammed Alresayes' publication *The History of Plastic Arts* in Saudi Arabia serves as a key resource for tracing historical developments in the arts of the kingdom. He starts with the historic 1953 school art exhibition at the Makkah Institute of Sciences which featured several notable artists, including Abdulhalim Radwi who was only fourteen years old at the time. Just a few years later, in 1958, the year the late King Saud bin Abdulaziz inaugurated the first school art

هي لحظاتٌ فارقة فـي التاريخ السـعودي، لم تكن هنـاك عدسـاتٌ تصوير منتشـرة بين النـاس تلتقط التاريـخ وتحفظه كمـا نفعـل الآن، لم تكـن هناك شاشات تنقل الإحساس كشاشاتنا الآن، كانت هناك ريشةُ الفنان ونظـره ونظرته.

بدأت فصول حكاية المشـهد الفني السعودي الموثقـة عـام 1953م مـن خـلال المعهـد العلمي السعودي بمكة المكرمة لإبراز مجموعة من الشباب الموهوبيـن في أول معرض للنشـاطات المدرسـية المختلفـة في تاريخ التعليـم الحكومـي المبكر، بعد تلـك الفتـرة اسـتمرت الروايـة فـي التواتـر إلـى أن وصلنا إلى عامنـا الحالي 2023م، وسيسـتمر بإذن الله النمـو والازدهار للمشـهد الفني السـعودي في ظل ما نشـهده مـن دعـم واهتمام كبيريـن لقطاع الثقافـة والفنون.

لحظات تاريخية شـاركت في تكوين الفن التشكيلي بالمملكة العربية السعودية

وثـق د. محمـد الرصيـص فـي كتابـه "تاريـخ الفن التشكيلي فـي المملكة العربية السـعودية" أبـرز اللحظـات التاريخيـة التي شـاركت في تكويـن الفن التشـكيلي في المملكة العربية السـعودية. ففي عام 1953م شـهدت المملكة أول معرض فني مدرسي، أقيـم في المعهد العلمـي بمكة المكرمـة. ومـن أبـرز الأسـماء التي شـاركت فيه الفنان عبـد الحليم رضـوي وكان عمـره آنـذاك أربعة عشـر عامـاً، وفي

for many solo and collective exhibitions to be held. Alsoliman notes that these included solo presentations by Ahmad Alzahrani, Saad Al-Obeid, Dr. Mohammed Alresayes, Mounirah Mosley, Abduljabbar Alyahya, Mohammed Almunif, Abdullah Hammas, Faisal Samra, Faisal Almashari, Ali Alsaffar, and Abdulhamid Albaqshi.

The 1980s saw the emergence of individual efforts within the art movement. The decade was marked by the inauguration of several museums and art galleries, established with support from the private sector, to whom the positive societal impact of art had become apparent. In 1979, the efforts of artist Mohammad Alsaleem saw the establishment of the Saudi Arts House, whose exhibition hall was host to *The First Collective Exhibition*. Some years later, in 1985, the Abdel Raouf Hassan Khalil Museum was established in Jeddah. That year also saw the launch of the GCC Art Friends Group with Saudi participation marked by cofounders Abdulrahman Alsoliman and Dr. Fouad Mougharbel, and the launch of the exhibition *Riyadh Yesterday and Today* in Germany (which was later known as *Saudi Arabia Yesterday and Today*) and its subsequent world tour. In 1988, the Saudi Center for Fine Art was founded.

In this exhibition, Misk Art Institute presents the discourse and developments in the arts of the kingdom that took place between 1959 and the 1980s, highlighting a group of Saudi artists who contributed to shaping the identity of the local art movement. Informed deeply by their roots, and influenced by their environments, the works in this exhibition are a testament to how artists take inspiration from nature, history, architecture, tradition, and customs, and respond to contemporary events and societal circumstances, cultural and literary trends, as well as economic, cultural, and social factors.

عـام 1958م بـدأت تنتشـر مناهـج التربيـة الفنيـة في المـدارس، وشـهدت تلك السـنة افتتـاح الملك سـعود بن عبد العزيز (رحمه الله) أول معرض فني مدرسـي علـى مسـتوى المملكة والذي أُقيم في بهو وزارة المعـارف بمدينـة الرياض.

ظهـر الدعـم الحكومـي الـذي كان لـه بالـغ الأثـر علـى الحركـة الفنيـة في نهايـة الخمسـينيات الميلاديـة، حيـث قُدِّمت منح دراسية لدراسة الفنون في مجـال التربية الفنية والفن التشـكيلي، ذكر ذلك عبـد الرحمـن السـليمان فـي كتابـه "مسـيرة الفـن التشـكيلي السعودي".

وفـي السـتينيات؛ وجـد الفنانـون مسـاحة للظهـور إلـى العلـن فانطلقـت المعـارض الفرديـة لـكل من عبـد الحليم رضـوي، وعبد العزيـز الحمّاد، ومحمـد السـليم، وصفية بـن زقر، ومنيـرة موصلي فـي مختلف مـدن المملكة مثل جـدة، والظهران، والدمـام، والريـاض، وذكر ذلك د. محمـد الرصيص في كتابـه، وفي عام 1965م تم إنشاء معهد التربية الفنيـة للمعلمين وكان له أثر ملحوظ علـى تطوّر الفنانيـن؛ يقـول د. الرصيص فـي كتابـه تاريخ الفن التشـكيلي فـي المملكة العربيـة السـعودية "بالرغم مـن أن الهـدف الأساسـي مـن إنشـاء المعهـد كان تعليميـاً وتربويـاً، إلا أن تأثيـره الفنـي يمكـن وصفه بأنـه حجـر الزاوية أو الأسـاس فـي تكويـن الخلفية الفنيـة الأولـى لعـدد كبيـر مـن فنانـي المملكـة من الجيـل الثاني".

في بدايـة السبعينيات شهدت المملكة الطفرة النفطيـة التي أدت إلى انتعاش المجتمع السعودي، وازدهار اقتصاده؛ الأمر الذي انعكـس على مختلف القطاعـات، فنالـت الحركـة الفنية نصيبها من هذا التطـوّر والرخـاء الاقتصـادي، ومـع وجود الرئاسـة العامـة لرعايـة الشـباب وإنشـاء الجمعيـة العربيـة السـعودية للثقافة والفنون في عام 1973م بمقرها الريـاض، وفروعهـا الثلاثة عشـر فـي مـدن المملكة المختلفـة، فُتح الباب لإقامة العديد من المعارض الفنيـة الفرديـة والجماعيـة، واسـتمرت المعـارض

exhibition with kingdom-wide participation at the Ministry of Education gallery in Riyadh, arts education curricula began to be adopted widely in schools.

In *The Journey of the Saudi Fine Arts Movement*, Abdulrahman Alsoliman emphasizes that the disbursement of academic scholarships by the government in the fields of arts education and fine arts in the late 1950s had a tremendous impact on the development of artistic discourse. Alresayes' research goes on to highlight the emergence of artist-led exhibition spaces in the 1960s, which hosted solo exhibitions—such as that of the works of Abdulhalim Radwi, Abdulaziz Alhammad, Mohammed Alsaleem, Safeya Binzagr, and Mounirah Mosley—throughout the kingdom, in cities such as Jeddah, Dhahran, Dammam, and Riyadh.

In 1965, the Institute of Art Education was established, impacting artist development significantly. Alresayes writes:

"Despite the primary goal behind the establishment of the academy being an educational and pedagogical one, its impact on the arts may be described as that of a cornerstone in the formation of a fundamental arts foundation for a large number of second-generation artists in the kingdom."

The oil boom experienced by the kingdom in the early 1970s led to a revitalization of Saudi society and to economic prosperity, both of which were reflected across all sectors. The art movement, in turn, had its share of this economic development and prosperity. With the support of the General Presidency of Youth Welfare and the establishment of the Saudi Arabian Society for Culture and Arts in Riyadh in 1973, and its thirteen branches across the kingdom, the door was opened

الفردية لكل من أحمد الزهراني، وسعد العبيد، ود. محمد الرصيص، ومنيرة موصلي، وعبد الجبار اليحيا، ومحمد المنيف، وعبد الله حماس، وفيصل سمرة، وفيصل المشاري، وعلي الصفار، وعبد الحميد البقشي، كما وثقه الكاتب عبد الرحمن السليمان في كتابه"مسيرة الفن التشكيلي السعودي".

فترة الثمانينيات؛ ظهرت جهود الأفراد في الحركة الفنية، فامتاز هذا العقد بافتتاح عدد من المتاحف وصالات العرض الفنية التي انطلقت بدعم من القطاع الخاص حين ظهر أثر الفن بشكل إيجابي على المجتمع، فعلى سبيل المثال انطلقت دار الفنون السعودية التي أسسها الفنان محمد السليم في الرياض عام 1979م وتشمل صالة عرض أُقيم فيها "المعرض الجماعي الأول"، وفي عام 1985م افتتح متحف "عبدالرؤوف حسن خليل للتراث الإنساني" بجدة وفي العام ذاته انطلقت جماعة أصدقاء الفن التشكيلي بدول مجلس التعاون الخليجي وشارك في تأسيسها من المملكة الفنان عبدالرحمن السليمان ود. فؤاد مغربل، وافتتح معرض "الرياض بين الأمس واليوم" في ألمانيا، والذي عُرف لاحقاً بـ(المملكة بين الأمس واليوم)، وبعد ذلك تنقّل إلى دول مختلفة عالمياً، وشهد عام 1988م تأسيس المركز السعودي للفنون التشكيلية بجدة.

واليوم يساهم معهد مسك للفنون في توثيق الحركة الفنية بين ستينيات وثمانينيات القرن العشرين بهذا المعرض الذي يضم نخبة من الفنانين السعوديين الذين ساهموا في تشكيل هوية الفن التشكيلي المحلي من خلال ارتباطهم بجذورهم المتينة وتأثرهم بالبيئة المحيطة بهم، فالبيئة هي كل ما يحيط بالإنسان وبالتالي يستلهم الفنان من الطبيعة وتضاريسها والتاريخ والعادات والتقاليد والعمران والأحداث المعاصرة والحالة المجتمعية والتوجهات الثقافية والأدبية ومختلف التغييرات بإيجابياتها وسلبياتها، وتشمل العوامل والظروف المختلفة الاقتصادية والثقافية والاجتماعية.

To understand this trajectory, one cannot separate the artist from their environment and the role it has in shaping creative minds. *Echoing the Land* showcases the diversity and divergence among the environments that have influenced these artists, expressed through the distinct styles of works produced from 1959 to the 1980s. The artworks on view touch upon numerous subjects, including natural and urban landscapes, and people and their relation to the environment, culture, and tradition. The exhibition curation was grounded in research and study of the available sources, as well as interviews with the artists and their families, and with specialists in the field.

ولفهـم هـذا السـياق لا يمكـن فصـل الفنـان عـن بيئتـه والدور الـذي تلعبه فـي تشـكيل إبداعه، فيعـرض هـذا المعـرض التنـوع والاختـلاف بيـن البيئـات التـي أثـرت على هـؤلاء الفنانيـن، والتي تم التعبيـر عنهـا من خـلال أنماطهم المختلفـة ابتداءً من عـام 1959 إلـى الثمانينيـات، وتتنـاول الأعمال الفنيـة المعروضة العديد مـن المواضيـع، بما في ذلـك المناظـر الطبيعيـة والحضرية، والأشـخاص، وعلاقتهـم بالبيئة والثقافة والتقاليـد، وارتكز تنظيم المعـرض على البحـث ودراسـة المصـادر المتاحة، بالإضافة إلى المقابلات مع الفنانين وعائلاتهم ومع المتخصصيـن فـي هـذا المجال.

مما جـــرى في بطحِــاء مكة
ألفـــن قريباً من الحيـــاة*
What Went on in Makkah's Batha:
Art Proximate to Life[1]

عبدالعزيز عاشور
Abdulaziz Ashour

The documentary film, *What Went on in Makkah's Batha*, narrates an aspect of the life of the late Saudi thinker and writer, Hamza Shehata (1909-1972).[2] Directed by Mahmoud Sabbagh,[3] the work features testimonials by local intellectuals and writers, contemporaries of Shehata who stood up for the positions he held in the 1940s. These stances were epitomized in 1940, when a lecture Shehata gave in his hometown of Makkah formed a historic cultural milestone for Saudi society.

In 1940, influenced by Socrates' philosophy of beauty, Shehata penned six articles for the newspaper, *Sawt Al-Hijaz*, under the title, "Beauty and Criticism."[4] In them, he discussed the process of art appreciation, including sensory perception and its relation to feeling and emotional response. He explained that enjoyment and emotion, or the splendor of imagination, reveal new meanings with the passing of time. Time itself, he said, is nothing but our sense of movement and transformation; and perception is comparable to body warmth—that is, the body's own sense of that warmth. Perception, in his view, is akin to the gathering of information or images and their interpretation via one's sensory and optical systems.

مما جرى فـي بطحاء مكة، فيلـم وثائقي من إخراج الأسـتاذ [1] محمود صباغ يروي فيـه جانباً من حياة المفكر والأديب السـعودي[2] حمزة شـحاته 1909 – 1972م، رحمـة الله عليـه، يوثق الفيلم شـهادات مثقفيـن وأدبـاء محلييـن ممـن عاصروا شـحاته أو انتصروا لمواقفه في الأربعينيات من القرن الماضي، والتـي بلغـت ذروتهـا فـي محاضـرة ألقاهـا عـام 1940م، بمسـقط رأسـه مكة المكرمة شكلت علامة بارزة فـي تاريخ الثقافة في المجتمع السـعودي.

كتـب شـحاته فـي صحيفـة[3] صـوت الحجاز عـام 1940 م سـت مقـالات تحـت عنـوان "بيـن الجمـال والنقـد" متأثراً بفلسـفة سـقراط الجمالية، تنـاول خلالهـا مفاهيـم عمليـة التـذوق الفني مثل الإدراك الحسّـي وعلاقته بالشـعور والتأثـر، موضحاً أن المتعة والحس أو طوبى الخيال الخلاب تكشف عـن معـانٍ جديـدة كلّمـا تقـادم بهـا الزمـن، وأن الزمن ليـس إلا إحساسـنا بالحركة والتحول ويشبّه شـحاته الإدراك بحـرارة الجسـد وذلـك مـن خلال إحسـاس الجسـد بها، والإدراك في نظره مثل جمع المعلومـات أو الصور يتم تأويلها مـن خلال الجهاز الحسـي والبصري.

يأتـي ذكر حمزة شـحاته رحمـه الله فـي هذا المقـام باعتبـاره مفكـراً تبنـى الفلسـفة والمفاهيـم الجمالية فـي الأربعينيات من القرن الماضي قال[4]

Therefore, the Italy-based programs they had attended did not yield their potential results, and the artistic spark was soon snuffed out in the hearts of some upon their return and submission to the routine of daily life. Their new responsibilities kept them exceedingly busy and swept them away from their envisaged purposes.

At the time, the country was moving forward, taking steps on a path toward growth and development across all sectors of life, and though art production, within the institute and elsewhere, emerged with great dynamism, there was a need for someone to recognize the artists' achievements. This is where the General Presidency of Youth Welfare (GPYW) took on a pioneering role by sponsoring art and artists.[8] It was the only organization to believe, with keen awareness, in the importance of art's presence in the local cultural ecosystem. The GPYW therefore took a bold stance, aware that it was responsible for fostering and protecting this emerging field. This adoption would become pivotal in defining how the arts were to be approached. The GPYW would become the spiritual home for artists as well as the most beloved institution in their hearts. It played a pivotal role in supporting the visibility of artists' work on the ground, holding central exhibitions with earmarks dedicated to related events in its yearly programing. With all its power, the GPYW sought to keep art directly visible and tangible while simultaneously offering legitimacy for artists. It also aimed to uphold artists' rights to create visual works, which were regarded as civilizational wealth to be presented to both local and international communities. The organization ultimately succeeded in planting the foundation stone for the legitimacy of fine art in the country.

The early exhibitions helped to shed light on art itself in addition to artists and their creativity. As exhibitions took their natural place in cultural life more broadly, and as art and its creators began to be taken

عنـه الدكتور سـعيد السـريحي إن شـحاته كان يريد للأمـة أن تفكـر بطريقـة سـقراط وشـجاعة المتنبي وجـرأة العقـاد، لقـد أدرك بوعـي يسـبق عصره أن مجتمعـه وبيئته كانت بحاجة إلـى الذوق والجمال في ذلك الوقت، معتبراً أن نشـأة الفنـون يجب أن تبـدأ من أحضان الفلسـفة، ودعا آنـذاك مثله مثل مفكريـن عـرب إلى طـرح مفاهيـم فكرية كالعروبة أو التعريـب والتأصيـل بحثـاً عـن الهويـة، إن دعوة شـحاته بمثابـة رد فعـل واقعـي لدحـض الصـورة النمطيـة التي تـروّج عـن ثقافتنا، بأننا دولة نشـأت بيـن فكي ثروة بترولية وفكر محافـظ، وأن تلك الصـورة إنما كانت مرحلـة فحسـب، وأن واقع فكر الفـن التشـكيلي فـي السـعودية لم يكـن يتيمـاً، بل سـبقت التجـارب التشـكيلية السـعودية مكتسـبات فكريـة نظريـة عـزّزت مـن بنيتهـا الثقافية.

في مقابل ما طرحه شـحاته فـي الأربعينيات بـدأ الفـن التشـكيلي فـي السـعودية بجهـود ذاتية من الفنانين أنفسـهم، فبين 1965 و1974 توجه(5) معظم الرّواد السـعوديين الذين نعرفهم إلى إقامة المعـارض الفرديـة الأولى فـي مدن كبـرى مختلفة مـن البـلاد، لتعطيهم هـذه المعـارض أكثـر مـن مجـرد اعتـراف الجمهـور العـام بهـم، فقـد تمكنوا فـي نهاية المطاف مـن الاعتـراف ببعضهم البعض وأدركـوا أنهـم لـم يكونـوا لوحدهـم، غيـر أن تلـك الجهـود كانـت بحاجـة إلـى الاعتـراف بها وبالفن معـاً، وعندمـا افتتح معهد التربية الفنيـة بالرياض 1965م علـى الأرجـح لـم تكـن الفنـون التشـكيلية بمفهومهـا الأوروبـي مرحبـاً بهـا، فالمعهد أنشـئ مـن أجـل تخريـج معلميـن لمـادة التربيـة الفنيـة، فيمـا لم يكـن(6) مهيـاً للفنانيـن وللمبتعثيـن منهم عند عودتهـم غير العمـل في حقل التعليم والذي يبـدو لنا أنـه شـكّل اسـتنزافاً لطاقاتهـم، فلم تعط عمليـات الابتعـاث إلـى إيطاليـا النتائج التـي يمكن أن تعطيها، إذ لـم تلبـث شـعلة الفـن أن انطفأت في أنفـس بعض أولئك الذين ابتعثوا واستسلموا لتيار الحيـاة اليوميـة التـي شـغلتهم بضـراوة عـن بلـوغ الغايـات المتوخاة، آنذاك كانت البلاد تتطلع

The late Shehata is invoked in this context because he was a thinker who adopted a philosophy and conceptualization of aesthetics in the 1940s. Dr. Saeed Alseraihi notes[5] that Shehata wished for the nation to think using the methods of Socrates, the courage of Almutanabbi, and the boldness of Alaqqad, a viewpoint that was ahead of its time. Moreover, he argued that his contemporaries and the environment needed sophistication and beauty, and he believed that art must be born into the embrace of philosophy. According to Alseraihi, Shehata, like other Arab thinkers, called for the introduction of concepts, such as Arabness, or Arabization, along with authentic rooting, as part of the quest for identity. This call constituted a realistic response aimed at dismantling the prevailing claim that we are a state born between petroleum wealth and conservative thought. That stereotype, believed Shehata, represented a mere phase. The state of thought and conceptualization within Saudi fine art is therefore not a detached phenomenon; rather, it has been preceded by intellectual and theoretical gains that served to bolster its cultural foundations.

Following what Shehata had put forward in the 1940s, fine art in Saudi Arabia emerged as a function of the individual efforts of artists themselves. Between 1965 and 1974, most of the artists we now know as the field's pioneers held the first solo exhibitions across the country's major cities.[6] They thus earned more than recognition from the public; they eventually gained the attention of their peers and the realization that they were not alone, that their efforts needed recognition, as did art itself. The Institute of Art Education was established in Riyadh in 1965 to train art education professionals. At the time, fine art, in its European conception, was mostly unwelcome.[7] Meanwhile, Saudi artists returning from their studies abroad were only presented with the option to teach.

إلى خطواتها التنموية في مختلف مجالات الحياة، وفيما بدأ إنتاج الفنانين في المعهد وخارج إطار المعهد حيوياً للغاية، كانت منجزاتهم بحاجة إلى من يعترف بها، من هنا اتخذت الرئاسة العامة لرعاية الشباب دورها الطليعي[7] في تبني الفن والفنانين معاً، وهي المؤسسة الوحيدة التي آمنت بوعي مطلق بأهمية حضور الفنون في المناخ الثقافي المحلي، لقد اتخذت الرئاسة العامة لرعاية الشباب موقفاً شجاعاً أدركت من خلاله أن عليها أن ترعى هذا المولود من دون أن ينال منه أحد، وقد شكل هذا التبني منعطفاً جذرياً في التعاطي مع الفنون، فأصبحت الرئاسة العامة لرعاية الشباب هي المؤسسة الروحية الأكثر حظوة في قلوب الفنانين، فقد لعبت دوراً رئيسياً في دعم حضور منجزاتهم على أرض الواقع وأقامت معارض مركزية مخصوصة استحدثتها في برامجها السنوية، وسعت بكل ما تملك لأن يكون للفن حضور فعلي ومباشر وظلّت مثل غطاء شرعي تبنى الدفاع عن حق الفنانين في استحضار منجزاتهم البصرية باعتبارها قيمة حضارية أمام أنظار المجتمع المحلي والدولي، وقد نجحت في تأسيس اللبنة الأولى لنواة مشروعية الفنون التشكيلية في البلاد.

أسهمت المعارض التشكيلية المبكرة في تسليط الضوء على الفن والفنانين وإبداعاتهم، وعندما أخذت المعارض شكلها الطبيعي في الحياة الثقافية العامة وصار ينظر إلى الفن والفنانين على محمل الجد، شعر الفنانين بأن عليهم أن يبرهنوا لأنفسهم وللمجتمع والواقع الذي ينتمون إليه بأنهم جديرون بصناعة مكتسباتهم المحلية وعوضاً عن مطالبهم في بنى تحتية أكثر احترافية تسير جنباً إلى جنب مع تطلعاتهم وطموحاتهم، وعوضاً عن غياب مراجع الفنون التي تنطوي على الفكر الفلسفي والجمالي والتي لم تكن حاضرة بينهم ضمن المقررات التعليمية أو منصات المثاقفة البصرية، فضلاً عن ندرة كتب علم الجمال التي لم تكن حاضرة ليتدارسوا من خلالها هيجل وكانط وشوبنهاور وسقراط، لقد أدرك الفنانون أن الفلسفة لم يكن مرحباً بها في

to resolve some artistic problems facing their age, failing often, and succeeding occasionally. That is how the first cohort of pioneering artists responded to the harshest of circumstances and the blows dealt to their hopes and aspirations; they worked assiduously, in silence, and without fuss, to preserve those hopes and achievements.

The expressive modes and techniques that artists employed in their practices were in accord with the art movements of the Renaissance and the modern age, subject, in their essence, to a balance among heritage, authenticity, the contemporary, and identity. To them, these concepts were akin to an ideology that many opted not to abandon. The GPYW, for its part, incentivized artists to work with these concepts, while at the same time representing a defense of identity. Though some were at absolute peace with the notion—discovering within it a means to express that identity—others found the question of acculturation in relation to their work more significant than merely continuing along the given path. Their works introduced a deluge of questions, either with the aim of preserving heritage and its authenticity through their practices, or of depicting the past and bolstering its presence for future generations, such that they, as artists, amplified their sensory experiences of the lives they lived as well as their environments. Some, meanwhile, tended toward exploring alternative aesthetics, diverging from those set formulas. Needless to say, those practices combined, in one way or another, would contribute to bolstering the artists' envisaged local identities, with the most significant implication being that they were expressions proximate to life itself.

According to Charles Lalo, artistic expression takes many forms, as evidenced by art's ability to be close to life, distant from it, or avoid it altogether.[10] In all of these eventualities, art cannot be said to be life

واقعنــا المحلي إلــى عهـد قريـب وأن مطالبهم في تلك اللحظة الزمنية ضلّت طريقها بفعل أسباب من بينها حساسية موجة الصحوة، عندها بقيت آمالهم معلقـة ومتمركـزة علــى مكتسـباتهم ومعطياتهـم الجمالية التـي كانـوا يستبسـلون من أجـل الحفاظ عليها بكل ما يملكون، لقد نجحوا لكي تستمر العجلة في التنامـي حتى تثمر.

لقـد أدرك الفنانـون عـن بكرة أبيهـم أن تاريخ الفـن[8] ليـس بالضـرورة تاريخ الانتصـار المسـتمر والتحـرر الدائم بل هو تاريخ شـاق حافـل بالعثرات الأليمة والمحاولات الفاشلة والخبرات المتوالية التي قد تصيب مـرة وتخيب مرات، وهذا مثلاً ما لاحظه المـؤرخ الفرنسـي جورج ديتـوي حينما قـال إن في وسعنا أن نسـتعيض عن صورة "الإنسـان المنتصر" التي قدمها لنـا مالرو في كتابه "سـيكولوجية الفن" بصورة ذلك الإنسان المتواضع الذي يسعى جاهداً في سبيل إشـباع حاجات عصره، فيعمل على القيام بمحـاولات متعـددة (لا تخلو مـن تـردد وتعثـر وخطـأ) مـن أجـل تحقيق ضرب مـن التكيـف بينه وبين المقتضيات الفنيـة لذلك العصر، فليس الفنان فـي نظـر الناقد بمثابة مـارد جبار يعيـش بمعزل عـن بيئتـه ومجتمعـه، بـل هو إنسـان يحـاول حل بعـض المشـكلات الفنية التـي يواجهها فـي عصره فيفشـل أحياتاً كثيـرة وينجح فـي بعـض الأحيان، هكـذا كانت ردود فعل فناني الريـادة والرعيل الأول في أشد المواقف التي نالت من تطلعاتهم وآمالهم المنشـودة، لقـد عملـوا بصمت وصلابة ومن دون جلبة حفاظاً على آمالهم ومكتسـباتهم.

كانـت طرائـق وأسـاليب التعبيـر فـي تجـارب الفنانين البصرية متصالحة مع تيارات عصر النهضة والحداثة وتخضـع في جوهرها لحل معادلة التراث والأصالـة والمعاصرة والهوية، كانت تلك المفاهيم بالنسـبة لهـم مثـل أيديولوجيـا آثر كثيـر منهم ألا يغـادروا منصاتهـا، فمن جهة كانت الرئاسـة العامة لرعايـة الشباب مصـدر تحفيـز لهـم فـي التعاطي مـع هـذه المفاهيـم، ومن جهة ثانية كانت أقرب للدفـاع عـن الهويـة، فيمـا آخـرون تصالحـوا معها

seriously, artists felt the need to prove to themselves, to society, and to the reality to which they belonged, that they were worthy of their local gains. This came in lieu of their demands for a more professional infrastructure that would meet with their aspirations and ambitions. This arose amid an absence of arts resources grounded in philosophical and aesthetical thought, not found in either the established curricula or the visual culture resources available to them. Also rare were books about aesthetics through which they could study; Hegel, Kant, Schopenhauer, and Socrates. Artists were aware that philosophy had long been unwelcome in their society and that their demands had thus been misplaced due to factors that included the sensitivities engendered by the Sahwa movement. Their aspirations therefore remained suspended and focused on their aesthetic achievements and gains, for which they had fought valiantly to preserve. They eventually succeeded in tending to and developing their sown seeds, so that fruit could be born.

Saudi artists of this time came to realize that the history of art is not necessarily one of persistent triumph and liberation.[9] Rather, it is a struggle, replete with painful setbacks, botched attempts, and successive experiences that may succeed once and fail multiple times. French historian Georges Didi-Huberman noted that we must replace the image of the "triumphant human being" presented to us by André Malraux in *Psychologie de l'art* (The Psychology of Art) with that of the modest human being who strives toward fulfilling the needs of their age, and so embarks on numerous attempts—trepidation, pitfalls, and error not excluded—to achieve some adaptation to the artistic imperatives of the age. The artist in the eye of the critic is not some mighty genie who exists irrespective of their environment and society, but rather a human being attempting

إلى مـا لانهايـة وبشـكل مطلق، فقد كانت بالنسـبة لهؤلاء تعبيراً عن هويتهم المنشودة، آخرون وجدوا أن الوقـوف عنـد أسـئلة المثاقفـة حـول منجزاتهم كان أمـراً أكثـر أهمية من المضي فـي الطريق، كانت منجزاتهـم تطـرح سـيلاً متدفقـا مـن الأسـئلة إمـا بقصـد اسـتبقاء التـراث وأصالتـه ليكـون ماثـلاً في منجزاتهم أو بقصد محاكاة الماضي وتعزيز حضورها للأجيال القادمة ليضاعف شعورهم كفنانين بالحياة أو بالبيئة التي عاشـوا فيهـا، وفضـلاً عـن ذلك فقد ذهب نفرٌ منهم لتقصي أبعاد جمالية مغايرة بعيداً عن تلك المعـادلات الثابتة. ومن نافل القول إن كل تلـك التجارب مجتمعة كانت بشـكل أو بآخر تنصب علـى تعزيز هويتهم المحلية المنشـودة وأن أهم ما تنطوي عليـه التعبير القريـب من الحياة.

يقول شـارل لالـو إن التعبير فـي[9] الفن يتخذ صـوراً عديـدة بدليـل أن الفـن قـد يكـون قريبـاً من الحيـاة أو بعيـداً عنهـا أو فـراراً منها. وفـي كل هذه الحالات لا يمكن أن نقول إن الفن هو الحياة بعينها أو إن الفن ليـس من الحياة في شـيء؛ بل لا بد من الاعتراف بأن الفن دائماً شـيء من الحياة، وقد يعمد بعـض[10] الفنانيـن أحياناً إلى التعبير عـن نوازعهم الخاصة ورغباتهـم الشـخصية مـن خـلال أعمالهم الفنيـة، فيكـون إنتاجهـم الفنـي فـي هـذه الحالـة مطابقـاً لحياتهـم، وكأن كل مهمـة الفـن عندئـذ لا تكاد تعدو مضاعفة الحياة عن طريق الإنتاج، وهكذا قـد يكـون الفـن مجـرد أداة موضوعية يصـوغ فيها الفنـان حياته الخاصة دون أدنى تحيّـز، أو قد يكون مجـرّد مظهر من مظاهر الأنانية وحب الذات، أو قد يكـون تعبيـراً عـن رغبة الفنـان في إعـادة قصة حبه مـن أجل التمتّع بما فيها من سـعادة للمـرة الثانية. تلـك هـي الأوجـه المختلفة لاتصال الفـن بالحياة علـى نحو مـا صورهـا لنا لالـو فـي ثالوثـه الجمالي المأثور (التعبير عن الحياة فـي الفن) و(الفن بعيداً عـن الحيـاة) و(الفـن قريبـاً مـن الحياة) وهـو بهذا يؤكد بـأن ثمة ازدواجاً بين الفـن والحياة بمعنى أن هناك روابط متغيرة تجمـع بينهما دون أن يندمج الواحد منهمـا في الآخر، إن الفـن لا يمكن أن يكون

Aesthetic action is not about "recreation and luxury." Instead, it is at the core of the quotidian behavior of the creative human being who undertakes a continuous process of adaptation to their surroundings and the natural or civilizational factors therein.[13] Both appreciation and creativity are responses within the process of adaptation to life and environment, effected by the artist with a basis in their experiences with the sociocultural ecosystem, including heritage, custom, tradition, and doctrine. Scholars and artists are at the forefront of introducing change to a given milieu,[14] and the role of the artist, according to Hungarian-French artist Victor Vasarely (1908–1997),[15] is to provide opportunity for the fulfillment of our need for beauty.

Beginning in the mid-1960s and throughout the 1970s, Saudi artists were involved in producing aesthetics that spoke to authenticity and the Arabization of art, arriving at their envisaged identity—one whose aesthetic calculus would stir them without mercy. Heritage, tradition, custom, environment, desert culture, archaeological ruins, and ancient cities, in all their vitality, would become fertile and safe harbor for the artists' aesthetic considerations. If Shehata had sensed authenticity and Arabization via the philosopher and thinker's spirit in the theoretical realm, then that first cohort of pioneering artists undertook through their work to aesthetically conjure, root, and Arabize their visual practices. Many among them dedicated themselves tirelessly to innovating boundless aesthetic articulations. They tenaciously augmented the visibility of their work to an astonishing degree at a time when art was unwelcome in Saudi Arabia and philosophical and aesthetical acculturation theory was absent from the visual fora. They believed that the wheel would continue to turn and that their bet would pay off thanks to the nuance of their aesthetic input,

هـو الحيـاة نفسـها، ومـن الخطـأ أن نقـول إنه ليس مـن الحيـاة في شـيء لأن من المؤكـد أن الفن يعبّر عن جانـب من جوانـب الحياة.

إن العلاقـة الجدليـة بيـن[11] الإنسـان وبيئتـه وثقافتـه قديمـة قدم الإنسـان نفسـه، والفنون من هـذه الزاويـة تسـتهدف التكيـف وحـل مشـكلات الحيـاة، والفنان الـذي يمارس نشـاطاً إبداعيـاً ذاتياً محضـاً إنمـا يشـبع احتياجـاً لديه متأثـراً بظـروف المـكان والزمـان والثقافة وكلّمـا تغيـرت البيئـة وثقافـة المجتمـع بإضافـات الفنانيـن والمفكريـن، تكشـفت للمبدعين مشـكلات تكيفية جديدة تسمى احتياجـات ثقافية جمالية علـى الفنانيـن المبادرة بالخـوض فيهـا لإعـادة الاتـزان إلـى الحياة.

إن الفعـل الجمالـي[12] لا يرتبـط "بالتسـلية والترف، بل يدخل في صلب السلوك اليومي للإنسان المبدع، فهو يقوم بعملية تكيف مستمرة مع البيئة المحيطـة ومـا تحفل بـه مـن عوامـل طبيعية أو حضاريـة، فكلّ مـن التـذوق والإبـداع هـو رد فعل لعمليـة التكيف مـع البيئة والحياة يؤديهما الفنان مسـتنداً إلـى خبراتـه مـع البيئـة الحضارية وثقافة المجتمع بتراثها، وعاداتها، وتقاليدها، وعقائدها؛ إن العلمـاء والفنانين[13] هم أكثر الذين يدخلون التغييّر علـى البيئـة وقـد قـال فيكتـور[14] فازاريلـي 1908- 1997م إن وظيفـة الفنان هي إتاحـة الفرصة لتلبية حاجاتنا إلـى الجمال.

لقد انشغل الفنانون السعوديون منذ منتصف الستينيات والسبعينيات بإنتاج صيغ جمالية تتصل بالأصالـة وتعريب الفـن وصولاً لهويتهم المنشـودة حتـى قضّـت معادلاتهـا الجماليّـة مضاجعهـم بـلا رحمة، كان التراث والتقاليد والعادات والبيئة وثقافة الصحـراء والأطـلال والمـدن القديمة بـكل حيويتها مـلاذاً خصبـاً وآمنـاً لمعطياتهـم الجماليـة، إذا كان شـحاته استشـعر الأصالة والتعريب بروح الفيلسوف والمفكـر نظريـاً فإن فناني الريادة والرعيل الأول تبنوا فـي منجزاتهم الجمالية استحضار وتأصيل وتعريب تجاربهـم البصرية جماليـاً، لقـد امتثـل كثيـر منهم

itself; it is also not entirely removed from life. Rather, it must be acknowledged that art is always *of* life. Artists may sometimes choose to express their personal impulses and desires through their work—their outputs thus corresponding to their lives—as though the objective of art in such cases were no more than a magnification of life by way of creation.[11] In this way, art may be a mere impartial instrument into which the artist inserts their personal life without the least bit of bias. Alternatively, art may simply be a facet of egoism and vanity, or an expression of one's desire to revisit a past love story, hoping to relish anew what that may contain a path of happiness. These are the facets of art's relation to life, as described to us by Charles Lalo in his trilogy on aesthetics: *L'expression de la vie dans l'art* (The Expression of Life in Art), *L'art loin de la vie* (Art at a Distance from Life), and *L'art près de la vie* (Art Proximate to Life). With these works, he confirms that a life-art duality does exist, in that varying links connect the two, although one does not meld entirely into the other. He also argues that art cannot be life itself, and we would be mistaken to say that it is entirely divorced from life, as art most certainly expresses a certain aspect of life—as the dialectical relationship between human beings and their environment and culture is as old as humanity itself.[12]

From this perspective, art aims for adaptation in addition to the ability to resolve life's problems, while the artist who practices a purely personal creative endeavor fulfills a need they have, moved by the circumstances of place, time, and culture. As the environment and culture change with the contributions of artists and intellectuals, new adaptive challenges—referred to as cultural and aesthetic needs—emerge to face the creatives, thereby requiring that artists take the initiative to address them, so as to bring life back into balance.

مـن دون كـل لإبداع صيـغ جماليـة لا تنتهـي عند حـد، لقد عـززوا بضراوة مـن حضـور منجزاتهم إلى حـدّ الدهشـة، وفي وقت كان الفـن فـي بلادنا غير مرحب به، وفي وقت غابت فيه المثاقفة الفلسفية والجماليـة ونظرياتهـا عن المنصـات البصريـة، لقد آمنوا أن العجلة سـتمضي وأن كسـب الرهان بفضل رهافـة معطياتهم الجماليـة التي كانت تتنامى جيلاً بعد جيل سـيكون من نصيبهـم، ويمكننـا القول إن الفنـون البصريـة في بلادنا منذ تلـك المرحلة وحتى يومنا هذا أخذ عودها يشـتد بفضل الدعم المستمر لها ثم بشـجاعة المحاربيـن القدامى مـن المبدعين وكثير ممن يقتفـي آثارهم.

لقـد كان الفنانـون في المحتـرف المحلـي يتعاطـون مـع عناصر التـراث والأصالة والمعاصرة كلّ وفق ما تملـيه عليه ثقافة بيئته، وكانت الفوارق الجماليـة بيـن تجربة محافظة هنا وأخرى منفتحة هنـاك كلهـا تتمظهر بقـدر ما يسـمح لهـا الرقيب، حاضرة بكل معاييرهـا الجمالية، لقد تخلى الفنانون عن رسـم ذات الأرواح أو ما يعرف بالموديل لأنها لم تكـن مهضومة فـي مجتمعهـم، ناهيـك عن موقف المؤسسـة الدينيـة والتعليميـة منها وهذه مسـألة كانت محل شـد وجذب في معظم البـلاد العربية، لهـذا كانـت تجـارب رسـم ذات الأرواح مقننـة أو قليلة قياسـاً إلى رسـم الطبيعة الصامتة والصحراء، والأطـلال القديمـة، والبيئـة والتـراث والزخرفـة الإسلامية، وصولاً إلى الحروفية، آخر حصن للوصول للهويـة، أو لنقل الأكثـر حظوة فـي مفاهيمها.

وهكذا أصبحـت معادلـة التـراث والأصالـة والمعاصرة بـل ولازالـت زمنـاً طويـلاً تتداعـى في مخيـلات الفنانيـن مثل أيديولوجيا ينبغـي عليهم أن يتدارسـوا طقوسـها كل بطرائقـه الخاصة، كانت مسـألة التوصل إلى أسـلوب خاص لكل فنان تشكل فارقاً مـا فـي تجاربهم الجماليـة طالمـا أنها ترضي ذائقتهم وأن مضامينها أقرب إلى واقعهم وبيئتهم وفـي كل الأحـوال كانت تلـك المعطيـات تعزّز من مفاهيمهم عـن الهوية، لقد كانت تلـك المتخيلات بالنسـبة إلى جيل بأكمله مثـل سـد حصين ضد

in arriving at aesthetic elements and works of the utmost technical virtuosity, with some among them creating vivid, inspirational aesthetics imbued with breathtaking and mind-bending delicacy.

Many of these artists excelled at representing village customs and traditions, painting Arab coffee pots, palm trees, and tents as one would depict national icons. Some found boundless imagination in desert life and camels, and others brilliantly represented houses, *roshans*, the sea, and fishing boats, as though they had been sources of eternal passion. Some had a role in unique representations of the horse as a subject, with aesthetic choices that varied in step with the equestrian realm. Among these was an artist who, through painting horses, drew inspiration for his lifelong practice, based on different aesthetics. And when he began simplifying the horse's features, he would not cease reciting Pablo Picasso's famous phrase, "Learn the rules like a pro, so you can break them like an artist," until, like a horseman, he found his calling in abstracting the Arabian horse.

There are those artists who arrived at their own unique formulas, involving the blending of common elements. They represented what they imagined of architecture, life, women, and love. Others tended toward expressions regarding central Arab issues, such as the Palestinian cause. Some painted works related to national occasions, while others represented situations and events as though they had been present to witness them. Needless to say, there are those who, through all of these experiences, found their own unique and emotive styles. Some chose the strictest of modern art trends, considering them to be havens for conveying the refinement of their work. They left no trend unexplored, including abstraction, surrealism, cubism, impressionism, and so on, until all of these schools became safe harbors for their aesthetic

التغريـب، مـن هنـا انتصـر غيـر فنـان فـي التجربة المحليـة فـي الوصـول إلـى معطيـات ومنجـزات جمالية فـي منتهى البلاغـة التقنية ووقف بعضهم علـى جماليـات نابضة وملهمة فيها مـن الرهافة ما يأسـر الروح والعقـل معاً.

لقـد أبدع كثير من الفنانين في تصوير طقوس وتقاليد القرية ورسموا دلال القهوة العربية والنخلة والخيمـة مثل أيقونـات وطنيـة فيمـا وجد بعضهم فـي حيـاة الصحراء والجمال متخيـلات لا حصر لها، وأبـدع نفـرٌ منهـم فـي تصويـر البيـوت والرواشـين والبحـر ومراكـب الصياديـن كما لـو كانت عشـقهم الأبـدي، ولعب بعضهـم دوراً فـي توظيـف الخيل بفـرادة وفـق صيـغ جماليـة متغيـرة تتشـأ بعوالم الفروسـية كيفمـا كانـت، كان أحـد أولئـك الفنانين يسـتلهم مـن رسـم الخيول طقوسـه الأبديـة وفق صيـغ جماليـة مختلفـة وعندمـا بـدأ فـي تبسـيط ملامـح الخيل لم يكن ينفـك عن ترديد عبـارة بابلو بيكاسـو الشـهيرة (أتقن قواعد الفن كمحترف حتى تتمكن من كسـرها كفنـان) حتى وجـد ضالته في تجريـد الخيل العربـي مثله مثـل فارس.

ثمّـة فنانـون وجدوا معادلاتهـم الخاصة في دمج عناصر مشـتركة وصـوروا متخيـلات عن العمارة والحيـاة والمـرأة والحـب فيمـا ذهـب بعضهـم إلى التعبيـر عـن القضايـا العربيـة المصيريـة مثـل قضية فلسـطين ونحوها؛ كما رسـم بعضهم أعمـالاً تتصل بالمناسبات الوطنية وصور آخرون المواقف والأحداث كما لـو كانوا بينها، ومـن نافل القـول أن ثمة فنانين وجدوا من خلال كل تلك الخبرات أسـاليبهم الخاصة والمؤثرة واختار بعضهم أشـد تيـارات الحداثة الفنية باعتبارها ملاذاً للتعبيـر عن بلاغة منجزاتهم ولم ينجُ تيـار فنـي إلا وخاضوا فيه لعل من بينهـا التجريدية والسـريالية والتكعيبيـة والانطباعيـة ونحوهـا، حتى أصبحـت كل تلـك المدارس مـلاذاً آمنـاً لمتخيلاتهم الجمالية، لقد أنتج بعض الفنانين أعمالاً متفردة في حيوية حضورها فـي الذاكرة المحليـة بعضها كانت مثل شـوكولاتة لا تستطيع مقاومة حضورها الجمالي مهما مضى عليها الزمن.

which continued to develop from one generation to the next. We can safely say that since that period, Saudi visual arts have gained robustness, thanks to continued support as well as the courage of the veteran artists and many of those who have followed in their footsteps.

Local professional artists have dealt with elements of heritage, authenticity, and the contemporary, each in accordance with what their cultural milieu imposed. Moreover, the aesthetic variations among practices, which ranged from the conservative to the more liberal, manifested to the degree that the censors permitted, but also within their own comprehensive aesthetic frameworks. Artists forwent depicting human figures, as such depictions were not tolerated by their society or religious and educational institutions; the question was also debated among Arab countries broadly. Practices involving the depiction of human figures were therefore limited and sparse in relation to the representation of still life, the desert, ancient ruins, nature, heritage, Islamic ornamentation, and, eventually, hurufism, the last fortress on the path to identity or the communication of that which is conceptually most desirable within it.

The heritage-authenticity-contemporary equation thus endures in the imagination of these artists, like an ideology whose rites they must consider, each with their own modality. The arrival of each artist at a unique style would form some distinction among aesthetic practices, so long as those practices satisfied the artists' own tastes and their content was close to their realities and environments. Nevertheless, these conditions bolstered their conceptualizations of identity, with those imaginaries constituting for an entire generation a fortified dam against Westernization. In this way, artists triumphed through their local practices

لقد وجد عبـد الحليم رضوي 1939-2006م رحمه الله إبان دراسـته في روما ضالتـه في تقنيات وألـوان فـان جـوخ 1853-1890م الآسـرة وأنتـج أعمـالاً عزّزت من نبوغه مسـتلهماً من ضربات جوخ البليغـة طقـوس أعمالـه التـي صـوّر فيهـا رقصاتنا الشـعبية فيما وجد محمد السـليم 1939-1997م يرحمـه الله في فلسـفة وعبـارات فان جـوخ عندما قال هـذا الأخير أنا لا أرسـم [15] الطبيعة كما هي بل أقـوم باخـتـزال الصـور فـي الطبيعة ومن ثـم أصل إلـى تحريرهـا ولعـل هـذا مـا فعلـه السـليم عندما اسـتلهم من فلسـفة جوخ أعماله عن الصحراء فهو بالمحصلة لم يكن يرسـم الصحراء كما هي وإنما كما كانـت تتداعى فـي متخيلاتـه البصرية التـي اختزلها برهافـة حساسـيته حتى وجـد فيهـا آفاقه السـرابية النابضة بالحياة.

من الطبيعي أن تجد في بلادنا فنانين مؤثرين مثل كهنـة مُحّصنين بالفن وألاعيبه السـاحرة حتى أنـا حفظنـا تجـارب بعضهم عـن ظهر قلـب، إنها تجـارب اسـتفادت مـن خبراتهـا التـي انسـلت مـن واقعهـم الأقرب للبيئـة والحياة والفن معاً.

(1) The essay's main title is taken directly from the documentary film *What Went on in Makkah's Batha* (2013). The subheading is taken from Charles Lalo's trilogy, referenced in note 10.

(2) Hamza Shehata was a Saudi writer, and among the most renowned of the modernizing poets. He was influenced by Gibran Khalil Gibran and Elia Abu Madi, gaining notoriety in the wake of a lecture he gave in Makkah.

(3) Mahmoud Sabbagh (1983) is a Saudi film director, producer and screenwriter, and was the director of the Red Sea Film Festival until 2020. Sabbagh studied documentary filmmaking in New York, with his most well-known works being *Barakah Meets Barakah* and *Amra and the Second Marriage.*

(4) Paraphrased from the six-article series, "Beauty and Criticism," which appeared in the book, Hamza Shehata, *Hamza Shehata's Donkey* (Dar Almarreekh, 1977).

(5) Stated by Saeed Alseraihi in the aforementioned documentary film, *What Went On in Makkah's Batha* (Riyadh/Cairo, 2013).

(6) Dr. Eiman Elgibreen, "Art That Begins at Home: A Dream of Saudi Artists," in ed. Sam Bardaouil and Till Fellrath, *That Feverish Leap into the Fierceness of Life*, exh. cat. (Riyadh: Misk Art Institute, 2018).

(7) Dia Aziz Dia, *The Enigmatic Journey of an Inspired Artist*, trans. Adla Kosseim (Jeddah: Al-Mansouria Foundation for Culture and Creativity, 2004), 27.

(8) Abdulrahman Alsoliman, *The Journey of the Saudi Fine Arts Movement*, 2nd edition (Riyadh: Saudi Arabian Ministry of Culture, 2011). In 1974, the General Directorate for Youth Welfare was transformed into a government institution with a dedicated fine arts department and renamed the General Presidency of Youth Welfare. It held its first exhibition in 1976.

(9) Zakaria Ibrahim, *Art Philosophy in Contemporary Thought* (Cairo: Dar Misr, 1966).

(10) Zakaria Ibrahim, *The Problem of Philosophy* (Cairo: Dar Misr, 1971).

(11) Ibid.

(12) Mokhtar Alattar, *Fine Arts: Between Benefit and Enjoyment* (Cairo: General Egyptian Book Organization, in cooperation with the Egyptian Art Critics Society, 1994).

(13) Ibid.

(14) Ibid.

(15) Victor Vasarely was a Hungarian-French artist and innovating pioneer of the op art movement. He abandoned medical school two years after beginning his studies and was interested in the Bauhaus school. He heavily employed spatial and color dimensions in his work.

(16) This saying has been paraphrased from the dramatic portrayal of Van Gogh during his final years, in the 2018 biographical drama, *At Eternity's Gate*, directed by Julian Schnabel and starring Willem Dafoe.

Abdulaziz Ashour (b. 1962, Saudi Arabia)

Abdulaziz Ashour is a fourth-generation Saudi artist and critic. Despite lacking formal arts education, he devoted himself to art and writing, participating widely in biennials and local/international exhibitions and winning numerous awards. In 2006, he started working as a consultant and curator at the Ministry of Media. His works have been exhibited in major cities like New York, London, Moscow, Paris, Frankfurt, Cairo, Dubai, Doha, and Tunis. Some of his pieces were sold at esteemed auctions houses including Christie's, Sotheby's, and Bonhams. He authored the book *Saudi Artists Today* (2011) and contributed to various local and Arab newspapers.

(*) العنوان مقتبس في شَقِه الأول من الفيلم الوثائقي مما جرى في بطحاء مكة، اما الشقُ الثاني فهو من ثالوث عن الفيلسوف شارل لا لو التي تمت الإشارة الى مصدره في المرجع (9).

(1) محمود صباغ، 1983م مخرج أفلام سعودي، ومنتج، وكاتب سيناريو، ومدير مهرجان البحر الأحمر السينمائي الدولي حتى 2020م درس السينما الوثائقية في نيويورك، أشهر أفلامه بركة يقابل بركة، وعمرة والزواج الثاني.

(2) حمزة شحاته شاعر وأديب سعودي، من أبرز الشعراء المجددين، تأثر بجبران خليل جبران وإيليا أبو ماضي ذاع صيته بعد محاضرة القاها عام 1940 م في جمعية الإسعاف الخيري بمكة المكرمة.

(3) كتاب حمار حمزة شحاته - دار المريخ للنشر- 1977م - تم اقتباسه بتصرف من 6 مقالات بين النقد والجمال.

(4) من الفيلم الوثائقي مما جرى في بطحاء مكة - شهادة عن سعيد السريحي.

(5) د. ايمان الجيبرين - فن يبدأ من البيت - حلم الفنانين السعوديين - كتالوج معرض خوض غمار حياة ضروس - نظره الى خمس جماعات فنية 2018م .

(6) كتاب ضياء عزيز ضياء – مقدمة د. سعيد السريحي – سيرة غامضة لفنان واضح – مؤسسة المنصورية للثقافة والإبداع ص 27.

(7) عبد الرحمن السليمان – مسيرة الفن التشكيلي – وزارة الثقافة والإعلام الطبعة الثانية 1433هـ في عام 1974م تحولت الإدارة العامة لرعاية الشباب إلى مؤسسة حكومية باسم الرئاسة العامة لرعاية الشباب وأنشئ قسم الفنون التشكيلية. فيما بدأت أول معارضها عام 1976م .

(8) د. زكريا إبراهيم – فلسفة الفن في الفكر المعاصر – دراسات جمالية (1) – دار مصر للطباعة 1988م.

(9) (10) د. زكريا إبراهيم - مشكلة الفن – مشكلات فلسفية (3) – مكتبة مصر – دار مصر للطباعة.

(11) (12) (13) مختار العطار - الفنون الجميلة بين المتعة والمنفعة – دراسات في نقد الفنون الجميلة (7) – الهيئة المصرية العامة للكتاب بالتعاون مع الجمعية المصرية لنقاد الفن التشكيلي– 1994 م.

(14) فيكتورفازرايلي فنان فرنسي من أصل هنغاري أول من ابتدع فن الخداع البصري ترك دراسة في كلية الطب بعد عامين من الالتحاق بها، اهتم بمدرسة الباهاوس. تعتمد اعماله على الأبعاد اللونية والبصرية.

(15) العبارات مقتبسة بتصرف من فيلم (عند بوابة الخلود) والذي يحكي دراما – سيرة ذاتية عن آخر أيام حياة الفنان فينسنت فان جوخ الفيلم من إخراج جوليان شنابل وبطولة ويليم دافو.

عبد العزيز عاشور (مواليد 1962م، المملكة العربية السعودية)

فنان تشكيلي سعودي قيم وناقد من الجيل الرابع، لم يتلقَّ أية دراسات علمية متخصصة في الفنون، متفرغ للفن والكتابة، وعمل مستشاراً وقيماً فنياً في وزارة الثقافة والإعلام عام 2006م ، وشارك في العديد من البيناليات والمعارض المحلية والدولية، وحقق العديد من الجوائز المحلية والدولية كما عرضت أعماله في محطات عالمية وعربية مثل نيويورك، لندن ، موسكو، باريس، فرانكفورت، والقاهرة ودبي، والدوحة، وتونس، بيعت مجموعة من أعماله في مزادات عالمية مثل: كريستيز وسوزبيز، وبونهامز، ألَّف كتاب (تشكيليون سعوديون اليوم) 2011م، وكتب عنه في العديد من الصحف المحلية والعربية.

imaginations. Some produced works that are unique in their vivid presence in local memory, among them examples whose aesthetic presence is irrepressible, regardless of the passage of time.

During his studies in Rome, the late Abdulhalim Radwi (1939–2006) found his calling in the captivating techniques and palette of Vincent van Gogh (1853–1890). Inspired by the Dutch painter's graceful strokes, Radwi produced works that cemented his brilliance, creating rituals of his own practice through which he represented popular Saudi dances. For his part, the late Mohammed Alsaleem (1939–1997) found inspiration in Van Gogh's philosophy, including that he did not paint nature, but rather found the picture within it and set it free.[16] That is, perhaps, what Alsaleem did with his works on the desert. At the end of the day, he did not paint the desert as it was, but rather, as it unraveled in his visual imagination, reduced with his delicate sensibility into his mirage-swept horizons that heave with life.

It is only natural to find influential artists in Saudi Arabia, akin to priests shielded by art and its enchanting play. So much so, that we have learned the practices of some by heart, ones that stem from experiences that flow from realities at once proximate to environment, life, and art.

الفنانون وأعمالهم

Artists
& Artworks

أحمــد فلمبــان

أحمــد فلمبــان هـو رسـام معـروف بتصويـره للأفـراد المنخرطيـن فـي مأسـاة إنسـانية، تلقـى منحـة دراسـية لدراسـة الفنـون الجميلـة فـي Accademia delle Belle Arti في رومـا وتخرج بدرجـة البكالوريـوس عـام 1971م، بـدأت حياتـه المهنية كمعلم فـي عام 1974م، وفي عام 2002م أصبـح مديـرا فنيـاً فـي مدرسـة ثانوية، وكتـب أكثر مـن 400 مقـال وقـراءات جماليـة باللغـة العربيـة والإيطاليـة والإنجليزيـة منشـورة فـي الصحـف السـعودية والإيطاليـة والنمسـاوية؛ هـو عضـو فـي الأكاديميـة الإيطاليـة للفنـون وعضـو فـي رابطـة الفنانيـن العالمييـن.

عـرض أعماله على نطاق واسـع على مدى خمسة عقـود، حيث شـارك في مئات المعارض الجماعية في المملكـة العربيـة السـعودية وخارجهـا، كما أقـام أكثر من ثلاثة وعشـرين معرضاً فرديـاً فـي المملكة العربية السـعودية، وإيطاليا والنمسـا وسـوريا، وكان معرضه الفـردي الأول فـي جدة عام 1976م، وكان آخر معرض لـه فـي صالة تجريد للفنون بالرياض عام 2021م.

فـاز فلمبـان بجوائـز متعـددة بمـا فـي ذلـك وسـام نجمـة إيطاليـا برتبة فـارس، الـذي منحه له الرئيـس الإيطالي السـابق عام 2007م، وحصل على درجة الماجسـتير في الفن من الأكاديمية الإيطالية فـي رومـا، ودرع معهد مسـك للفنون كأحـد رواد الفـن التشـكيلي السـعودي في عـام 2018م، والمركز الأول في البينالي الأوروبي والبحر الأبيض المتوسط الثلاثيـن بإيطاليا عام 2005م كما أصدر سـتة كتب عن الفـن التشـكيلي السـعودي منهـا "التشـكيليون السـعوديون" (2007) "فـن في نصـف قرن أضواء على توهجات الفن التشـكيلي السـعودي" (2016)، و"لمـاذا ومـاذا؟" (2016)، و"إضـاءة للذكـرى" (2015)، و"حكايـة أجيال" (2022).

تعتبـر أعمال فلمبان الفنيـة جـزءاً مـن مجموعـات متعـددة خاصـة وعامـة في المملكة العربيـة السـعودية بمـا فـي ذلـك وزارة الخارجية السـعودية ومؤسسـة المنصورية، وكذلك في عدة كيانـات في إيطاليا أبرزها وزارة الخارجية الإيطالية ومكتـب جامعـة الـدول العربيـة برومـا؛ والمتحف الوطنـي لفنـون الجرافيك بروما.

تجسّـد أعمال الفنّان أحمد فلمبان حسّـاً مرهفاً بالقضايا الإنسـانية والاجتماعية، مركـزاً بالتحديد على صعوبة المعاناة البشـرية بأسـلوبه الفني، يولي أهمية للقضايا أكثر من الشكليات لتسليط الضوء على أهميتها.

فـي السـبعينيات، خطـا فلمبـان خطـوة غيـر مسـبوقة بعرض أعمال فنيّـة مجـرّدة باسـتخدام تقنية النقـش الحمضـي علـى ألـواح الزنك مجسـداً عناصر مـن المناظـر الطبيعيـة؛ كمـا اسـتخدم الزيـت على اللوح واسـتلهم بعضها من وسـائل الإعـلام الغربية، ومـن أبـرز أعمـال فلمبـان خـلال تلك الفتـرة "ضحايا بيافرا" 1971، والتي يصور فيها الفنان فرداً يعاني من المجاعة بسـبب الإبادة الجماعية التي حلّت بالقبيلة فـي غـرب أفريقيـا. و"عيـد ميـلاد بائـس" 1976م، و"الضريبة" 1976م، و"صرخـة للضمائـر" 1977م، تنقل هـذه الأعمـال بوضوح مشـاعر الفقـر المدقع لمجموعـة من الأطفال والأفراد وهم يتوسلون للبقاء على قيد الحياة ويعانون من سـوء التغذية، ويعتمد فـي أعمالـه على اسـتخدام درجـات الألوان الباهتة مـن الأخضـر والبرتقالي والبنـي ليعكس عمـق الألم والمعانـاة؛ حيـث تضفي هذه الألـوان طابعاً عاطفياً عميقـاً مـن خـلال الخلفيـات الباهتـة والمـزج بيـن الأصفر والبرتقالي والأبيض والأخضر لتسـليط الضوء على مسـائل الظلـم الاجتماعي فـي العالم، وتتميز أعمـال فلمبان بأنها مفعمة بالمشـاعر لأنه يسـلط الضـوء علـى الظلم المجتمعـي دافعاً المشـاهدين لمواجهة هـذه القضايا الملحّة والتجاوب معها.

Ahmed Felemban

(b. 1951, Saudi Arabia)

Ahmed Felemban is a painter known for his evocative portrayal of individuals immersed in human tragedy. Felemban received a scholarship to study fine arts at the Accademia delle Belle Arti in Rome, Italy, and graduated with a bachelor's degree in 1971. His career as an art educator began in 1974, and in 2002, he became an art supervisor at a secondary school. Felemban also worked as a journalist and wrote over four hundred articles and art critiques in Arabic, Italian, and English published in Saudi Arabian, Italian, and Austrian newspapers. He is now a full-time artist living between Rome and Jeddah. Felemban is a member of the Italian Academy for Art and a member of the World Artists Association.

The artist has exhibited widely throughout the decades, having participated in numerous group exhibitions in Saudi Arabia and abroad. He has also held over twenty-three solo exhibitions in Saudi Arabia, Italy, Austria, and Syria. His first solo exhibition was in Jeddah (1976) and the latest exhibition was at Abstract Art Gallery, Riyadh (2021).

Felemban was honored by Misk Art Institute as a pioneer of Saudi art (2018); he won multiple awards including first place at the 30th Euro-Mediterranean Biennale in Italy (2005), the Order of the State of Italy with the rank of Knight, awarded by the former President of Italy (2007). Felemban has also published six books including *Story of Generations* (2022), *Art in Half a Century, Lights Glow on Saudi Art* (2016), *Why and What?* (2016), *Illumination of the Memory* (2015), *Saudi Plastic Artists* (2007).

Felemban's artworks are part of multiple private and public collections in Saudi Arabia including the Saudi Ministry of Foreign Affairs and the Al-Mansouria Foundation; and they can be found in several entities in Italy notably the Italian Ministry of Foreign Affairs, the League of Arab States office, and the National Museum of Graphic Arts, Rome.

Ahmed Felemban's artworks demonstrate a profound sensitivity towards social and humanitarian issues, particularly portraying the complexities of human suffering through portraits. In his artistic approach, Felemban prioritizes the subject matter over stylistic considerations to emphasize on the importance of narrative.

During the 1970s, Felemban ventured into creating abstract prints using an acid etching technique on zinc plates. Within these prints, he incorporated elements of the landscapes. Additionally, Felemban employed oil on canvas to depict themes of poverty, hunger, and oppression. Some of his sources for these portrayals were from Western mass media. In *Biafra Victims* (1971), the artist depicts an individual suffering from starvation from the genocide of the Biafra tribe in West Africa.

Other notable examples of his work from this period include *Poor Birthday* (1976), *Tariff* (1976), and *Crying for Heart* (1977). These paintings vividly portray real-life scenes of children and individuals living in poverty, begging for survival, and struggling with inadequate nutrition during humanitarian crises. Felemban's deliberate use of dull greens, oranges, and browns in his color palette serves to convey the depth of pain and suffering he wishes to reflect. These colors imbue his paintings with an intense emotional atmosphere. The backgrounds are out of focus and blend shades of yellow, orange, white, and green, emphasizing that these paintings could represent social injustices around the world.

Through his evocative portrayals, Felemban sheds light on societal injustices, inviting viewers to confront and engage with the pressing issues of our time.

أحمــد فلمبــــان

(ولد عام 1951م في المملكة العربية السعودية)

ضحايا بيافرا، 1971

ألوان زيتية على قماش
70 × 45 سم
بإذن من صالة تجريد للفنون

Ahmed Felemban

(b. 1951, Saudi Arabia)

Biafra Victims, 1971

Oil on canvas
70 × 45 cm
Courtesy of Abstract Art Gallery

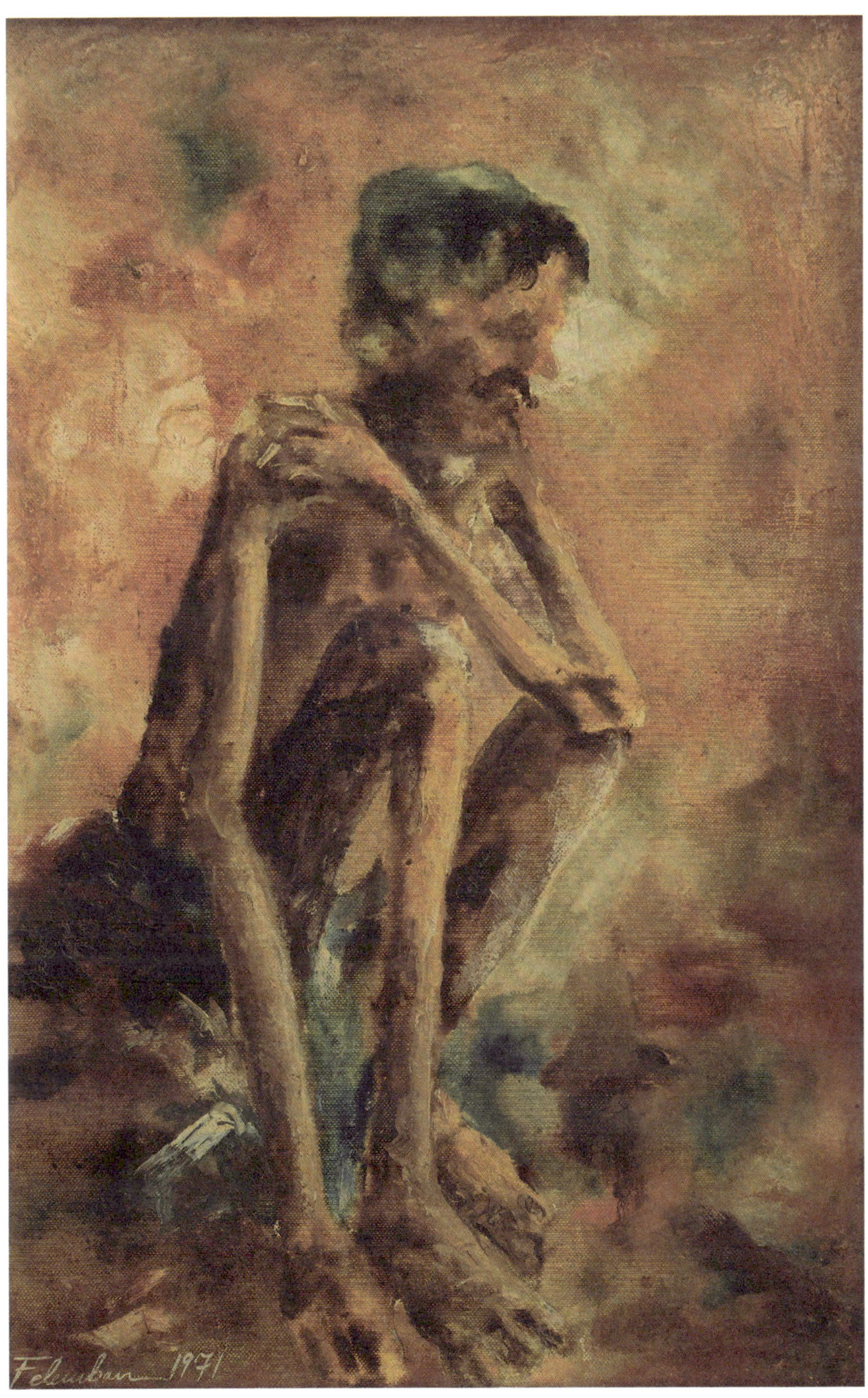

Feluban 1971

أحمــد فلمبـــان

(ولد عام 1951م في المملكة العربية السعودية)

صرخة للضمائر، 1977

ألوان زيتية على قماش
68 × 47.5 سم
بإذن من حوار جاليري

Ahmed Felemban

(b. 1951, Saudi Arabia)

Crying for Heart, 1977

Oil on canvas
68 × 47.5 cm
Courtesy of Hewar Art Gallery

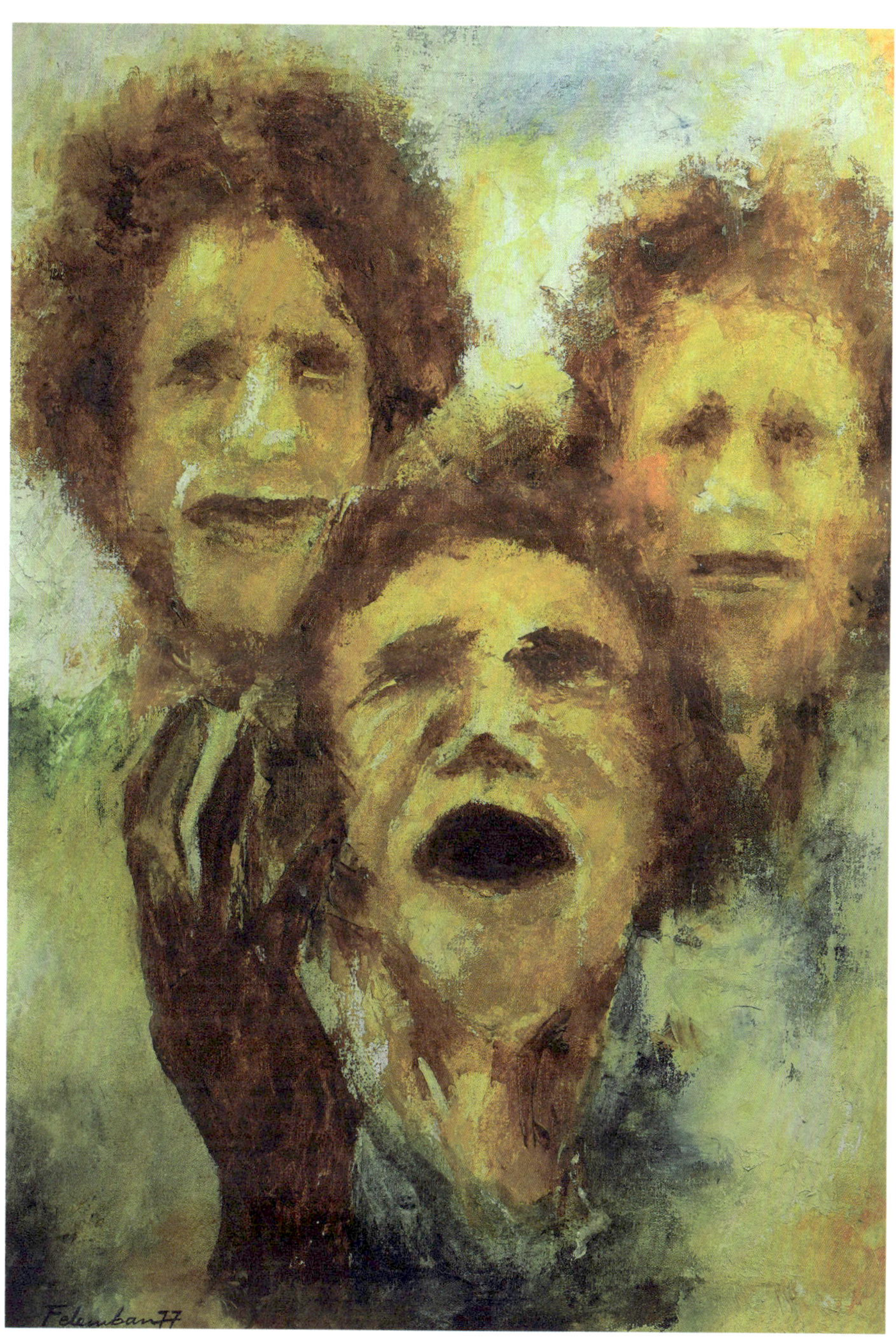

أحمـــد فلمبـــــان

(ولد عام 1951م في المملكة العربية السعودية)

الضريبة، 1976

ألوان زيتية على قماش

68.5 × 49 سم

بإذن من حوار جاليري

Ahmed Felemban

(b. 1951, Saudi Arabia)

Tariff, 1976

Oil on canvas
68.5 × 49 cm
Courtesy of Hewar Art Gallery

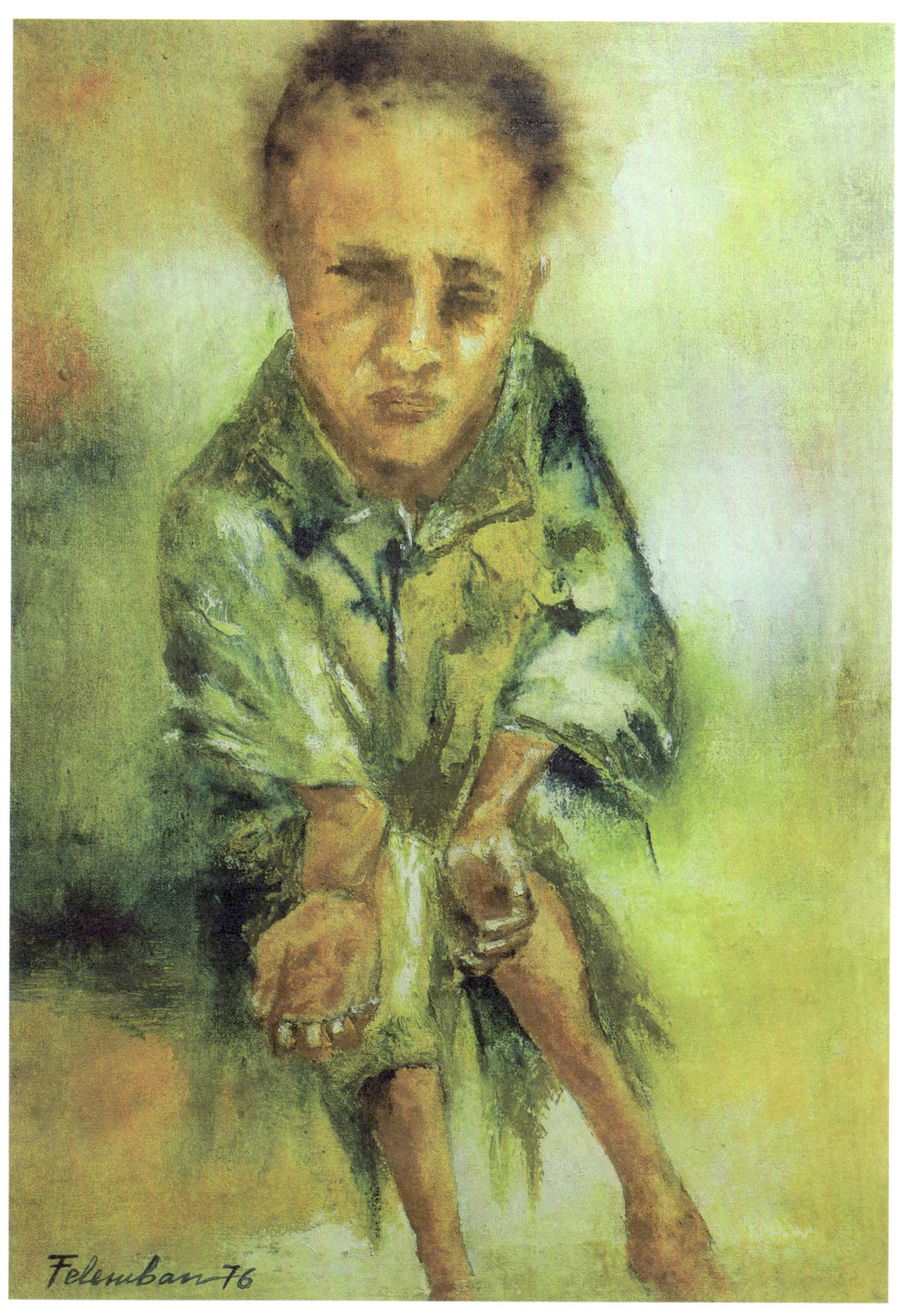

أحمــد فلمبـــان

(ولد عام 1951م في المملكة العربية السعودية)

عيد ميلاد بائس، 1976

ألوان زيتية على قماش
68 × 48 سم
بإذن من حوار جاليري

Ahmed Felemban

(b. 1951, Saudi Arabia)

Poor Birthday, 1976

Oil on canvas
68 × 48 cm
Courtesy of Hewar Art Gallery

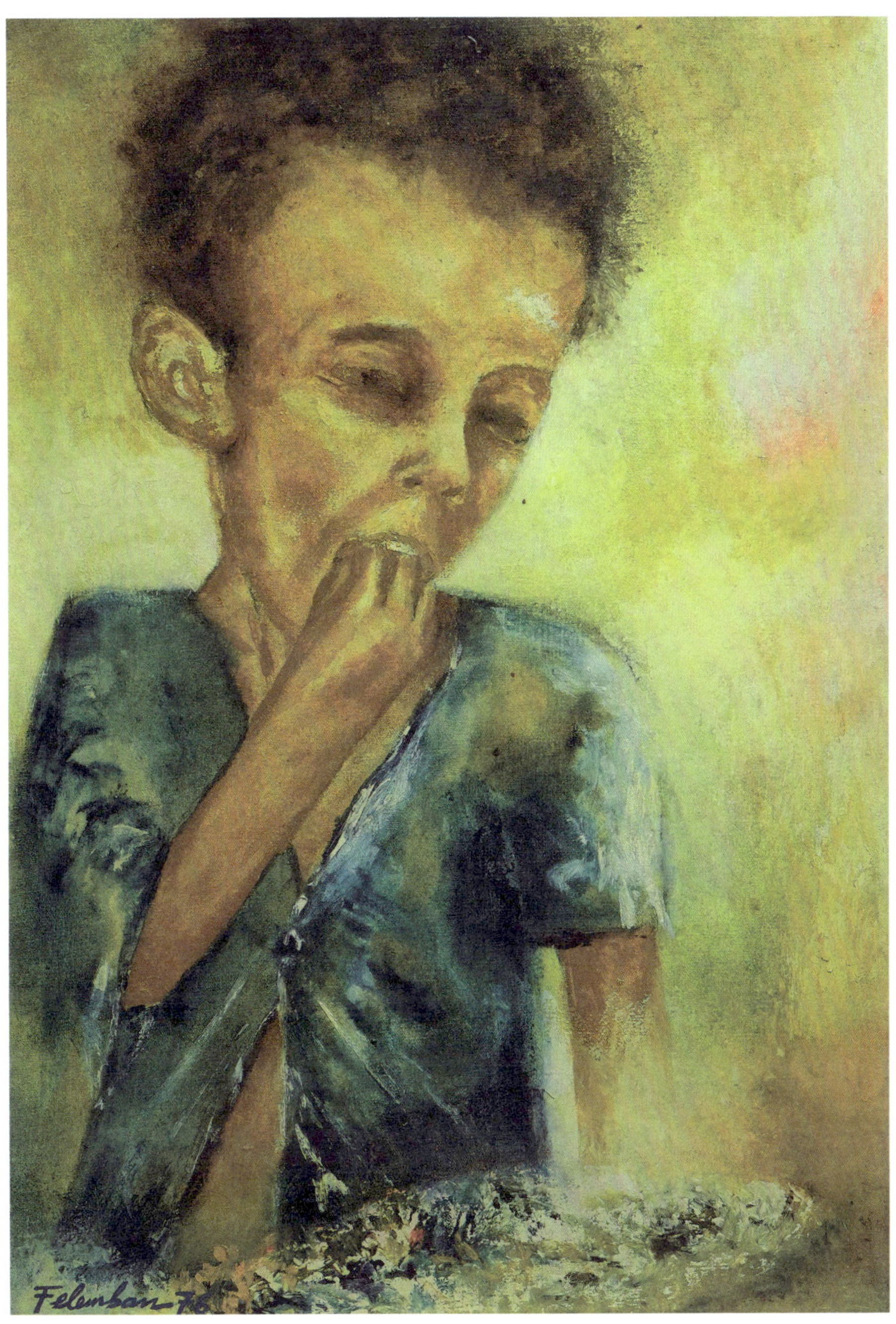
Felemban 76

سعد المسعري

(ولد عام 1953م في المملكة العربية السعودية)

سعد المسعري فنان ونحات وخزاف، ومعلم للتربية الفنية ثم مشرفاً تعليمياً حتى عام 2005م، وحصل على دبلوم التربية الفنية في عام 1971م، وحصل على البكالوريوس من دنفر كولورادو في الولايات المتحدة الأمريكية عام 1979م ثم الماجستير عام 1982م ثم الشهادة العليا MFA في الفنون التشكيلية عام 1983م من جامعة ولاية يوتا، وحصل على جائزة المبتعث من الملحقية الثقافية السعودية في أمريكا لأفضل بحث أو رسالة في عام 1983م، وحصل على دراسة عليا في متحف اللوفر في فرنسا عام 1980م، وفي متحف الفاتيكان، في مدينة الفاتيكان عام 1979م، وفي متحف برادو في إسبانيا عام 1979م.

عُرضت أعماله في العديد من المعارض الداخلية وفي أكثر من خمسين محفلاً ومعرضاً خارجياً منها ما هو في مصر والجزائر والمغرب وليبيا وجميع دول الخليج وفرنسا وألمانيا وإيطاليا وإسبانيا وبريطانيا وأمريكا واليابان وكندا والهند، وبنجلاديش، وأوزباكستان، وأذربيجان، أقام المسعري أربعة معارض شخصية في الولايات المتحدة الأمريكية، وشارك في ندوة التربية الفنية ودورها في بناء المواطن العربي في دول الخليج عام 1985م، وفي مؤتمري النحت الحادي عشر والثاني عشر عام 1980م وفي عام 1982م في الولايات المتحدة الأمريكية.

حصل المسعري على عدة جوائز، منها جائزتا الرئاسة العامة لرعاية الشباب في الفن التطبيقي المعاصر في الأعوام 1984م و1989م، وجائزة عام التراث الإسلامي 1990م، وشارك في العديد من لجان التحكيم المحلية والعربية والدولية، هو حالياً متفرغ لمرسمه ومحترفه ومعرضه الشخصي في محافظة المزاحمية بمنطقة الرياض.

تغطّي أعمال الفنان والنحّات سعد المسعري مجموعة واسعة من الأساليب والأنماط بما في ذلك مجسمات السيراميك، والمنحوتات البرونزية، واللوحات الزيتية، والألوان المائية، وألوان الأكريليك؛ كان المسعري غالباً ما يستوحي أفكار أعماله من ذكريات الماضي والتراث المحلي والعمارة وكل ما يتصل ببيئته ومجتمعه في المملكة العربية السعودية وتحديداً في مدينة الرياض؛ يبرز في أعماله تأثره الواضح بالفن الإسلامي القديم حيث يستخدم أسلوب التسطيح ويدمجه بأنماط معاصرة تتضمن خداعاً بصرياً إلى جانب الأشكال الهندسية التي تمثل جزءاً لا يتجزأ من أعماله في تصوير فني للطابع المعماري للمجتمع.

يصور المسعري في لوحة "أرضنا العطاء نبع الكرم" 1980م جوهر المشاهد المحلية مثل الأرض والكثبان الرملية والجبال بطريقة مجرّدة مستخدماً درجات الأحمر والأزرق مع أشكال هندسية وخطوط رفيعة للتناسق بين المساحات، تساهم الأشكال الهندسية في تحقيق الوهم البصري الذي يرغب المسعري في إيصاله.

يصور المسعري المشهد المعماري السعودي في عمله "المد والجزر (مناظرة بين البعدين والثلاثة أبعاد)" 1983م وهو يرسم المباني والمساجد والممرات المظللة. تهيمن الألوان الترابية على اللوحة، وتعكس الألوان الطبيعية داخل المناظر الطبيعية السعودية. وبينما تتعمق هذه القطعة في المزيد من التمثيل التصويري، فإنها تظل متوافقة مع أسلوب الفنان.

Saad Almasari

Saad Almasari is a painter, sculptor, and art educator who later became an educational supervisor until 2005. Almasari holds several degrees and certificates from the Institute of Art Education, Saudi Arabia (1971), the University of Colorado, Denver, United States (bachelor's 1979, master's 1982), and an MFA in fine arts from the University of Utah, United States (1983). He also received postgraduate certificates from the Vatican Museums, Vatican City (1979); The Prado Museum, Spain (1979); and the Louvre Museum, France (1980). The artist received the Scholarship Award in 1983 for best research, thesis, or dissertation submitted to the Saudi Cultural Attaché. He is now a full-time artist active in several art committees with a private gallery located in Mazahmiya, Riyadh.

Almasari's artworks have been exhibited in over fifty local and international exhibitions in Egypt, Algeria, Morocco, Libya, Kuwait, Qatar, the United Arab Emirates, Oman, France, Germany, Italy, the United Kingdom, Japan, Canada, India, Bangladesh, Uzbekistan, and Azerbaijan. He has held four solo exhibitions in the United States. The artist participated in the Regional Symposium on Art Education in Qatar (1985) and the 11th and 12th Sculpture Conferences in the United States (1980 and 1982).

Almasari received numerous awards, including prizes from the General Presidency of Youth Welfare and the Applied Arts Award at the Saudi Contemporary Art Exhibition (1984 and 1988); and the Islamic Heritage Year Award (1990).

Saad Almasari's works span various mediums and styles, including ceramics, bronze sculptures, oil paintings, watercolors, and acrylics. Almasari often draws inspiration from the past, personal memories, local heritage, architecture, society, and his immediate environment in Saudi Arabia, specifically Riyadh. He acknowledges the influence of traditional Islamic art, which employed flatness, and infuses modernity by incorporating optical illusions into his work. Geometry plays a significant role in his paintings, and he intertwines architectural depictions with society.

In Our Generous Land (The Spring of Generosity) (1980), Almasari captures the essence of local scenes, depicting the land, desert dunes, and mountains in an abstract way. Employing a color palette of reds and blues, with geometric shapes and sharp lines, he harmonizes the convergence of spaces. The geometric shapes also contribute to the overall optical illusion that Almasari seeks to achieve.

Almasari captures the Saudi architectural landscape in *Tides (A Debate Between Two and Three Dimensions)* (1983) as he paints the buildings, mosques, and the shaded walkways. Earthy tones dominate the palette, mirroring the desert hues and natural colors within the Saudi landscape. While this piece delves into more figurative representation, it remains faithful to the artist's style.

سعد المسعري
(ولد عام 1953م في المملكة العربية السعودية)

المد والجزر (مناظرة بين البعدين
والثلاثة أبعاد)، 1983

ألوان زيتية على قماش
80 × 120 سم
مجموعة خاصة

Saad Almasari

(b. 1953, Saudi Arabia)

*Tides (A Debate Between Two and
Three Dimensions), 1983*

Oil on canvas
80 × 120 cm
Private Collection

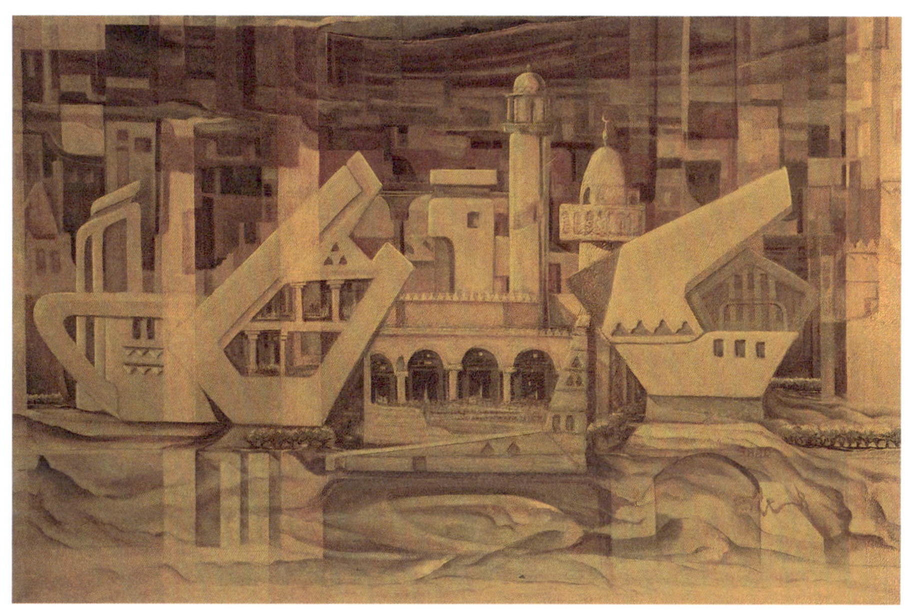

Saad Almasari

(b. 1953, Saudi Arabia)

Our Generous Land (The Spring of Generosity), 1980

Oil on canvas
55 × 70 cm
Courtesy of Abstract Art Gallery

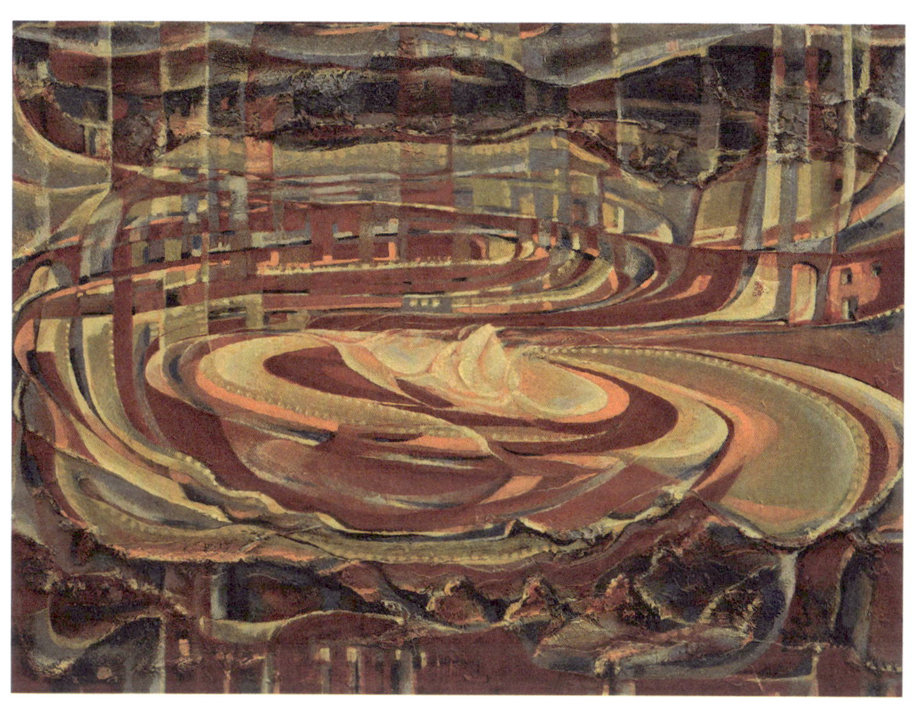

صفيـــة بــن زقـــر

(ولدت عام 1940م في المملكة العربية السعودية)

اشتهرت صفية بن زقر بأعمالها المستوحاة من العناصر الاجتماعية والثقافية والمعمارية الحجازية؛ نشأت في مصر وحصلت على دبلوم في الفنون عام 1960م، ثم توجهت إلى لندن والتحقت بمدرسة الإتيكيت لمدة ثلاث سنوات، وحصلت على شهادة في الرسم والجرافيكي عام 1976م من كلية سانت مارتن في لندن، المملكة المتحدة، وكتبت عن الفن في الصحف المحلية، وألقت محاضرات في السعودية ومصر، وقامت بتحكيم العديد من مسابقات فنون الأطفال، وفي عام 2000م افتتحت "دارة صفية بن زقر" وهي مساحة فنية نشطة تقام فيها ورش عمل ومحاضرات، وتحتوي على مكتبة ومعرض تُعرض فيه أعمالها.

تعد صفية بن زقر، أولى النساء اللواتي أقمن معارض فنية مشتركة عامة للجمهور في المملكة العربية السعودية في عام 1968م في مدرسة دار التربية الحديثة، وبعد هذا المعرض شاركت في العديد من المعارض الجماعية من بينها معرض الماضي كمقدمة في المملكة العربية السعودية عام 2014م، ومعرض اليوم الوطني للمملكة في بلدة نوي سور سين في فرنسا بدعم من مؤسسة المنصورية عام 2005م، ومعرض متنقل بعنوان "المملكة بين الأمس واليوم" عام 1985م، ومعرض الفنانات السعوديات في المملكة العربية السعودية عام 1983م، ومعرض قاعة ردك للفنون في المملكة العربية السعودية عام 1982م، ومعرض جامعة الملك عبدالعزيز في المملكة العربية السعودية عام 1969م وغيرها، ولها 18 معرضاً شخصياً من بينها جاليري دي آرت دي فيشن في سويسرا عام 1980م، وجاليري دورون في فرنسا عام 1980م، وجاليري باترك سيل في المملكة المتحدة عام 1980م، وجاليري وودستوك في المملكة المتحدة عام 1973م.

حصلت على العديد من الجوائز والتي كان على رأسها تكريم خادم الحرمين الشريفين الملك سلمان بن عبد العزيز آل سعود بميدالية الملك عبد العزيز لإسهاماتها في الفن السعودي في عام 2017م، وتكريم من الرئاسة العامة لرعاية الشباب باسم صاحب السمو الملكي الأمير فيصل ابن فهد عام 2003م، وتكريم من برنامج الأمم المتحدة للبيئة لمساهمتها في حماية التراث الوطني عام 1997م؛ وأصدرت كتابين بعنوان "رحلة ثلاثة عقود مع التراث السعودي" في عام 2000م، و"المملكة العربية السعودية: نظرة فنانة للماضي" في عام 1979م.

اقتنيت أعمالها ضمن مجموعات المتحف البريطاني في المملكة المتحدة، ومؤسسة المنصورية في المملكة العربية السعودية، والمتحف الوطني الأردني للفنون الجميلة في الأردن وغيرها.

تُغطي أعمال صفية بن زقر مجموعة واسعة من الفنون المتنوعة بما في ذلك الألوان الزيتية والمائية، والباستيل والرسم والنقش؛ خلال تجاربها لمختلف الأساليب على مر السنوات، كانت بن زقر تستلهم أسلوبها الفني من أعمال غوغان وجيوتو وسيزان، وتوثّق في أعمالها العادات والتقاليد المحلية والعمارة القديمة والاحتفالات والأنشطة اليومية لمنطقة الحجاز لتخليد ثقافة المنطقة؛ كانت رحلة بن زقر الفنية العامل الرئيسي الذي مكّنها من تطوير أسلوبها الخاص الذي يتلاءم مع رؤيتها الفنية.

"ملتقى 1 و 2" 1980م هي جزء من سلسلة من الأعمال الفنية التي تصور لحظة حميمية لزوجين يجلسان تحت شجرة، ويتجلى في الصورة جلوس المرأة وتحديقها المتواصل في الرجل مضفياً بذلك شاعرية أكبر على المشهد.

Safeya Binzagr

(b. 1940, Saudi Arabia)

Safeya Binzagr gained recognition for her work which draws inspiration from Hejazi social, cultural, and architectural elements. After spending her formative years in Egypt, Binzagr earned an art diploma in 1960, then headed to London and enrolled in a finishing school for three years. She graduated with a degree in drawing and graphics in 1976 from Saint Martin's College, the United Kingdom. Binzagr wrote about art in local newspapers, gave lectures in Saudi Arabia and Egypt, and served as a judge for children's art competitions. In 2000, the artist opened the doors to Darat Safeya Binzagr Gallery, an active art space that holds workshops, lectures, a library, and a gallery showcasing her work.

In 1968, Binzagr was one of the first women to exhibit art publicly in a joint exhibition in Saudi Arabia at Dar Al-Tarbia Al-Hadetha School. Following this exhibition, Binzagr participated in many exhibitions including *Past is Prologue*, Saudi Arabia (2014); the Kingdom's National Day exhibition in Neuilly-sur-Seine with the support of Al-Mansouria Foundation, France (2005); *Saudi Arabia Yesterday and Today*, traveling exhibition (1985); *Saudi Women Artists Exhibition*, Saudi Arabia (1983); RDC Art Hall, Saudi Arabia (1982); and King Abdulaziz University, Saudi Arabia (1969). She held eighteen solo exhibitions, their locations include Galerie d'Art du Vieux Chene –Bourgeries, Switzerland (1980); Galerie Drouant, France (1980); Patrick Seale Gallery, the United Kingdom (1980); and Woodstock Gallery, the United Kingdom (1973).

Binzagr received several awards and recognitions which include being honored by His Majesty King Salman bin Abdulaziz Al Saud with the King Abdulaziz Medal for her contributions to Saudi art (2017); recognition from the General Presidency of Youth Welfare, in the name of HRH Prince Faisal bin Fahd (2003); and recognition from the United Nations Environment Program (UNEP) for contributing to the protection of national heritage (1997). She published two books, *A Three-Decade Journey with Saudi Heritage* (2000) and *Saudi Arabia: An Artist's View of the Past* (1979). Binzagr's works have been acquired by the British Museum, the United Kingdom; the Al-Mansouria Foundation, Saudi Arabia; and the Jordan National Gallery of Fine Arts, Jordan, amongst others.

Safeya Binzagr has a multifaceted body of work that features various mediums including oil, watercolor, pastel, drawing, and etching. During her years of experimenting with style, Binzagr drew inspiration from Gauguin's palette, and Giotto and Cézanne's pictorial styles. In her works, she documents traditions, local customs, old architecture, ceremonies, daily activities, and the heritage of the Hejaz region. Binzagr's artistic journey led her to cultivate her own style that resonates with her chosen subject matter.

Wealth of Nations (1969) is part of a series of portraits made between 1968–1978 portraying female Bedouins. In this work, Binzagr depicts a Bedouin woman covered in traditional face coverings, embellished with gold jewelry, cradling a goat in her arms. The face mask, a cultural symbol of a woman's honor, and the goat, represents the Bedouin women's roles to herd livestock and weave wool for their tents. Beyond the surface, the painting holds profound symbolism, asserting that the moral and economic wealth of Saudi Arabia lies in its women.

Rendezvous 1 and 2 (1980) is part of a series of works and preparatory drawings that depict a moment between a couple seated beneath a tree. The distance between the two, the woman's pose and gaze upon the man add an air of mystery to the scene.

In *Al-Diriyah* (1980) and *Al Muusmak Palace* (1980), realized respectively with the technique of aquatint and etching, Binzagr accentuates architectural elements and preserves the grandeur of old, traditional buildings. These works pay homage to Saudi Arabia's heritage and the significance of its historical architecture.

"ثروة الأمم" 1969م هي جزء من سلسلة من الأعمـال التي رسـمت بيـن عامـي 1968 - 1978م لبدويـات؛ وتعـرض بـن زقر في هـذا العمل سـيدة بدويـة تغطي وجهها بالغطـاء التقليـدي المرصع بالجواهـر الذهبيـة وتحتضـن ماعـزاً بيـن ذراعيهـا، يُمثل غطاء الوجه رمزاً ثقافياً لشرف المرأة في حين تعكس الماعز الأدوار المهمة التي تلعبها نساء البدو في تربية الماشية ونسج الصوف لخيامهن، والجدير بالذكـر أن هـذا العمل يحمـل رمزية عميقة مؤكداً علـى أن الثـروة المعنويـة والاقتصادية للسـعودية تكمن في نسـائه.

أما فـي لوحتـي "الدرعيـة" و" قصـر المصمك" 1980م، اسـتخدمت فـن الطباعـة الغائـرة لإبـراز العناصـر المعماريـة وتخليـد روح المبانـي التراثيـة القديمة؛ كلّ ذلك بهدف تمجيد إرث المملكة العربية السـعودية وأهمية هندسـتها المعماريـة التاريخية.

صفيـــة بـــن زقـــر

(ولدت عام 1940م في المملكة العربية السعودية)

قصر المصمك، 1980

الطباعة الحجرية
45 × 63 سم
بإذن من حوار جاليري

Safeya Binzagr

(b. 1940, Saudi Arabia)

Al Muusmak Palace, 1980

Lithography
45 × 63 cm
Courtesy of Hewar Art Gallery

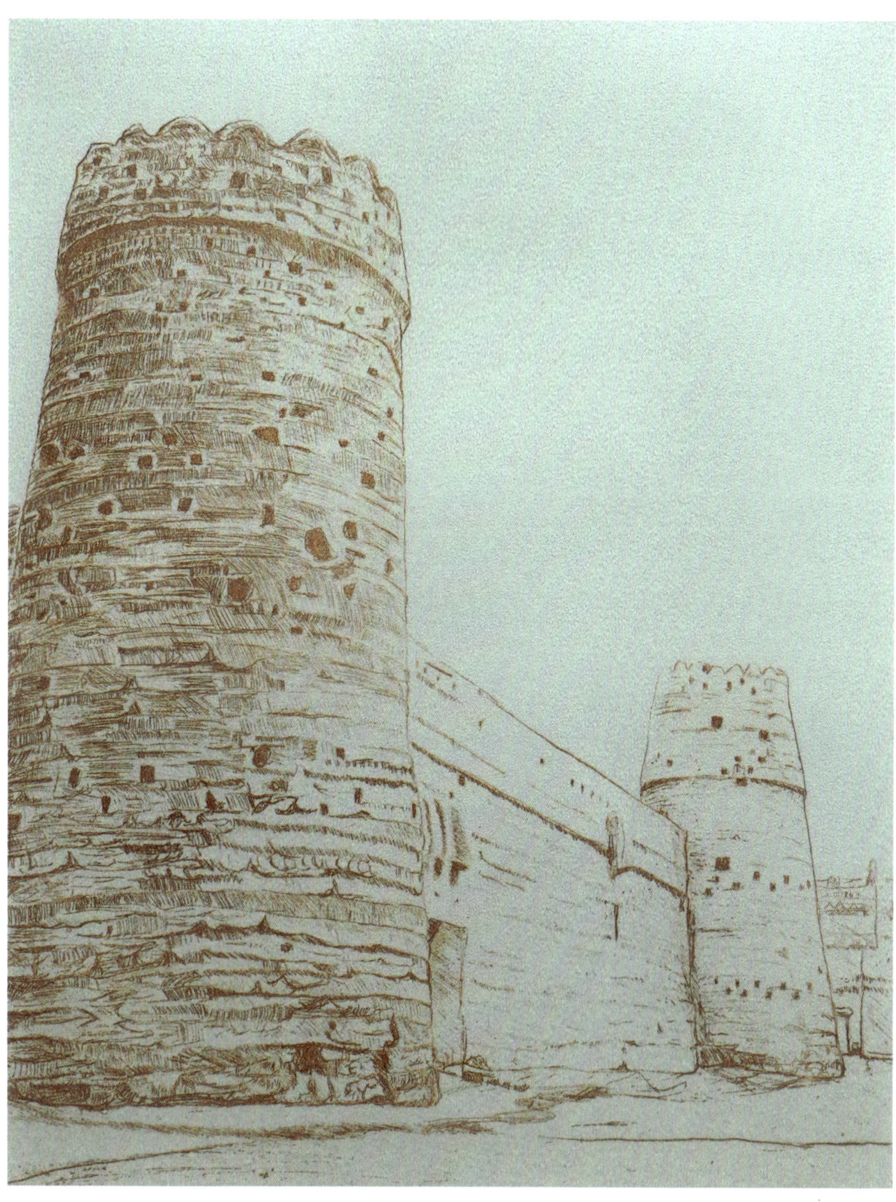

صفيــــة بـــن زقــــر
(ولدت عام 1940م في المملكة العربية السعودية)

ثروة الأمم، 1969

طبعة محدودة الإصدار
71 × 50 سم
بإذن من حوار جاليري

Safeya Binzagr

(b. 1940, Saudi Arabia)

Wealth of Nations, 1969

Limited edition print
71 × 50 cm
Courtesy of Hewar Art Gallery

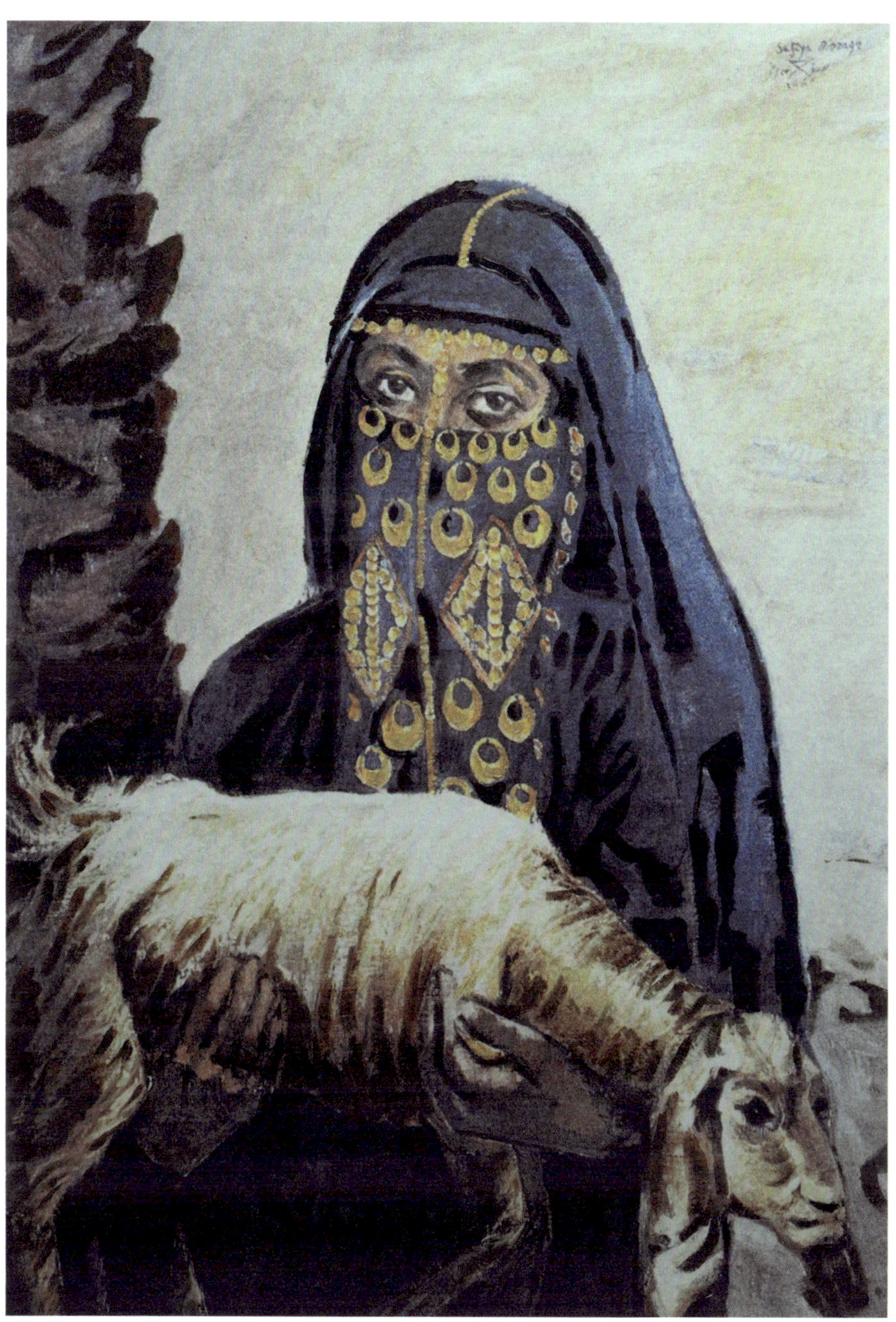

Safeya Binzagr

(b. 1940, Saudi Arabia)

Rendezvous 1, 1980

Lithography
63 × 86.5 cm
Courtesy of Hewar Art Gallery

صفيـــة بـــن زقـــر

(ولدت عام 1940م في المملكة العربية السعودية)

ملتقى *1*، 1980

الطباعة الحجرية
63 × 86.5 سم
بإذن من حوار جاليري

Safeya Binzagr

(b. 1940, Saudi Arabia)

Rendezvous 2, 1980

Lithography
63 × 86.5 cm
Courtesy of Hewar Art Gallery

صفيـــة بـــن زقـــر

(ولدت عام 1940م في المملكة العربية السعودية)

ملتقى *2*، 1980

الطباعة الحجرية
63 × 86.5 سم
بإذن من حوار جاليري

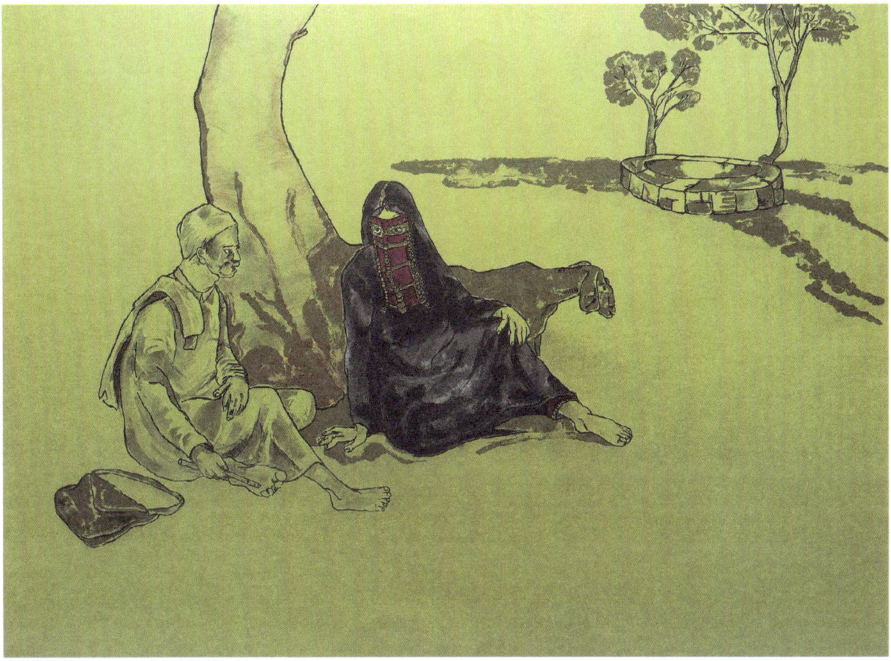

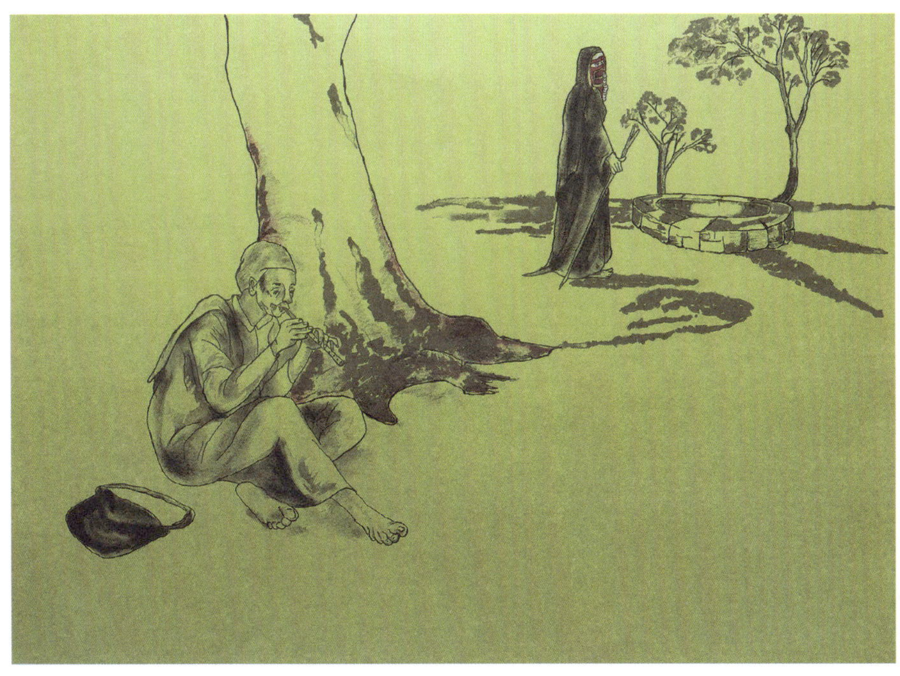

صفيــة بــن زقــر
(ولدت عام 1940م في المملكة العربية السعودية)

الدرعية، 1980

الطباعة الحجرية
40 × 57 سم
بإذن من حوار جاليري

Safeya Binzagr

(b. 1940, Saudi Arabia)

Al-Diriyah, 1980

Lithography
40 × 57 cm
Courtesy of Hewar Art Gallery

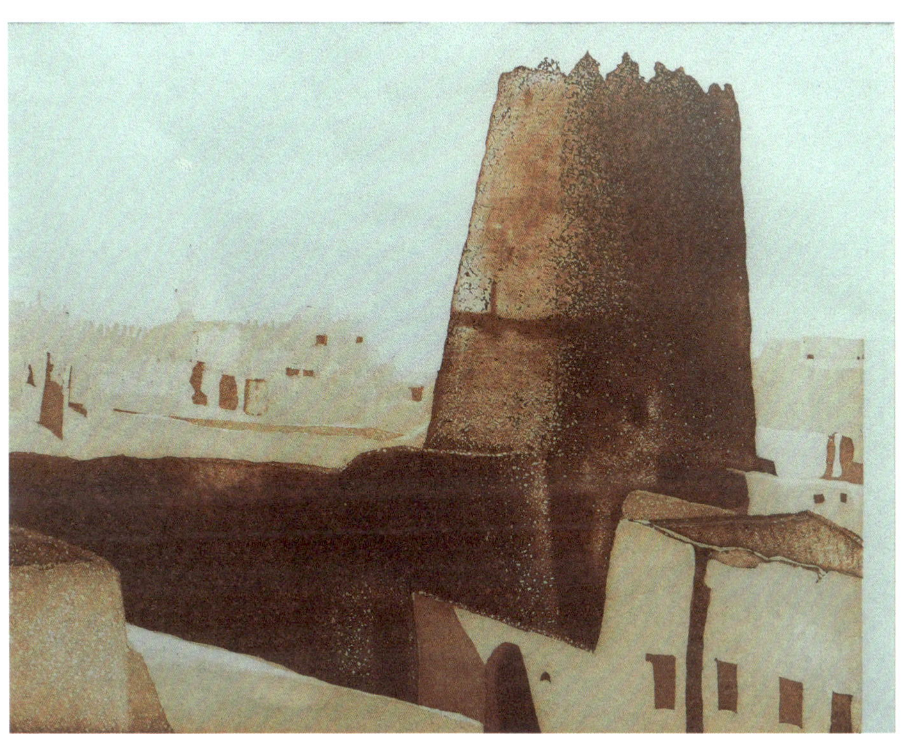

طـه الصبـان

(ولد عام 1948م في المملكة العربية السعودية)

طـه الصبـان فنـان تعلـم ذاتيـاً وحصـل علـى بعثة مـن وزارة الإعلام للدراسـة فـي المملكة المتحدة حيـث اسـتغل وقـت فراغـه -أثنـاء الدراسـة- في صقـل مهاراتـه كفنـان. واتسـم الفنـان بالعزيمة والنزعـة للتجـارب ما سـاعده فـي إنشـاء جداريات شاسـعة الأطراف فـي المسـاحات العامة وداخل المبانـي الحكوميـة والمطـارات، كان الصبان عضواً بـارزاً في عـدة مجموعـات فنيـة، فقـد كان رئيس قسـم الفنـون فـي الجمعيـة العربيـة السـعودية للثقافة والفنـون وعُيّن كأول رئيس لبيـت الفنانين التشكيليين بجـدة عـام 1993.

شارك الصبان بفاعلية في المعارض الجماعية التـي أقيمـت فـي المملكـة العربيـة السـعودية، وإيطاليـا، والهنـد، والمملكـة المتحـدة، والإمارات العربيـة المتحـدة، ومصر، وسويسـرا، وإيـران، ومن أبـرز مشـاركاته: بينالي إيـران فـي عـام 2002م، وبينالـي القاهـرة الدولـي للفنـون بمصر فـي عامي 1994م و1998م، وبينالي الشارقة بالإمارات العربية المتحـدة فـي عامـي 1993م و2001م، ومعـرض بنـك الريـاض بلندن فـي عامـي 1985م و1994م، ومعـرض الفن السـعودي المعاصر فـي الهند عام 1984م، والبينالـي الدولـي بإيطاليا عـام 1970م.

أقـام الصبـان عـدة معـارض فرديـة فـي أنحاء العالـم، مثل: إنجلترا في عام 1975م؛ وإسـكتلندا عام 1976م؛ وفي المملكة العربية السعودية عام 1993م (فـي صالة بيـت التشـكيليين) فـي المملكـة العربية السـعودية عـام 1997م، ولبنـان عـام 1999م، حـاز الصبـان علـى عدة جوائـز، منها جائـزة بينالي المحبة الأول والثالث للفنون التشكيلية في اللاذقية، سوريا في عامي 1995م و1999م وجائزة المفتاحة عام 1999م.

اقتنيـت أعمـال الصبـان من قبل عـدة جهات سـعودية مثـل: الحـرس الوطنـي فـي جـدة، مطار الملك عبـد العزيز في جدة، مطار الملك خالد في الريـاض، ومطـار الملك فهد في المنطقة الشرقية.

يسـتمد طـه الصبـان إلهامـه مـن الحيـاة الاجتماعيـة الحجازيـة والتـراث المحلي السـعودي والثقافة والعمارة والبحـر والبيئة العامة، وتشـمل أعماله مجموعة واسـعة من الأسـاليب بما في ذلك التجريد والتعبيريـة والتكعيبية، ومن بين مواضيعه المتنوعة، غالبـاً ما يركز على النسـاء، ويرسمهن لإبراز أدوارهـن المختلفة داخـل المجتمع.

تصور لوحة "منظر طبيعي" 1959م مشـهداً طبيعيـاً تقف فيه سـيدتان محجبتان تحت شـجرة كبيـرة، علامـات الأوراق على الشـجرة هـي خطوط سـريعة وحادة رُسـمت بدرجـات من اللـون الأزرق والأحمر والأصفر والأبيـض، وفي الخلفية تضيف طاحونـة الهواء التـي تذكرنـا بالهندسة المعمارية الهولنديـة لمسـة غير متوقعة للوحـة لتمزج عناصر من ثقافـات مختلفة.

في لوحته "سـباق الهجن" 1961م، يسـتخدم الصبـان مجموعـة ألـوان أكثـر بـرودة مـن أعمالـه اللاحقـة، ويهيمـن علـى اللوحة اللـون الأرجوانـي والقشـدي والرمـادي، وتُظهـر مقدمتها أربعـة جمال تتحرك فـي انسـجام تـام، ويمثل الفنان الجمـال باسـتخدام خطـوط مميـزة، بينما تعـزز ضربـات الفرشـاة العموديـة شـكلها، ويمتطي هذه الجمال رجال يرتدون الـزي التقليدي، الثوب الأبيض والعمامـة، ويتجاهل التفاصيل المعقدة، ما يسـمح للمشـاهد بالتركيـز علـى التكويـن العـام وإحسـاس الحركـة داخل المشـهد؛ تظهـر الخلفيـة والمقدمة فـي أعمـال الصبـان الفنيـة في حالة مـن الغموض، والـذي يخلق إحساسـاً بالعـوم ومن خـلال طمس الحـدود بيـن العناصر، يمكـن للمرء أن يتسـاءل عن المفاهيـم الثابتـة للزمان والمكان.

Taha Alsabban

(b. 1948, Saudi Arabia)

Taha Alsabban is a self-taught painter who was awarded a scholarship from the Ministry of Media to study in the United Kingdom; during his free time he learned to hone his skills as a painter. The artist's determination and proclivity for experimentation helped him create large-scale murals for public spaces, governmental institutions, and airports. Alsabban was part of multiple groups and served as the first president of the House of Artists in Jeddah in 1993, and the art department of the Saudi Arabian Society for Culture and Arts.

Alsabban actively participated in group exhibitions in Saudi Arabia, Italy, India, the United Kingdom, the United Arab Emirates, Egypt, Switzerland, and Iran. Notable among his participation history are the *Iran Biennale*, Iran (2002); *Cairo Biennale*, Egypt (1994 and 1998); *Sharjah Biennale*, the United Arab Emirates (1993 and 2001); *Riyadh Bank* exhibition, United Kingdom (1985 and 1994); *Contemporary Saudi Art Exhibition*, India (1984). His solo exhibitions were held in England (1975); Scotland (1976); The House of Artists Gallery, Saudi Arabia (1993); Saudi Arabia (1997), and Lebanon (1999). Alsabban won several awards, including the 1st and 3rd *AlMahaba Biennale* in Lattakia, Syria in 1995 and 1999, and the Muftaha Award in 1999.

Alsabban's artworks have been acquired by several Saudi organizations: National Guard, Jeddah; King Abdulaziz Airport, Jeddah; King Khaled Airport, Riyadh; and King Fahd Airport, Dhahran.

Taha Alsabban draws inspiration from Hejazi social life, local Saudi heritage, culture, architecture, the sea, and the general environment. Alsabban's oeuvre spans over a wide range of styles including abstraction, expressionism, and cubism. Among his diverse subjects, the artist frequently focuses on women, painting them to project their different roles within society.

The painting *Landscape* (1959) portrays a natural scene where two veiled ladies stand beneath a large tree. The markings of the leaves on the tree are quick, sharp lines, created by utilizing shades of blue, red, yellow, and white. In the background, a windmill reminiscent of Dutch architecture adds an unexpected touch to the landscape, juxtaposing elements of different cultures.

In *Camel Race* (1961), Alsabban employs a cooler color palette than his later works, the composition is dominated by purples, creams, and greys. The foreground of the painting showcases four camels moving in unison. Employing distinct lines, the artist represents the camels, while vertical brushstrokes further enhance their form. Men dressed in traditional attire, wearing white *thoub* and wrapped head garments ride atop the camels. Alsabban omits intricate details, allowing the viewer to focus on the overall composition and the sense of motion within the scene. The background and foreground in the artwork exist in a state of ambiguity, creating a sense of movement. By blurring the boundaries between the elements, one may question the fixed notions of time and space.

In *Thursday Market* (1980), Alsabban offers insight into the bustling Thursday Markets in Abha, where women engage in commerce. Against a backdrop of buildings and skyscrapers, the foreground highlights the women immersed in the market ambiance. Employing abstract geometric shapes, Alsabban interconnects architectural motifs, encapsulating the memory of the place. The color palette predominantly features monochromatic tones of browns, yellows, and subtle hints of blue, creating a heritage-filled structure. The human figures, positioned along the street, intertwine with the buildings, forming a harmonious visual narrative.

Untitled (1988) presents a night of jubilation, as men stand holding the *teeran*, a traditional Arabic percussion instrument. The painting is viewed from an elevated perspective, resembling a bird's-eye view. Warm hues dominate the canvas with reds, oranges, and blues harmoniously blending. The men, dressed in traditional attire, become part of a vibrant tableau. The focal point lies at the center of the composition, with men and their drums arranged in a flowing formation, while the background fades into a washed-out orange hue.

في لوحته "سوق الخميس" 1980م، يعرض الصبان لمحة من أسواق الخميس الصاخبة في أبها، حيث تشارك النساء في أنشطة البيع وعلى خلفية المباني وناطحات السحاب، تسلط المقدمة الضوء على النساء المنغمسات في أجواء السوق، وباستخدام الأشكال الهندسية المجردة، يربط الصبان بين الزخارف المعمارية، ويغلف ذاكرة المكان، وتتميز مجموعة الألوان في الغالب بدرجات أحادية اللون من البني والأصفر ولمحات خفيفة من اللون الأزرق مشكلة للتراث تتشابك الشخصيات البشرية، المتمركزة على طول الشارع، مع المباني لتشكل سرداً بصرياً متناغماً.

تقدم لوحة "بدون عنوان" 1988م ليلة ابتهاج، حيث يقف الرجال ممسكين بآلة الطيران، وهي آلة إيقاعية عربية تقليدية؛ يُنظر إلى اللوحة من منظور مرتفع يشبه منظور عين الطائر، وتهيمن درجات الألوان الدافئة على اللوحة القماشية، مع مزج الألوان الأحمر والبرتقالي والأزرق بشكل متناغم وأصبح الرجال الذين يرتدون الزي التقليدي، تقع النقطة المحورية في مركز اللوحة، حيث يُرتب الرجال طبولهم، بينما تتلاشى الخلفية لتتحول إلى تدرج برتقالي باهت.

طــــه الصبـــــان

(ولد عام 1948م في المملكة العربية السعودية)

منظر طبيعي، 1959

ألوان زيتية على قماش
60 × 71 سم
بإذن من الفنان

Taha Alsabban

(b. 1948, Saudi Arabia)

Landscape, 1959

Oil on canvas
60 × 71 cm
Courtesy of the artist

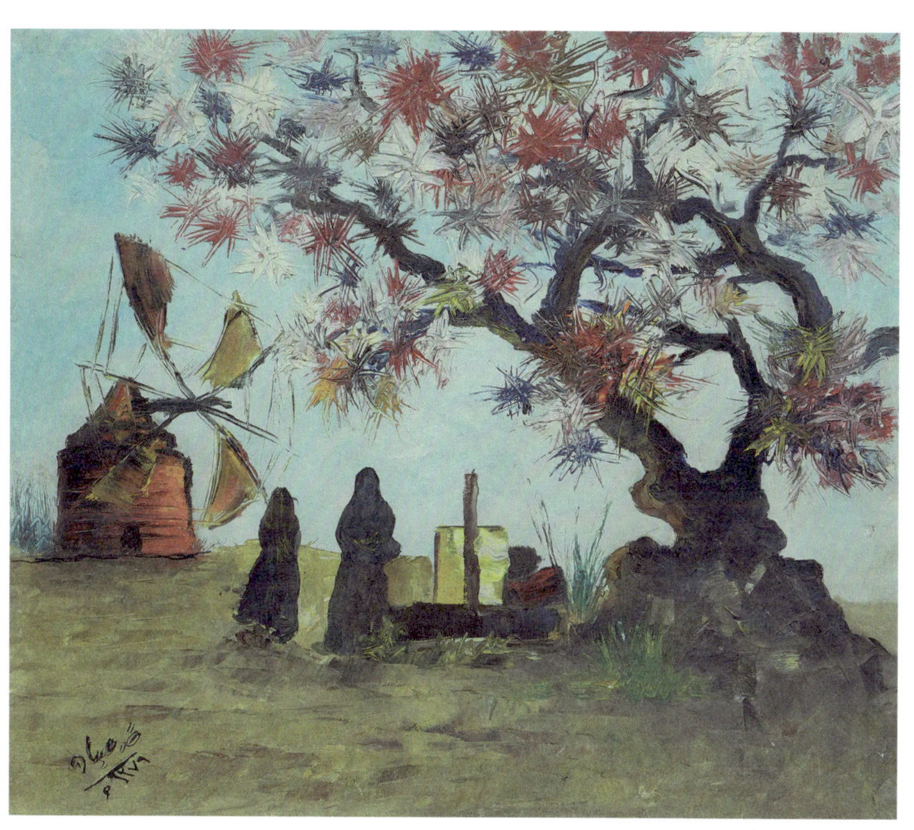

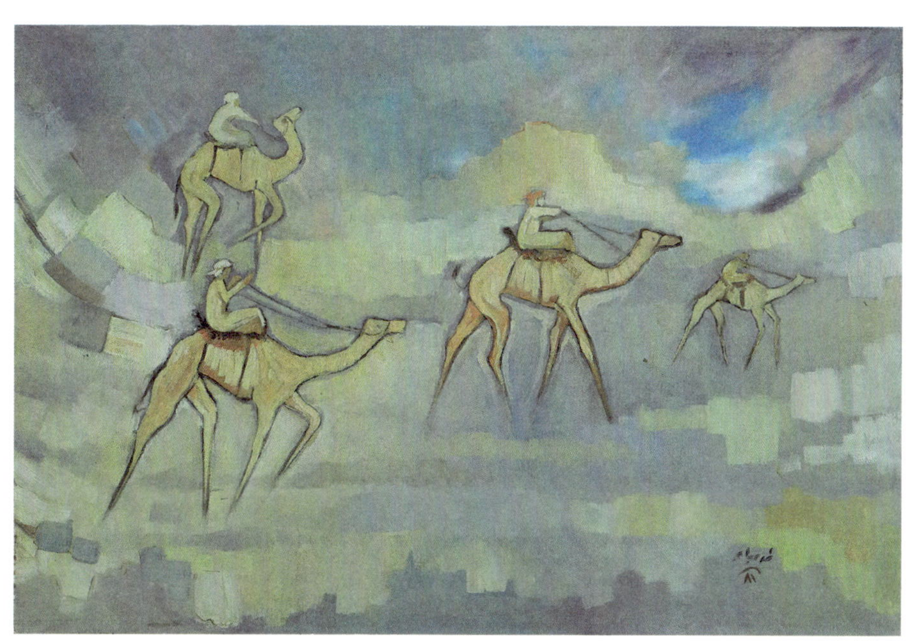

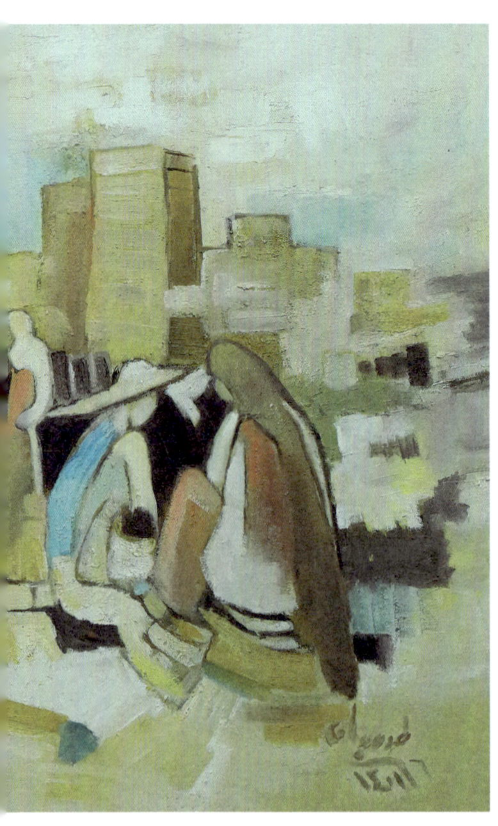

Taha Alsabban

(b. 1948, Saudi Arabia)

Thursday Market, 1980

Oil on canvas
60 × 120 cm
Courtesy of the artist

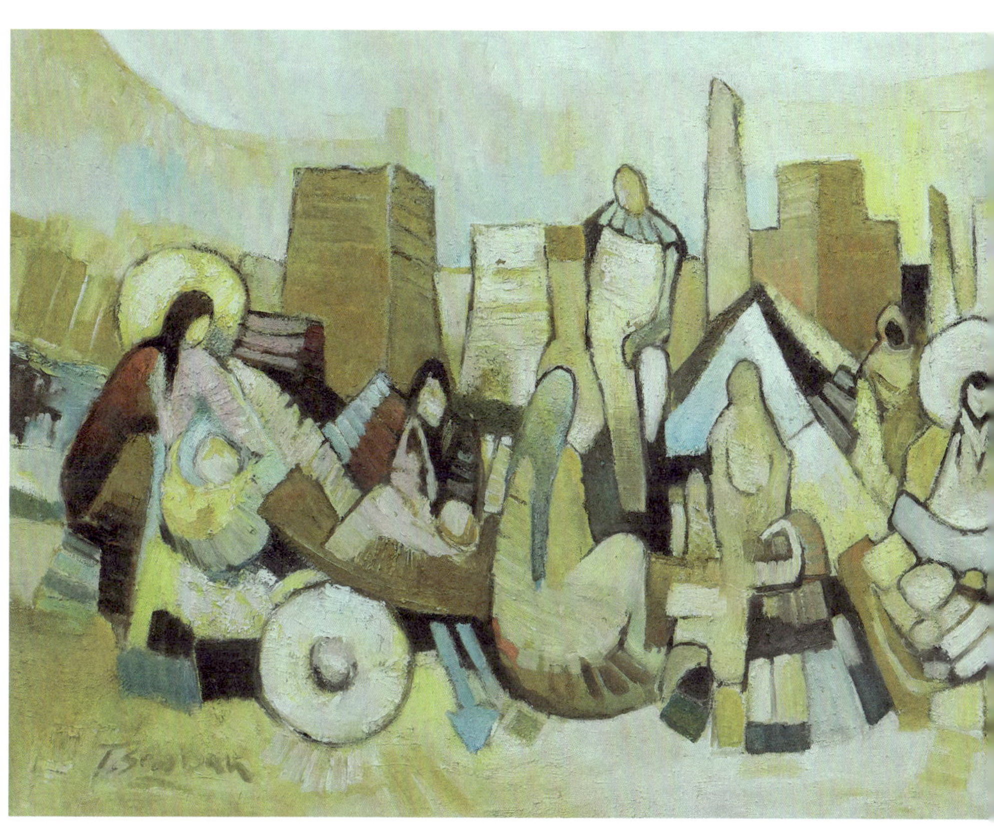

Taha Alsabban

(b. 1948, Saudi Arabia)

Untitled, 1988

Oil on canvas
75 × 120 cm
Courtesy of Abstract Art Gallery

طـــه الصبـــــان

(ولد عام 1948م في المملكة العربية السعودية)

بدون عنوان، 1988

ألوان زيتية على قماش
75 × 120 سم
بإذن من صالة تجريد للفنون

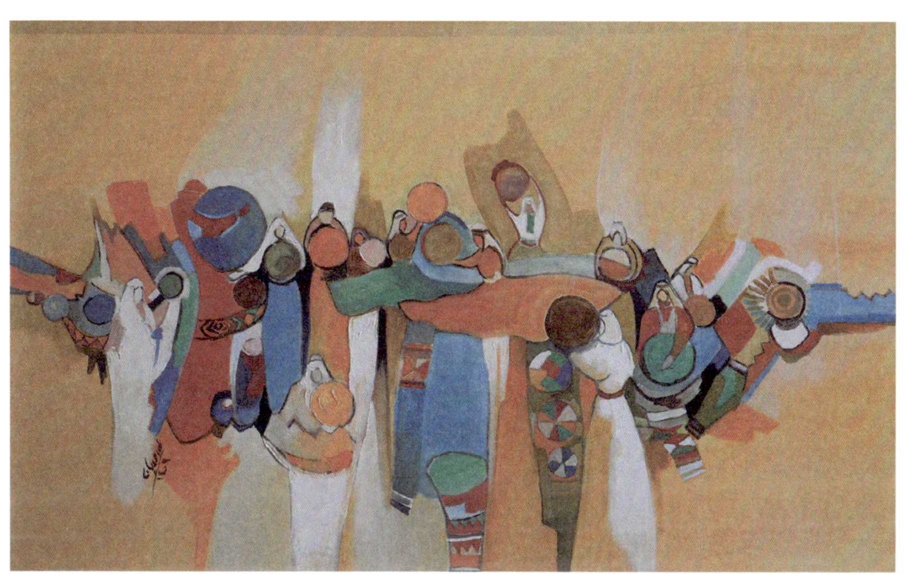

عبـد الجبّـار اليحيـا

(ولد عام 1931م في العراق وتوفي عام 2014م في المملكة العربية السعودية)

كان عبـد الجبـار اليحيـا رسامـاً عصاميـاً علّـم نفسـه الفن وطوّر شـغفه مع الثقافة المحلية، بعد دراسـته الهندسـة فـي أتلانتا جورجيا، الولايـات المتحدة عام 1951م عـاد اليحيا إلى جدة وانخرط في العديد من الأنشطة الإبداعية، حيث صمم شعارات للقوات الجوية وعمـل كمحـرر لقسـم الفنون التشكيلية فـي جريدة المدينـة، والتحـق بكلية لنـدن للطباعة عـام 1976م وكان آنذاك عضواً مؤسسـاً في جماعة ألوان بالرياض، وعضواً في جماعة أصدقاء الفن التشكيلي الخليجي، وتلقـى دعمـاً من الرئاسـة العامة لرعاية الشباب.

شـارك اليحيا فـي أكثر مـن خمسـين معرضاً محليـاً وعالميـاً، ويعتبـر أول فنان سـعودي يعرض أعمالـه دوليـاً في متحف فورسـت بارك في سـانت لويس بولاية ميسـوري، الولايـات المتحـدة عـام 1951م، ومـن بعـض المعـارض الفردية للفنان ما أُقيم في شـركة لوكهيد مارتـن الأمريكية في الرياض عـام 1972م، وفنـدق اليمامـة فـي الريـاض عـام 1973م، وطريق الشـمال في الرياض عام 1972م، وشـركة الواكد في الريـاض عـام 1971م، والسـفارة الفرنسـية فـي الرياض عـام 1998م، وآخـر معرض أقامـه كان حوار غاليـري في الرياض عـام 2009م، ويُعـدّ أول فنـان سـعودي يقيم معرضـاً منفـرداً نظمتـه جمعيـة الثقافة والفنون.

نشـر اليحيا كتاب "خمسـون عامـاً من الرسـم" عـام 1999م، وترجـم ("اللـون للفنان" لهانز شـوارز 1968م) إلى اللغة العربية عـام 2003م، واقتنيت أعمالـه من قبـل جهات محليـة ودولية.

عبـد الجبار اليحيا رسـام يتنقل بين مختلف الأسـاليب الفنية، بما فـي ذلك السـريالية والتكعيبية والفن التجريـدي بغض النظـر عن الأسـلوب، ظل استكشافه للإنسـانية في صميم أعماله الفنية.

تصور لوحـة "الصرخـة" 1975م شكلاً خارجياً بيدين تحاولان التمسك بما يكمن أدناه، وتحيط بهذا الشكل قضبان ملونة على كلا الجانبين، مؤكدةً حبسه. داخل الشكل، يصور شخصية بشرية تحتوي على أشـكال بلوريـة ملونة نابضة بالحيـاة، ووسطه شـخص يعـزف علـى البيانو وفـي الجزء السـفلي، يظهر شـيء يشبه مخطط الاهتـزازات الصوتية للألـوان، مكمـلاً العوالـم البلوريـة بداخلـه، فيبدو أن الشـكل يتحـرر من قيـوده، ويتحـول إلى ألوان و موسيقى .

توسـع التركيـز الفنـي لليحيا فـي السـنوات الأخيرة من حياته المهنية ليشـمل البيئـة المحلية، وتحديـداً الاسـتلهام مـن المناظـر الطبيعيـة الصحراوية، وظهر تصويـر المـرأة في العديد من أعماله، واستكشف العلاقات بين البشر ومحيطهم، ويمكـن رؤيـة التتويـج لهذه الممارسـة مـن خلال لوحـته "بناء" 1983م، حيـث يسـتخدم نهجـاً مبسـطاً، ولكنه تمثيلي؛ يصور العمل الفنـي تعاوناً بيـن رجـل وامـرأة، حيـث تمـد الشـخصية الأنثوية ذراعيهـا لتسـليم شـيء للرجـل، وكلاهمـا يرتديان ملابس غير رسـمية وتقليدية؛ هذه اللفتة البسـيطة هـي بمثابة رمز قوي يتحـدى الأعـراف المجتمعية ويسـلط الضـوء علـى الـدور المحـوري للمـرأة مـع التأكيـد علـى أهميـة الجهـود الجماعيـة فـي بناء مجتمـع متناغـم.

تُظهـر لوحـاته مـن الثمانينيـات أيضـاً ارتباطاً عميقـاً بمفهـوم الانتمـاء، سـواءً كان ذلك تجاه الذات، أو البشـرية، أو العائلة، أو الطبيعة، أو الأرض؛ في العمـل الفني "انتمـاء" 1983م، يعـرض اليحيا رجـلاً نائمـاً بهـدوء في الصحـراء، وتمـزج الخطوط المتدفقة في اللوحة بين الكثبان الرملية والشخصية البشـرية، طامسـاً الحدود بين الاثنين، تلخص هذه

Abduljabbar Alyahya

(b. 1931, Iraq – d. 2014, Saudi Arabia)

Abduljabbar Alyahya was a self-taught painter who developed a fascination with the local environment. After studying engineering in Atlanta, Georgia, United States in 1951, he returned to Jeddah and immersed himself in various creative endeavors, designing Air Force logos and serving as the editor of the "Plastic Arts" section in *Al Madina* newspaper. He attended the London College of Printing in 1976 and was a founding member of the Colors of Riyadh group, a member of the GCC Art Friends Group, and was supported by the General Presidency of Youth Welfare.

Alyahya participated in over fifty local and global exhibitions, he is considered to be the first Saudi artist to exhibit internationally at the Forest Park Museum in St Louis, Missouri, United States (1951). Some of the artist's Saudi solo exhibitions were held at the American company Lockheed Martin, Riyadh (1972); Al Yamamah Hotel, Riyadh (1973); North Road, Riyadh (1972); Al-Wakeed Company, Riyadh (1971); and the French Embassy, Riyadh (1998); his last exhibition took place at Hewar Art Gallery, Riyadh (2009). Alyahya was also the first Saudi artist to have a solo exhibition organized by the Arts and Culture Society.

Alyahya published *Fifty Years of Painting* (1999) and translated *Color for the Artist* by Hans Schwarz (1968) into Arabic in 2003. His work is part of multiple private local and international collections.

Abduljabbar Alyahya navigates various artistic styles, including surrealism, cubism, and abstract art. Regardless of style, his exploration of humanity remains at the core of his artworks.

The Scream (1975) depicts an outer form with two hands trying to cling to what lies below. Surrounding this form are colored bars on both sides, emphasizing its confinement. Within the form, a womb or a human figure is portrayed, containing vibrant colored crystal shapes and someone playing the piano. At the bottom, something akin to a chart of sound vibrations of colors is seen, complementing the crystal worlds within. The form seems to break free from its constraints, morphing into colors and music.

In the later years of his career, Alyahya's artistic focus expanded to include the local environment, specifically drawing inspiration from the desert land-scapes. The portrayal of women emerged in many of his works, exploring the relationships between human beings and their surroundings. A culmination of this practice is seen through his painting *Building* (1983), where he employs a simplistic yet representational approach. The artwork depicts a collaboration between a man and a woman, with the female figure extending her arms to hand an object to the man, both dressed in casual, traditional attire. This simple gesture serves as a powerful symbol, challenging societal norms and highlighting the pivotal role of women while emphasizing the importance of collective efforts in constructing a harmonious society.

His paintings from the 1980s also demonstrate a deep connection to the notion of belonging, whether it be to oneself, humanity, family, nature, or the land. In *Belonging* (1983), Alyahya presents a man serenely slumbering in the desert. The flowing lines in the composition merge the sand dunes and the human figure, blurring the boundary between the two. This surrealistic piece epitomizes Alyahya's ability to intertwine his distinct style with themes of belonging and local culture, inviting viewers to contemplate the symbiotic relationship between humans and their natural surroundings. In *Untitled* (1987), the relationship between the Arab man and his heritage and surroundings are depicted through portions of color. The transparent figure, draped in a cloak, gazes over the Najd village, blurring the lines between his identity and the landscape, symbolizing his relationship with his legacy. Beneath him, a curled-up female figure perhaps represents being grounded within tradition, identity, and heritage.

القطعــة الســريالية قدرة اليحيــا علــى التداخل بين أســلوبه المتميــز وموضوعـات الانتمـاء والثقافـة المحلية، ويدعو المشـاهدين إلى التفكير في العلاقة التكافليـة بين البشـر ومحيطهـم الطبيعي.

تصور لوحته "بـدون عنـوان" 1987م العلاقة بين الإنسـان العربـي وتراثه الأصيـل، فتتضمن رجلاً بـرداء تراثـي في قريـة نجديـة، وفي الأسـفل يصوّر امـرأة منحنيـة ويبـدو أنهـا تمثـل العلاقـة بالتراث والهويـة والتاريخ.

Abduljabbar Alyahya

(b. 1931, Iraq – d. 2014, Saudi Arabia)

Belonging, 1983

Oil on canvas
76.5 × 101.5 cm
Courtesy of Hewar Art Gallery

عبـــد الجبّـــار اليحيـــــا

(ولد عام 1931م في العراق وتوفي عام 2014م في المملكة العربية السعودية)

انتماء، 1983

ألوان زيتية على قماش
76.5 × 101.5 سم
بإذن من حوار جاليري

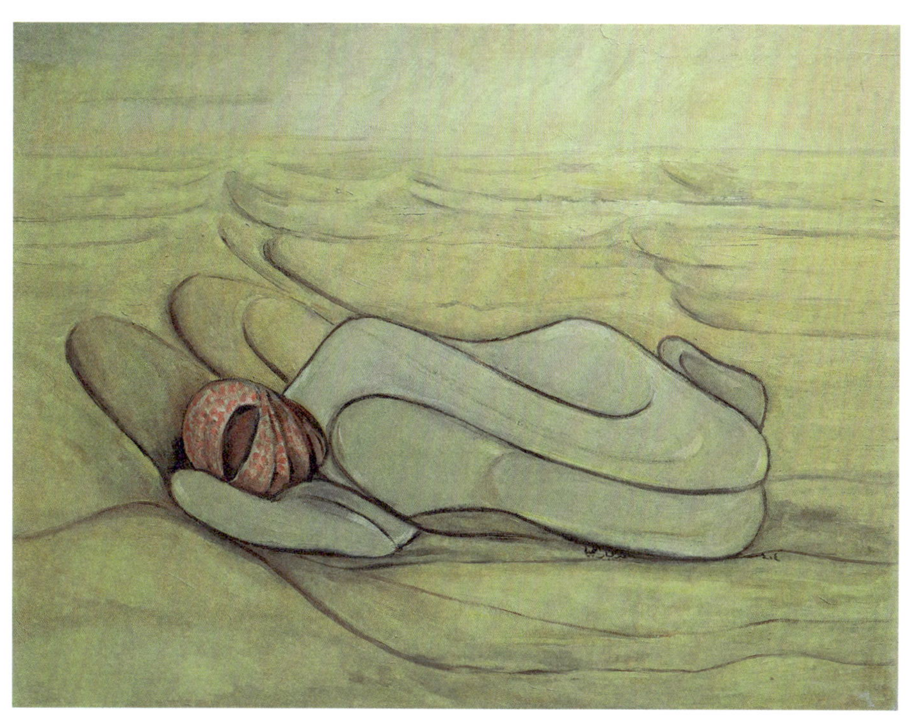

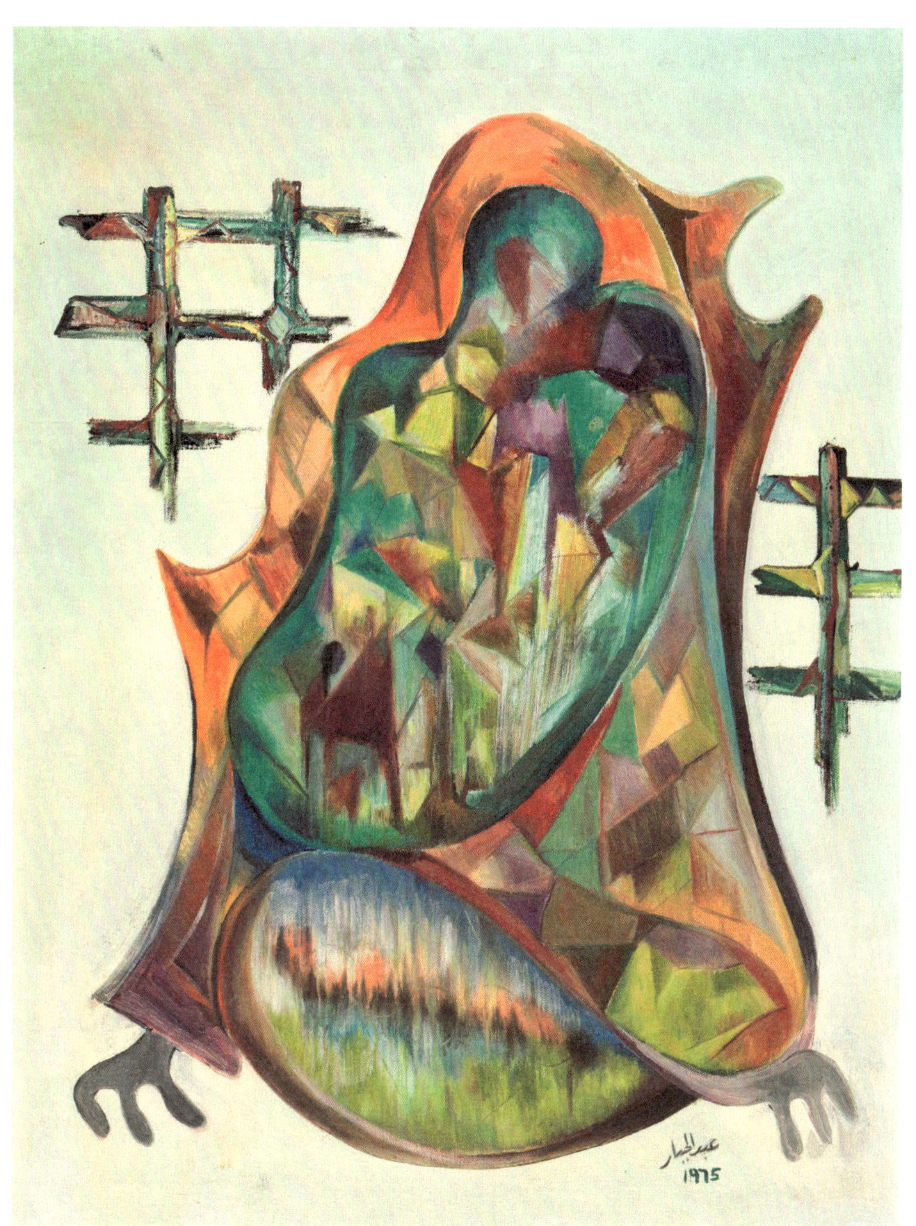
عبد الجبار
1975

Abduljabbar Alyahya

(b. 1931, Iraq – d. 2014, Saudi Arabia)

Building, 1983

Oil on canvas
122 × 90.5 cm
Courtesy of Hewar Art Gallery

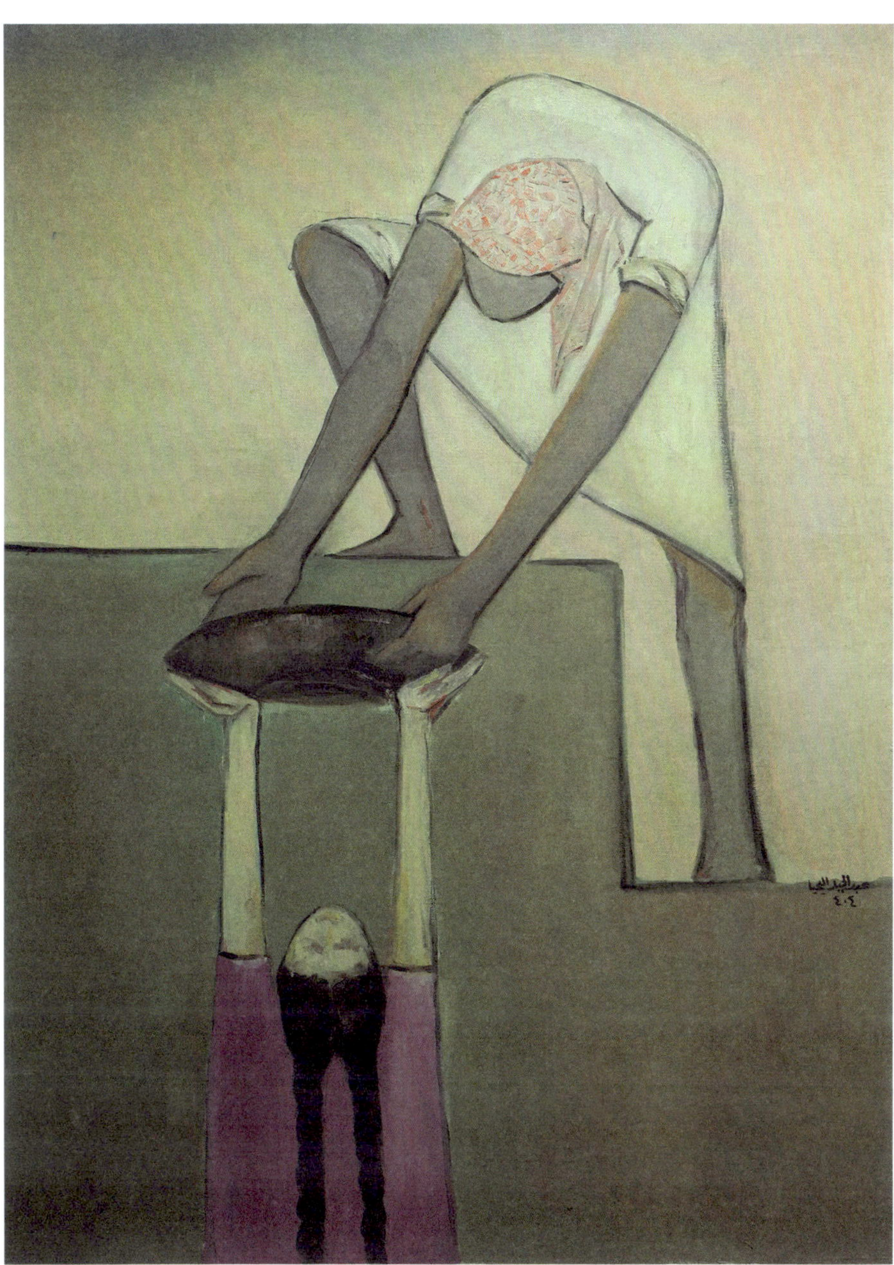

Abduljabbar Alyahya

(b. 1931, Iraq – d. 2014, Saudi Arabia)

Untitled, 1987

Oil on canvas
50 × 70 cm
Private Collection

عبــد الجبّــار اليحيـــــا

(ولد عام 1931م في العراق وتوفي عام 2014م
في المملكة العربية السعودية)

بدون عنوان، 1987

ألوان زيتية على قماش
50 × 70 سم
مجموعة خاصة

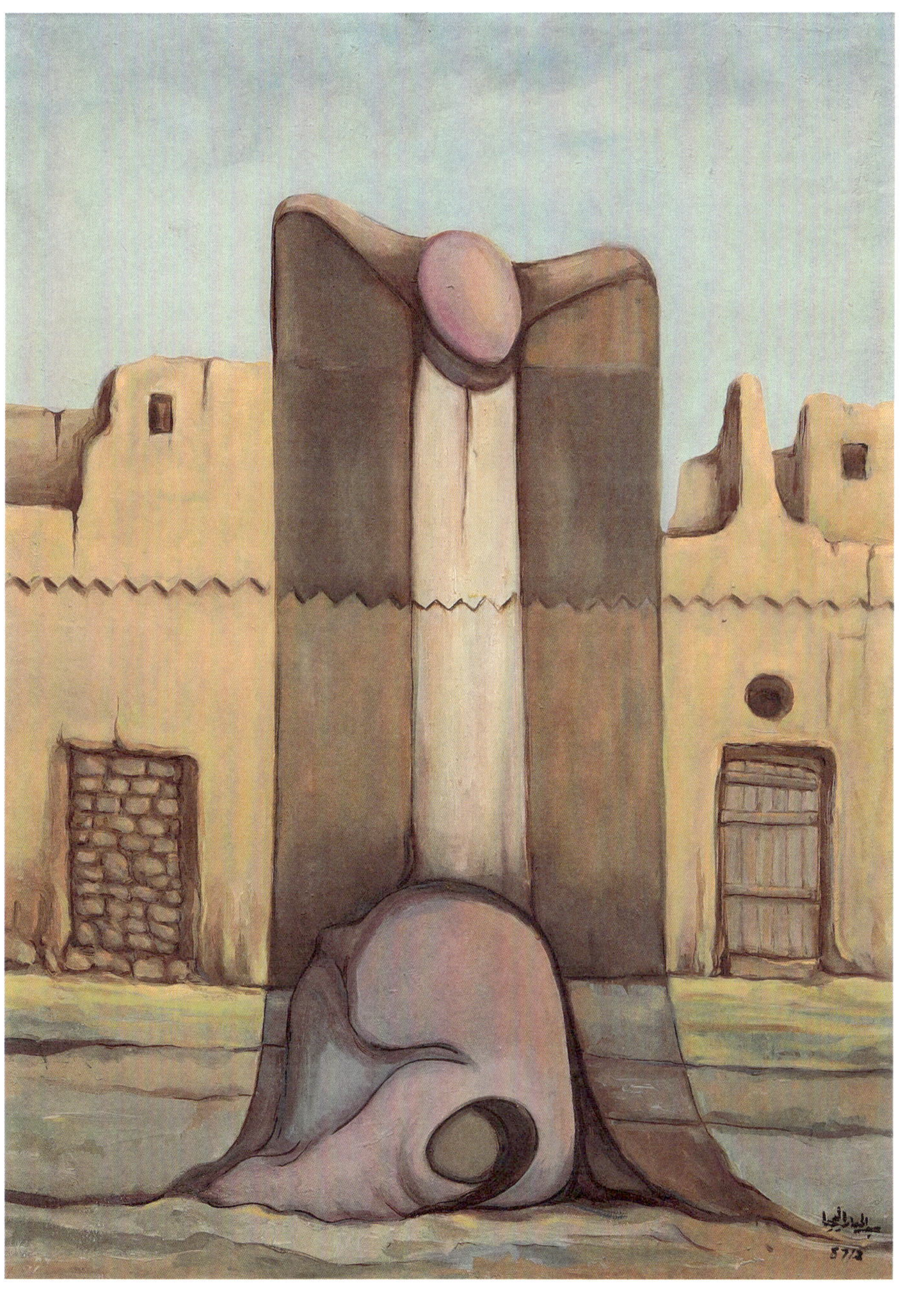

عبـد الحليــم رضــوي

(ولد عام 1939م، وتوفي عام 2006م، في المملكة العربية السعودية)

كان عبـد الحليـم رضـوي رسامـاً ومعلمـاً للتربية الفنيـة، وفي عـام 1964م حصل رضـوي على بعثة لأكاديميـة Accademia delle Belle Arti في رومـا بإيطاليـا، وبعدهـا حصـل على الدكتوراه من أكاديمية سـان فيرنانـدو الملكية للفنون في مدريد بإسبانيا في عام 1979م. وفي عام 1968م، أشرف ودرب رضـوي في مركز الفنـون الجميلـة في جدة حتى إغلاقه عام 1975م أنتج رضوي خلال مسـيرته الفنيـة 15 مجسـماً خارجيـاً في جدة.

من معارض رضوي الجماعية الأخيرة: معرض "أماكن" للمجلس الفني السـعودي فـي جدة ومن ثم نقل إلى مركز الملك عبدالعزيز الثقافي (إثراء) فـي الظهـران عـام 2022م، "معـرض مجموعـة متحـف، فهرس، جـزء 2" فـي المتحـف العربي للفـن الحديث في قطر عـام 2017م، معرض "البحر معلقـاً" في متحـف طهران للفن المعاصر فـي إيـران عـام 2016م، معرض "الطليعـة" فـي حافـظ جاليـري فـي المملكـة العربيـة السـعودية عـام 2014م، معـرض "ردّ الشـرق: نظـرة معمقة علـى الحداثـة فـي العالم العربي منـذ 1950 وحتى 1970" فـي مؤسسـة بارجيـل للفنون فـي الإمارات العربيـة المتحـدة عـام 2013م، كما شـارك رضوي فـي بينالي إسـبانيا عـام 1998م حيـث حصل على جائزة عن لوحته "يا قارئ القرآن"، ويُقال أن رضوي كان أول فنان سـعودي يُقيم معرضاً فرديـاً في جدة فـي عـام 1965م.

تم اقتناء الأعمال الفنية للفنان من قبل العديد من المتاحف، منها متحف الفن الحديث في إسبانيا، ومتحف الفن الحديث فـي البرازيل، ومتحف محمد السـادس للفـن الحديـث والمعاصـر فـي المغـرب، ومتحـف الفـن الحديث في تونس، والمتحـف العربي للفـن الحديـث في قطر.

على الرغـم من أن عبـد الحليم رضوي قضى الكثير من وقته في إسـبانيا، إلا أن ممارسـته الفنية تتميـز بلغة بصرية متجذرة فـي الثقافـة العربية، وتتفاعـل أعمالـه التـي غالبـاً ما تنقسـم إلى أقسـام، مع الحياة اليومية في المجتمعات السـعودية التي تعبر عـن الطاقـات البشـرية الفكرية والعاطفيـة، وغالبـاً ما تشـمل أعماله النسـاء، معبرة عن أدوارهن المتنوعـة، مثـل الأم أو القرويـة أو كرمـز للصمـود، ويرسـم رضوي بضربات الفرشـاة العريضة وأسـلوب ما بعد الانطباعية المرأة المزينة بالزي السـعودي التقليـدي والمجوهـرات فـي لوحـة "فتـاة عربية" 1975م، فالفستان المرسوم مشابه للطراز الأندلسي في إشـارة دقيقة إلى سنوات نشأته التي قضاها في مدريـد، حيث تأثر بشـدة بتراثها وثقافتهـا، والتأثير الأندلسـي حاضـر في أعمالـه الأخـرى لاسـيما تلك التي تشـمل العناصـر المعمارية.

تجسّـد التنـوع الفنـي فـي أعمالـه أثنـاء استكشـافه لنمط الطبيعـة الصامتة في "صورة زيتية مع سـمك" 1975م، اسـتخدم رضوي مزيجاً مـن الطـلاء والرمـل، نتـج عنه تصويـراً مسـطحاً لسـمكتين ضمن إطار هندسـي غير محكم الترتيب، يُظهـر هـذا الاستكشـاف للطبيعـة الصامتـة تحت المـاء انخـراط رضوي العميـق في بيئتـه، فهذه اللوحـة تحيـي أصـول نمط الطبيعـة الصامتـة، حيـث صُـورت الأسـماك في كثيـر مـن الأحيـان بالأسـلوب التقليـدي الذي يميـز تركيبـات الطبيعـة الصامتـة المبكـرة.

يقدم رضوي في لوحته "الأم" 1978م تصوّراً مميـزاً لعلاقتـه مـع والدتـه، حيـث تُظهـر اللوحة تباينـاً ملحوظـاً بين خلفيتهـا ومقدمتهـا، وتبرز في الخلفيـة ضربـات الفرشـاة المرئيـة بحـركات دائرية، بينمـا يعمـق رضوي في الجزء الأمامي مـن اللوحة

Abdulhalim Radwi

(b. 1939, Saudi Arabia – d. 2006, Saudi Arabia)

Abdulhalim Radwi was a painter and an art educator. Radwi received a scholarship to the Accademia delle Belle Arti, in Rome, Italy (1964) and he received a PhD from the Royal Academy of San Fernando in Madrid, Spain (1979). In 1968, Radwi directed and taught at The Center for Fine Arts in Jeddah, until it closed in 1975. Throughout his career, he had created fifteen monumental outdoor sculptures in Jeddah.

Radwi's recent group exhibitions include *Amakin*, by the Saudi Art Council in Jeddah, which traveled to King Abdulaziz Center for World Culture (Ithra), Dhahran (2022); *Mathaf Collection, Summary, Part 2*, Mathaf Arab Museum of Modern Art, Qatar (2017); *The Sea Suspended*, Tehran Museum of Contemporary Art, Iran (2016); *Al Taliaa*, Hafez Gallery, Saudi Arabia (2014); and *Re: ORIENT: Investigating Modernism in the Arab World 1950s – 70s*, Barjeel Art Foundation, the United Arab Emirates (2013). He also participated in the 1988 Biennale Arte in Spain, where he won a prize for his painting *Recitation of Qur'an*. It is speculated that in 1965 Radwi was the first Saudi artist to hold a solo exhibition in Jeddah.

The artist's artworks were acquired by the Museum of Modern Contemporary Art, Spain; Museum of Modern Art, Brazil; Mohamed VI Museum of Modern and Contemporary Art (MMVI), Morocco; Museum of Modern Art, Tunisia; Mathaf: Arab Museum of Modern Art, Qatar.

Although **Abdulhalim Radwi** spent a lot of his time in Spain, his artistic practice is characterized by a visual language rooted in Arab culture. Radwi's compositions, often divided into sections, interact with the daily life of Saudi societies expressing intellectual and emotional human energies. His oeuvre often encompasses women performing diverse roles such as mother, villager, or symbols of resilience. With broad brushstrokes and a post-impressionist style, Radwi paints the essence of an Arab woman adorned with traditional Saudi dress and jewelry in *An Arab Girl* (1975). The dress painted is similar to the Andalusian style, a subtle nod to Radwi's formative years spent in Madrid, where he was profoundly influenced by its heritage and culture. The Andalusian influence is also present in his other works, particularly those that encompass architectural elements.

Radwi's artistic versatility was exemplified as he explored the still-life genre. In *Still Life with Fish* (1975), Radwi employs a combination of paint and sand, resulting in a flattened portrayal of two fish within a loosely arranged geometric framework. This exploration of underwater realm reveals Radwi's deep engagement with his environment. *Still Life with Fish* pays homage to the origins of the still-life genre, as fish were frequently depicted in the traditional style that characterized early still-life compositions.

In *The Mother* (1978), Radwi offers a depiction of his relationship with his mother. The painting shows a contrast between the background and foreground. In the background, visible brushstrokes were created with circular motions, while, in the foreground, Radwi immerses the figure of his mother, emphasizing her significance through his dynamic style.

Untitled 11 (1982), showcases a fusion of landscape and human presence. The brushstrokes bring the landscape to life while incorporating figures within the composition. Inspired by the intricacies of Islamic architecture, the artist incorporates geometric patterns, intricate details, and symbolic, religious elements. These patterns are reminiscent of the architectural marvels found within the environment in Saudi Arabia. Notably, the monochromatic blue palette resonates with the hues associated with *Haj Day* (1987). Radwi often explores symbolic representations of Islamic motifs, in *Haj Day* the Kaaba is centrally positioned and encircled by a halo. Radwi merges perspective to highlight the Kaaba, intersecting mountains, and pilgrims, creating a sense of spiritual symbolism.

تصوير شخصية والدته، مُؤكداً على أهميتها وبروزها من خـلال أسـلوبه الدينامـي والمتجدد.

تعـرض لوحـة "بـدون عنـوان 11" 1982م اندماجـاً بين المناظـر الطبيعية والحضور البشـري، حيث تضفي ضربات الفرشـاة الحياة علـى المناظر الطبيعيـة مـع دمـج الأشـكال داخـل اللوحـة؛ كما يدمـج الفنـان أنماطـاً هندسـية وتفاصيـل معقدة وعناصـر دينيـة رمزيـة متأثـراً بتعقيـدات العمـارة الإسـلامية؛ هـذه الأنمـاط تعيـد إلـى الأذهـان العجائـب المعماريـة الموجـودة في بيئـة المملكة العربيـة السـعودية؛ يتناغم اللون الأزرق الأحادي مع الأشـكال في لوحـة "يـوم الحج" 1987م، ويستكشف رضـوي غالبـاً تمثيـلات رمزية للزخـارف الإسلامية، حيث توسـطت الكعبة لوحـة "يـوم الحج" محاطة بهالـة، ويدمج المنظور لتسـليط الضوء على الكعبة والجبـال المتقاطعـة والحجـاج ما يخلق إحساسـاً بالرمزيـة الروحية.

Abdulhalim Radwi

(b. 1939, Saudi Arabia – d. 2006, Saudi Arabia)

Untitled, 1969

Mixed media
48 × 80 cm
Private Collection

عبـد الحليـم رضـوي

(ولد عام 1939م في المملكة العربية السـعودية - وتوفي عام 2006م في المملكة العربية السعودية)

بدون عنوان، 1969

وسائط مختلفة
48 × 80 سم
مجموعة خاصة

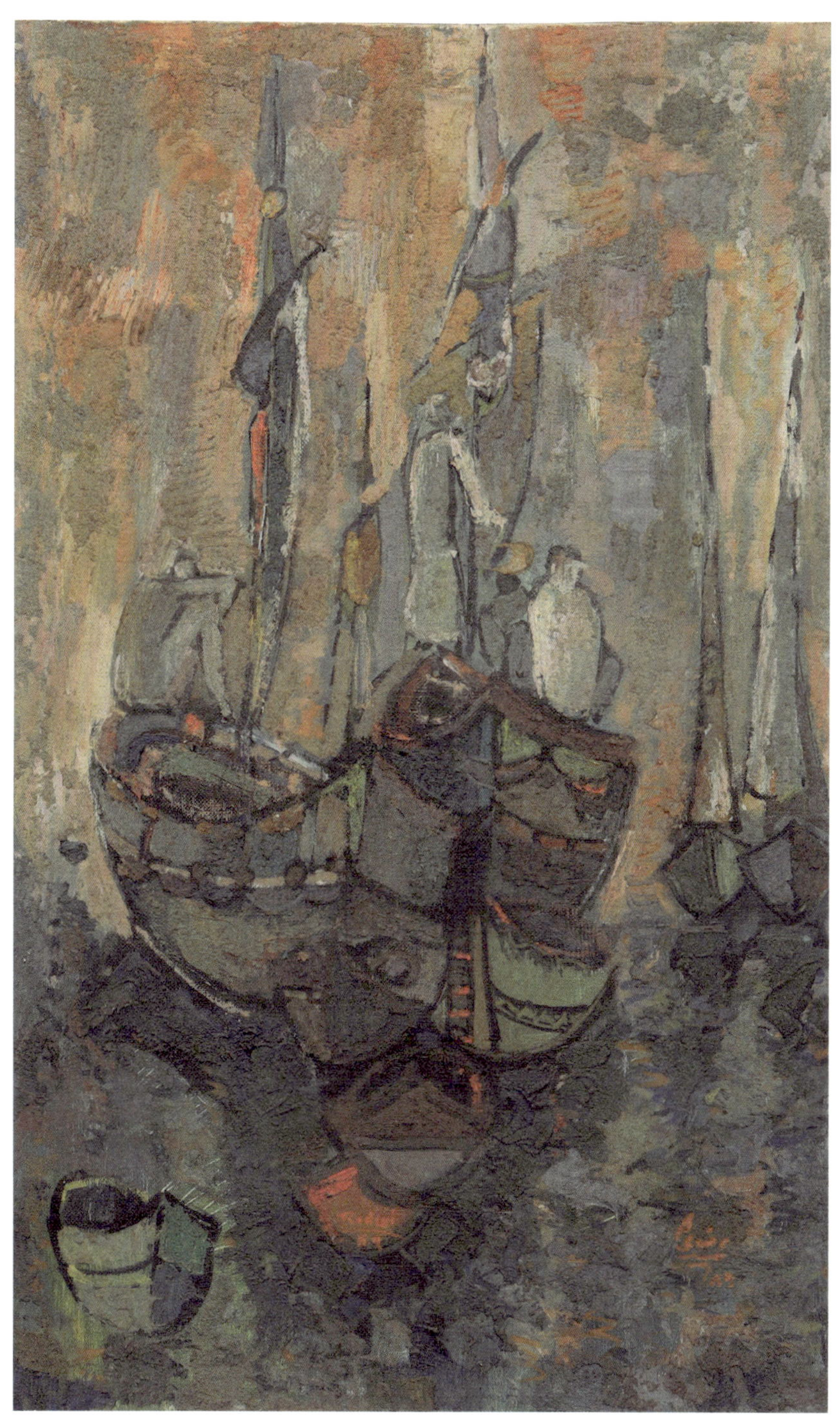

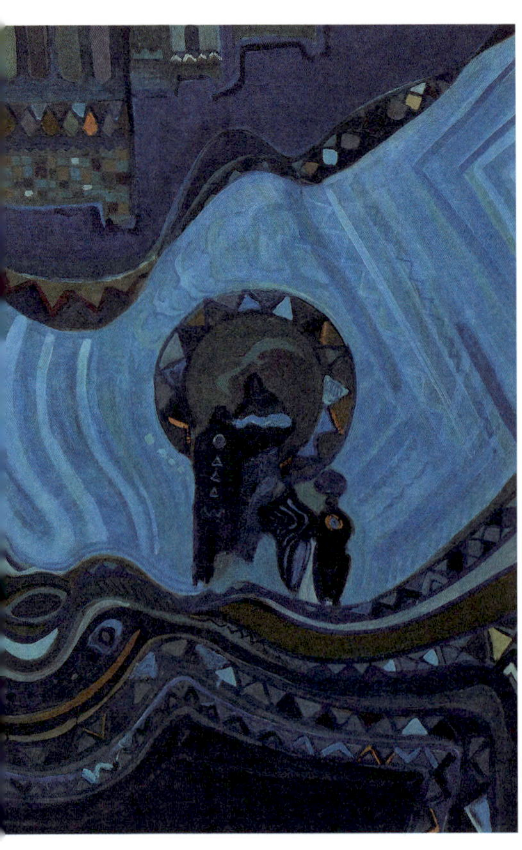

(ولد عام 1939م في المملكة العربية السعودية - وتوفي
عام 2006م في المملكة العربية السعودية)

بدون عنوان *11*، 1982

ألوان زيتية على قماش
100 × 200 سم
بإذن من حافظ جاليري

Abdulhalim Radwi

(b. 1939, Saudi Arabia – d. 2006, Saudi Arabia)

Untitled 11, 1982

Oil on canvas
100 × 200 cm
Courtesy of Hafez Gallery

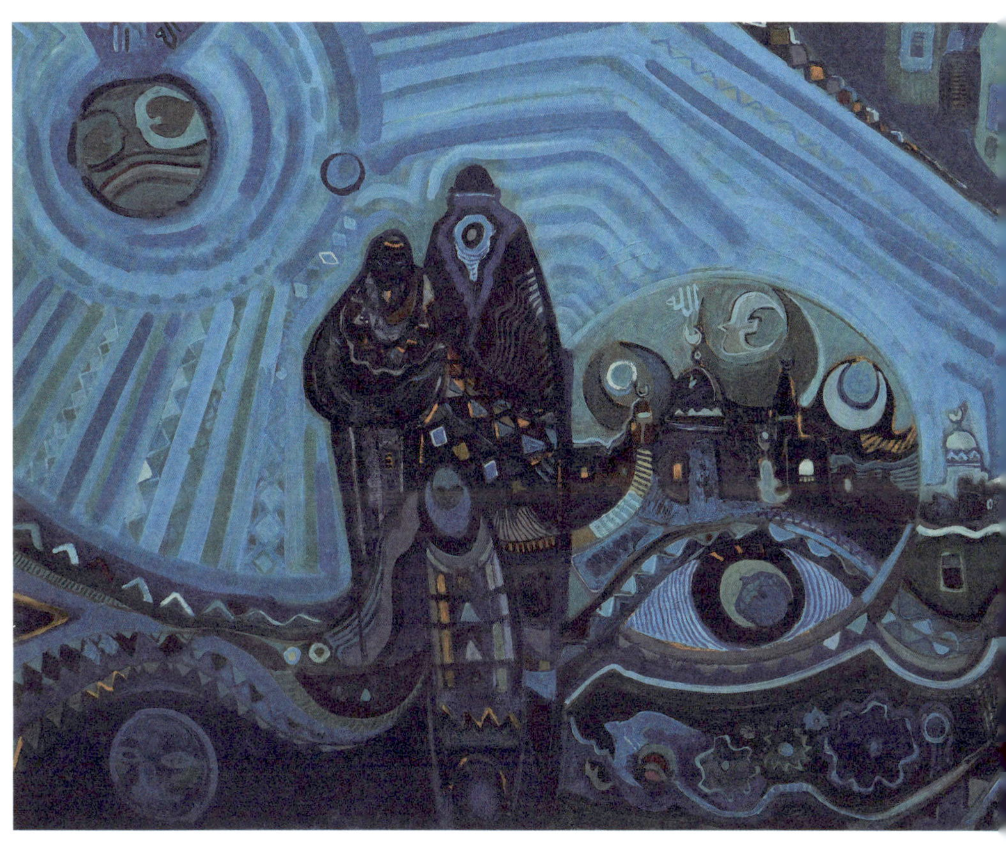

عبـــد الحليـــــــم رضـــــوي
(ولد عام 1939م في المملكة العربية السـعودية - وتوفي
عام 2006م في المملكة العربية السعودية)

يوم الحجّ، 1987

وسائط مختلفة على قماش
104 × 125 سم
بإذن مـن المتحف العربي للفن الحديث، الدوحة، قطر

Abdulhalim Radwi

(b. 1939, Saudi Arabia – d. 2006, Saudi Arabia)

Haj Day, 1987

Mixed media on canvas
104 × 125 cm
Courtesy of Mathaf: Arab Museum of Modern Art, Doha, Qatar

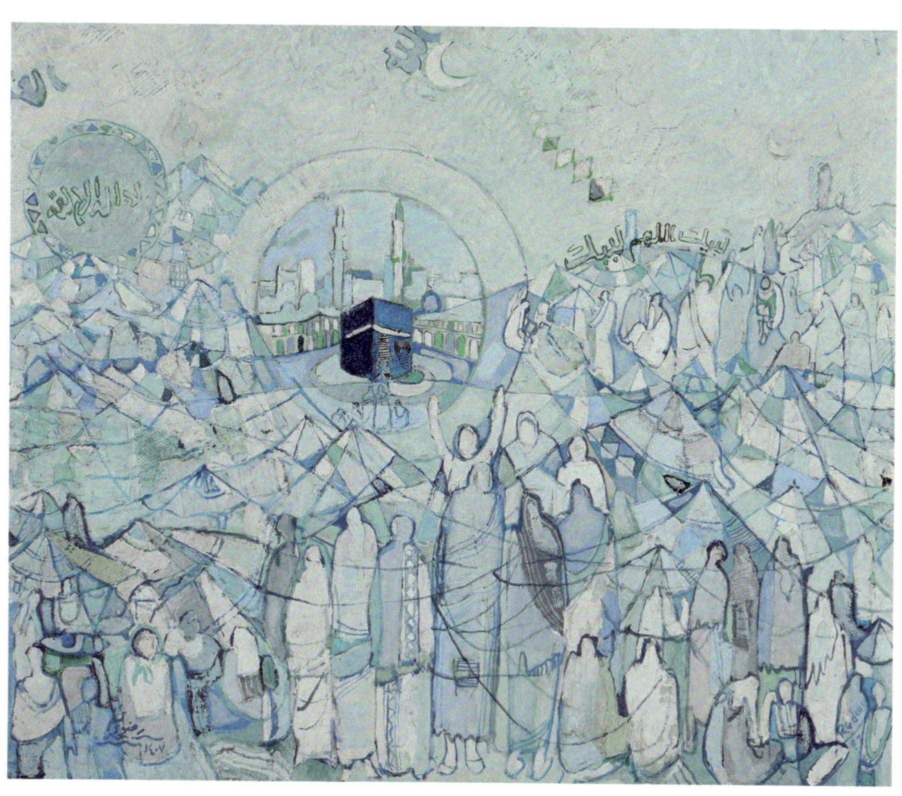

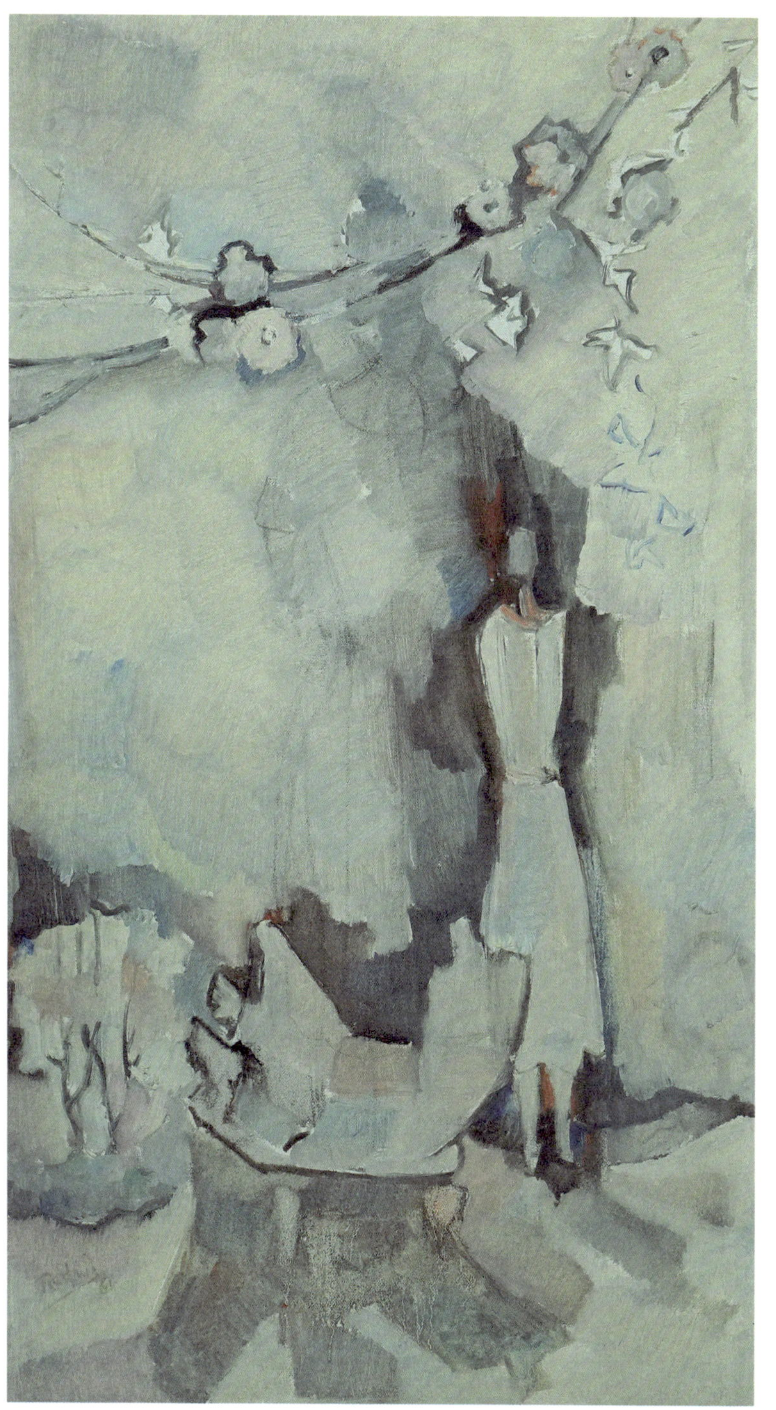

Abdulhalim Radwi

(b. 1939, Saudi Arabia – d. 2006, Saudi Arabia)

Still Life with Fish, 1975

Oil and sand on masonite
33 x 46 cm
Collection of Barjeel Art Foundation, Sharjah,
United Arab Emirates

عبـد الحليــــم رضــــوي
(ولد عام 1939م في المملكة العربية السـعودية - وتوفي
عام 2006م في المملكة العربية السعودية)

صورة زيتية مع سمك، 1975

ألوان زيتية ورمل على لوح ماسونيت
33 × 46 سم
مقتنيات مؤسسة بارجيل للفنون، الشارقة،
الإمارات العربية المتحدة

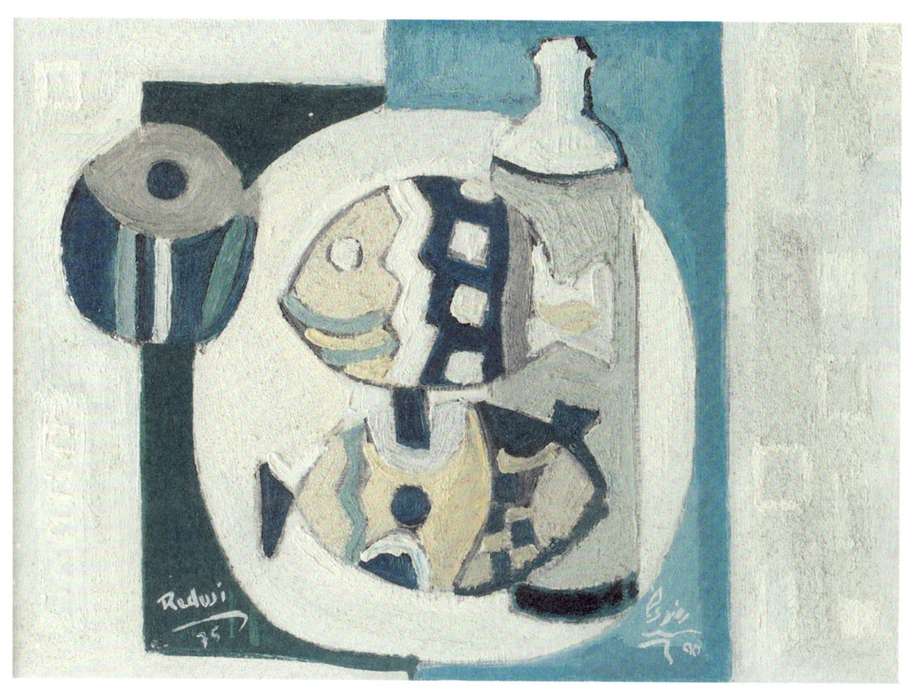

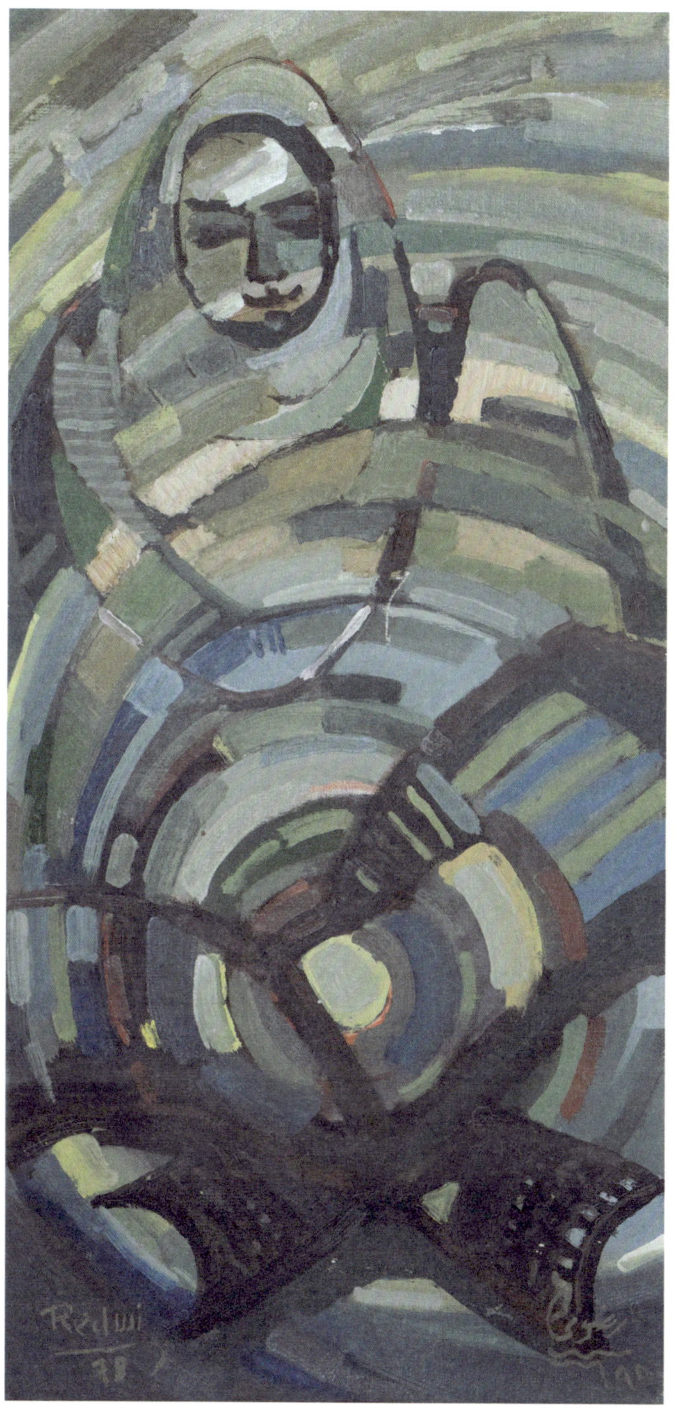

فتاة عربية، 1975

وسائط مختلفة على قماش
64 × 22.2 سم
بإذن مـن المتحف العربي للفن الحديث، الدوحة، قطر

عبــد الحليـــم رضــــوي

Abdulhalim Radwi

(b. 1939, Saudi Arabia – d. 2006, Saudi Arabia)

An Arab Girl, 1975

Mixed media on canvas
64 × 22.2 cm
Courtesy of Mathaf: Arab Museum of Modern Art, Doha, Qatar

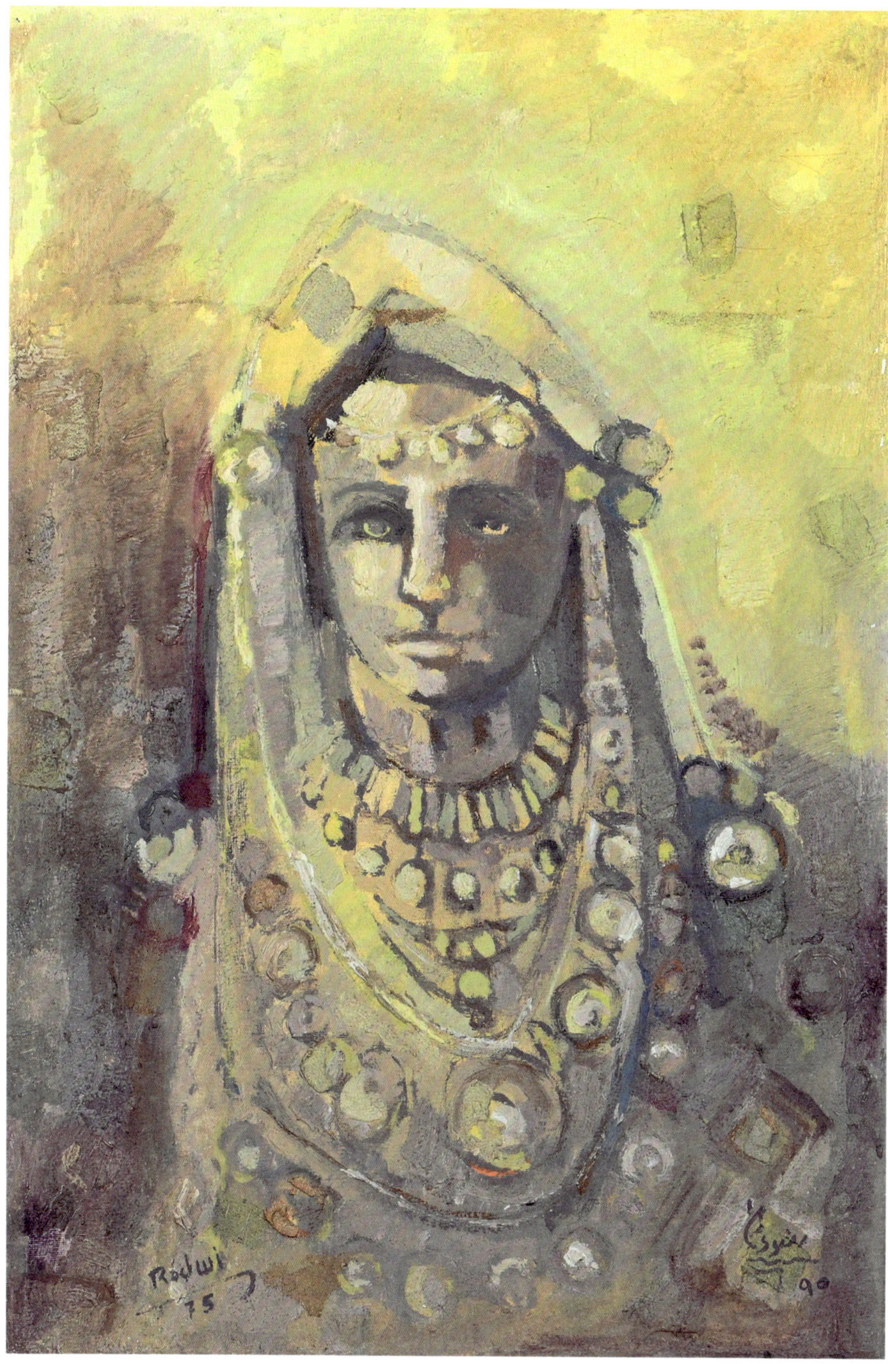

عبـد الحميـد البقـــشي

(ولد عام 1950م في المملكة العربية السعودية)

عبد الحميـد البقشي هـو رسـام اشـتهر بأعمالـه الفنية السـريالية، بدأ رحلته الفنية في معهد التربية الفنيـة بالريـاض، وتخرج بشـهادة الدبلـوم في عام 1974م، ثـم حصل على منحة دراسـية إلى الولايات المتحدة الأمريكية، حيث أكمل دراسـاته في جامعة كاليفورنيـا، إرفايـن، وحصل على درجة البكالوريوس فـي عـام 1985م، وبعد ذلـك عمل مدرسـاً للتربية الفنية في الأحسـاء قبـل أن يتفرغ تماماً للرسـم.

أثنـاء دراسـته فـي معهـد التربيـة الفنيـة، بدأ بالمشـاركة في المعـارض، حيث عرضـت أعماله في عدة معـارض نظّمتها الجمعية السـعودية للثقافة والفنون بالأحساء، وأبرز مشـاركاته كانت في معرض قاعـة محمد الصنـدل، بالمملكة العربية السـعودية عـام 2019م، و"معرض 23" فـي المملكة العربية السعودية عام 2018م، ومعرض "الماضي كمقدمة" في جدة بالمملكة العربية السـعودية عام 2014م، ومعرض "الأربعمائة" في المملكة العربية السعودية عام 2009م، ومعرض مؤسسـة العالـم الثالث في المملكـة المتحدة عام 1981م، ومعـارض متعددة نظمتها الرئاسـة العامة لرعاية الشباب، أقام العديد من المعـارض الشـخصية داخل المملكـة، ونظمت جمعيـة الفنـون والثقافة أول معرض شـخصي له في عام 1979م.

حاز الفنـان عبدالحميد البقشـي علـى العديد مـن الجوائـز خـلال مسـيرته المهنية، بمـا في ذلك مهرجـان الـروّاد العرب في الدوحة عام 2010م كما اقتنيت أعماله الفنية بشـكل خاص.

يتميـز عبد الحميـد البقشـي عـن غيـره مـن الفنانيـن بالعوالـم الخياليـة الحالمـة التي يعكسـها فـي أعماله؛ فقبـل أن يتعرف البقشـي علـى الحركة السـريالية، كان يرسـم مناظر طبيعيـة مـن وحـي خيالـه، فيدمـج فـي فنـه بيـن البيئـات المألوفة

والعناصر الخارجـة عـن المألوف ليقـدّم مناظر طبيعيـة تعكس أفكاره الداخليـة.

يعرض البقشـي في "عملة إسـلامية" 1987م. اتصالـه بالنصـوص الإسـلامية، ويتخطـى حـدود الأبعـاد الثنائيـة بأسـلوبه الخـاص وتبايـن الضـوء والظل لتظهر اللوحة وكأنها منقوشـة على النحاس أو الحجـر، وتمثّـل هـذه اللوحـة برهانـاً لديمومـة التـراث الثقافـي العربي والإسلامي.

Abdulhamid Albaqshi

Abdulhamid Albaqshi is a painter known for his surrealist style artworks. He began his artistic journey studying for a diploma at the Institute of Art Education in Riyadh, graduating in 1974. He then received a scholarship to the United States where he pursued further studies at the University of California, Irvine, completing his bachelor's degree in 1985. Afterward, Albaqshi worked as an art teacher in Al Ahsa before dedicating himself to painting.

While still a student at the Institute of Art Education, Albaqshi started participating in exhibitions. His works were showcased in multiple shows and exhibitions organized by the Saudi Association for Culture and Art in Al Ahsa. Notably, he took part in the Mohammed Al-Sandal Hall, Saudi Arabia (2019); *Exhibit 23*, Saudi Arabia (2018); *Past is Prologue*, Saudi Arabia (2014); *Al-Arba'ia*, Saudi Arabia (2009); *Third World Foundation Exhibition*, the United Kingdom (1981); and multiple exhibitions organized by the General Presidency of Youth Welfare. He held several solo exhibitions in Saudi Arabia, his first solo exhibition was organized by the Arts and Culture Society (1979).

Albaqshi's artworks have garnered recognition, and he has received multiple awards throughout his career, including the Festival of Arab Pioneers in Doha in 2010. His artworks are part of several private collections.

Abdulhamid Albaqshi delves into imaginative, dream-like realms through his paintings. While initially painting imaginary Western landscapes, Albaqshi's art began to resemble surreal formulations before discovering the surrealist movement. In his art, familiar environments intertwine with supernatural elements, creating mystifying landscapes that reflect his inner thoughts.

In *Islamic Currency* (1987), Albaqshi showcases his connection to Islamic texts. Through his signature style and a contrast of light and shadow, the artist transcends the two-dimensional surface and makes the work appear as though it is etched from bronze or rock. *Islamic Currency* serves as a testament to the enduring heritage of Arab and Islamic cultures.

Abdulhamid Albaqshi

(b. 1950, Saudi Arabia)

Islamic Currency, 1987

Acrylic on canvas
125 × 125 cm
Courtesy of the artist

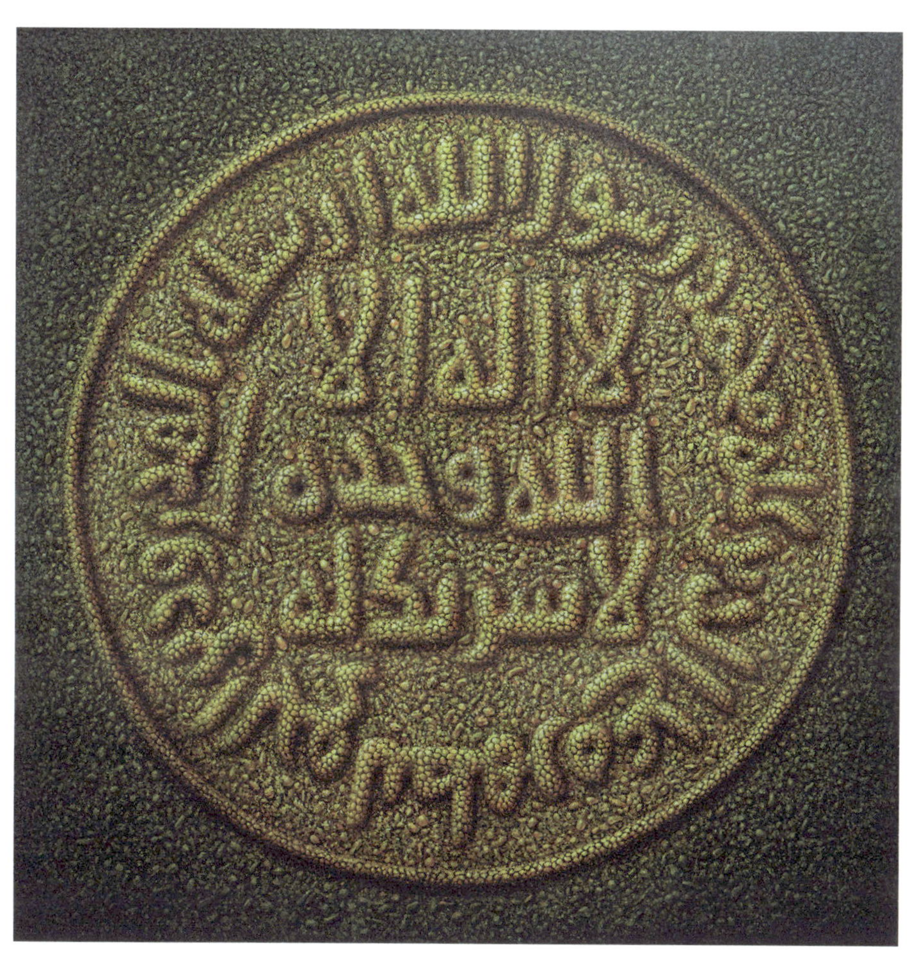

(ولد عام 1954م في المملكة العربية السعودية)

هو فنـان وكاتـب ومؤرخ فنـي، تعلّـم تعليمـاً ذاتيـاً واشـتهر بلوحاتـه التجريدية والهندسـية، تخرّج من كليـة المعلمين بالدمـام عـام 1991م في تخصص التربيـة الفنيـة، وعمل محـرراً بقسـم الفنون بجريدة اليـوم، وتـرأس قسـم الفنـون التشـكيلية بجمعيـة الثقافـة والفنون بالدمـام بيـن الأعـوام 1987-2000م، وشـغل منصـب رئيـس مجلـس إدارة الجمعيـة العربيـة السـعودية للثقافـة والفنون بين الأعـوام 2007-2012م وأسـهم في تأسـيس العديد مـن المبـادرات بما في ذلـك جماعة أصدقاء الفن التشـكيلي الخليجي وكان عضـواً نشـطاً في دار الفنون السـعودية.

شـارك في أكثـر من سـبعين معرضاً جماعيـاً في العـراق وسـوريا ولبنـان وتونـس والجزائـر والمغـرب وإسـبانيا وفرنسـا وألمانيـا وجمهوريـة الدومينيكان والولايـات المتحـدة الأمريكيـة والهنـد وبنغلاديـش، وإندونيسـيا، وتركيا، وروسـيا، كما شـارك في بينالي الشـارقة بدولـة الإمـارات العربيـة المتحـدة عـام 1997م، ومعـرض المملكة بيـن الأمـس واليوم وهو معـرض متنقـل بيـن عـدة دول كالولايـات المتحدة الأمريكيـة وفرنسـا وإنجلتـرا ومصـر بيـن الأعـوام 1983م-1992م، وأقـام أكثـر مـن عشـرة معارض فرديـة في فرنسا عام 2011م، والكويت عام 2004م، ومصر عام 2002م، والإمارات العربية المتحدة عام 1999م، والمغـرب عـام 1989م، والمملكة العربية السـعودية منذ عـام 1971م وغيرها.

حـاز السـليمان على العديـد من الجوائـز منها المركـز الأول في معارض الفن العام في السـعودية خـلال الأعـوام 1985م و1988م و1989م، وكتـب عـدة مقـالات في صحـف ومجـلات مثل الشـرق الأوسـط والبيـان والحيـاة والزمـان، ومـن مؤلفاتـه المنشـورة: "مسـيرة الفن التشـكيلي السـعودي" عـام 2000م، و"الفـن التشـكيلي السـعودي في

المنطقة الشرقية" 2018 و"تحولات الفن التشكيلي السعودي" عام 2021 و"عين على الفن في المملكة العربيـة السـعودية والوطـن العربي" عـام 2021م، وأصدر حول مسـيرته كتاب "عبد الرحمن السـليمان: لـون المكان.. عطر الذاكرة" عـام 2018م وفي نفس العام أصدر معهد مسك للفنون كتاب "عبد الرحمن السليمان إشارات ورموز" ضمن مبادرة (مكتبة الفن).

تعـد أعمـال السـليمان جـزءاً مـن العديد من المجموعـات الفنيـة مثل المتحف الوطني للثقافات في المكسـيك، والمتحـف الوطنـي الأردنـي للفنون الجميلـة فـي الأردن، وجمعيـة الثقافـة والفنون في المملكـة العربيـة السـعودية؛ ومكتبـة الملـك فهد الوطنيـة فـي المملكـة العربيـة السـعودية.

يسـتمد الفنان عبـد الرحمن السـليمان إلهامه من المناظر الريفية والعمرانية والصناعية بالمنطقة الشـرقية، حيـث يدمـج فـي أعمالـه بيـن الأسـاليب المختلفـة مثـل التكعيبيـة والواقعيـة والتجريـد والسـريالية أحيانـاً؛ طوّر في الثمانينات أسلوبه الفني الخـاص الذي يعكس الطابـع التاريخـي والتقليدي والاجتماعـي العربـي، وتمكّـن مـن خـلال أسـاليه المتنوعـة مـن تقديم أعمـال متناسـقة مـع التركيز على المنازل والأزقـة والمسـاجد والأسـواق والمزارع والاحتفـالات مـن طفولته.

في "البنايـة" 1977م، صـوّر السـليمان رجلين يرتديان الـزي التقليـدي ويحمـلان مـواد البنـاء، فاسـتخدم الأسـلوب التكعيبي لتحويلهمـا إلى زوايا تتقاطـع وتتداخـل، مجسـداً العمارة المحليـة في تداخـل بيـن العناصر المختلفة في اللوحة بشـكل يعكـس التعقيد الذي يحيط بمهنـة البناية والتاريخ المتعلـق بها.

يجسـد في سلسـلة لوحاتـه عـن المسـاجد العمـارة المحليـة فـي بيئتـه المحيطة باسـتخدام

Abdulrahman Alsoliman

(b. 1954, Saudi Arabia)

Abdulrahman Alsoliman is a self-taught artist, writer, and art critic known for his abstract and geometric paintings. Alsoliman graduated from the Teacher's College, Dammam in 1991, specializing in arts education. He worked as an editor of the fine arts section of the *Al Yaum* newspaper, headed the fine arts department at the Society for Culture and Arts, Dammam (1987–2000); and served as chairman of the Saudi Arabian Society for Culture and Arts (2007–2012). The artist co-founded several initiatives including the GCC Art Friends Group and was an active member of the Saudi Art House.

Alsoliman participated in over seventy group exhibitions held in Iraq, Syria, Lebanon, Tunisia, Algeria, Morocco, Spain, France, Germany, the Dominican Republic, the United States, India, Bangladesh, Indonesia, Turkey, and Russia. He participated in the 3rd Sharjah Biennale, the United Arab Emirates (1997); *Saudi Arabia Yesterday and Today*, traveling exhibition in the United States, France, the United Kingdom, and Egypt (1985–1992). He held more than ten solo exhibitions in France (2011); Kuwait (2004); Egypt (2002); the United Arab Emirates (1999); Morocco (1989); and Saudi Arabia since 1971 amongst others.

Alsoliman won many awards, including first place in the Saudi General Art Exhibitions in 1985, 1988, and 1989. He wrote articles for *Asharq Al-Awsat, Al-Hayat, Al-Bayan,* and *Zaman*; and published books: *The Journey of the Saudi Fine Arts Movement* (2000), *An Eye on Art in Saudi Arabia and the Arab World* (2018), *Saudi Fine Art in the Eastern Region* (2018), *Abdulrahman Alsoliman: The Color of Space and the*

Scent of Memory (2018), and *Transformations in Saudi Fine Arts* (2021). In 2021, Misk Art Institute published *Abdulrahman Alsoliman: Signs and Symbols* as part of The Art Library series.

Alsoliman's works are part of several collections including the Museo Nacional de las Culturas, Mexico; the Jordan National Gallery of Fine Arts, Jordan; the Association of Culture and Arts, Saudi Arabia; and the King Fahd National Library, Saudi Arabia.

Abdulrahman Alsoliman draws inspiration from various rural, urban, and industrial landscapes of the Eastern Province. His work navigates different styles including cubism, realism, abstract, and at times, surrealism. In his 1980s body of works, Alsoliman explores historical, traditional, and societal shifts in Saudi Arabia. Throughout his diverse styles, his subject matter stays constant and includes houses, alleys, mosques, markets, farms, and events from his childhood.

In *Builders* (1977), two builders within the environment are depicted wearing traditional attire as they carry construction materials. The artist employs a cubist style, characterized by the fragmentation of forms and the use of geometric shapes to transform the two builders into angular forms that intersect and overlap. This cubist approach highlights the physicality of the laborers and may suggest the complexity of their task and the layers of history that surround them.

In his series of mosques, Alsoliman illustrates his surrounding architecture and environment through cubist techniques which include *Early Transitions* (1980) and *Worshippers Leaving the Mosque* (1981).

In *Early Transitions*, Alsoliman observes the ruins, symbolizing the dawn of a transformative era and the gradual abandonment of old spaces. *Worshippers Leaving the Mosque* (1981) captures men leaving a mosque after Friday prayer. Through the geometric, abstract shapes and subtle colors, Alsoliman's use of light and shadow captures the groups' collective identity and the mosque's atmosphere. The choice of palette in both works may further hint at the Saudi environment, adding depth and contextual meaning to the artwork. Through this scene, Alsoliman highlights his personal memories within the sacred act.

In *Mosque Between Palms* (1983), Alsoliman's work takes on a different approach from his previous cubist style, embracing a more figurative approach. Inspired by the mosque's original location, he depicts the structure surrounded by palm trees. The dynamic brushwork in this painting sets it apart from his previous works, infusing the artwork with a sense of movement and life.

Abdulrahman Alsoliman

(b. 1954, Saudi Arabia)

Builders, 1977

Oil on canvas
60 × 80 cm
Private Collection

أسـلوب التكعيبية، وتشمل هذه الأعمال "التحولات المبكـرة" 1980م و"خروج المصلين من المسـجد" 1981م؛ يتعمـق السـليمان فـي لوحة "التحـولات المبكـرة" في الأنقاض مصوراً مطلـع تحول جديد وهجـر المسـاحات القديمـة تدريجياً.

تصوّر لوحـة "خـروج المصلين من المسـجد" 1981م رجالاً يغادرون المسجد بعد صلاة الجمعة؛ يعكس السـليمان الهوية الجمعيـة للمصلين والجو العام للمسـجد عبر اسـتخدام الأشـكال الهندسـية والتجريدية والألوان الدقيقة والضوء والظل، ويشير اسـتخدامه لدرجـات الألوان هـذه فـي كلا العملين إلى بيئة المملكة العربية السـعودية ما يضفي عمقاً وبعـداً سـياقياً للوحـات، ويخلّد جـزءاً مـن ذكرياته الشـخصية عبر هذه الطقوس المقدسـة.

يتبع السـليمان أسـلوباً فنياً آخر غيـر التكعيبي في لوحته "مسـجد تحفّه النخيـل" 1983م متبنياً الأسـلوب التصويري، فيصور البناء محاطاً بأشـجار النخيل مستلهماً ذلك من الموقع الأصلي للمسجد، وتتميز هذه اللوحة عن بقية لوحات السـليمان التي تتبع أسـلوب التكعيبية بضربات الفرشاة الديناميكية ما يضفي حسـاً بالحركة والحياة.

عبـــد الرحمـــن السليمـــان
(ولد عام 1954م في المملكة العربية السعودية)

البناية، 1977

ألوان زيتية على قماش
60 × 80 سم
مجموعة خاصة

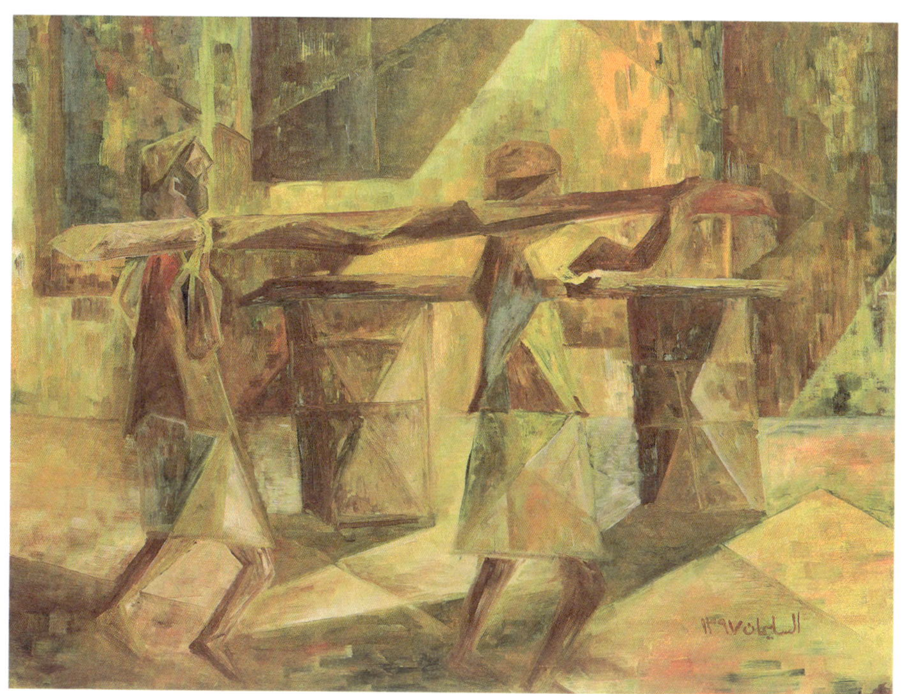

عبــد الرحمـــن السليمـــــان

(ولد عام 1954م في المملكة العربية السعودية)

خروج المصلين من المسجد، 1981

ألوان زيتية على قماش
76 × 101 سم
مقتنيات مؤسسة بارجيل للفنون، الشارقة،
الإمارات العربية المتحدة

Abdulrahman Alsoliman

(b. 1954, Saudi Arabia)

Worshippers Leaving the Mosque, 1981

Oil on canvas
76 × 101 cm
Collection of Barjeel Art Foundation, Sharjah,
United Arab Emirates

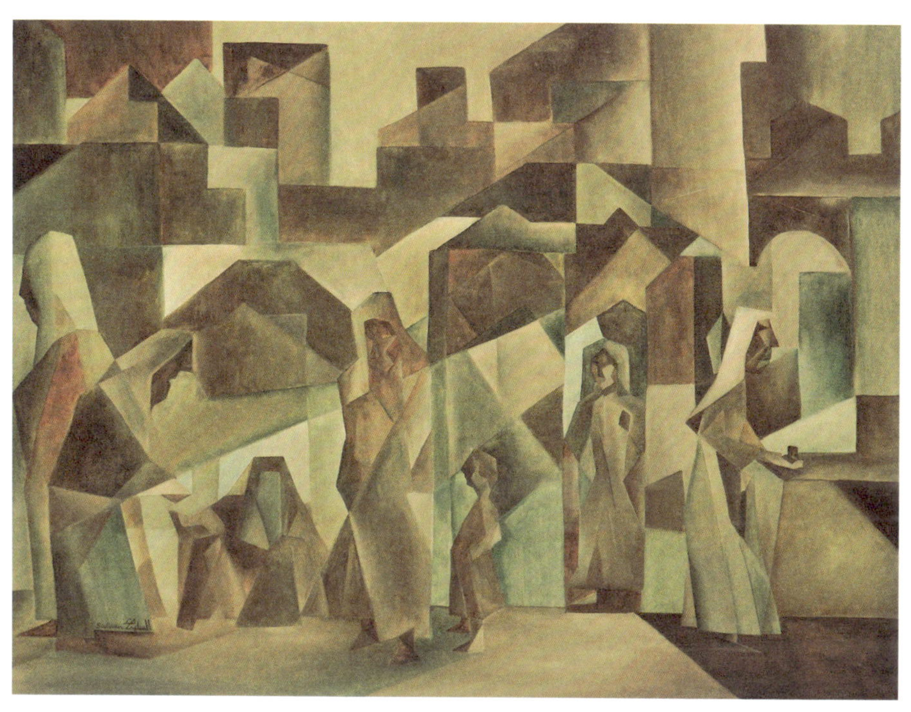

عبــــد الرحمـــن السليمـــــان

(ولد عام 1954م في المملكة العربية السعودية)

مسجد تحفّه النخيل، 1983

ألوان زيتية على قماش
90 × 120 سم
بإذن من الفنان

Abdulrahman Alsoliman

(b. 1954, Saudi Arabia)

Mosque Between Palms, 1983

Oil on canvas
90 × 120 cm
Courtesy of the artist

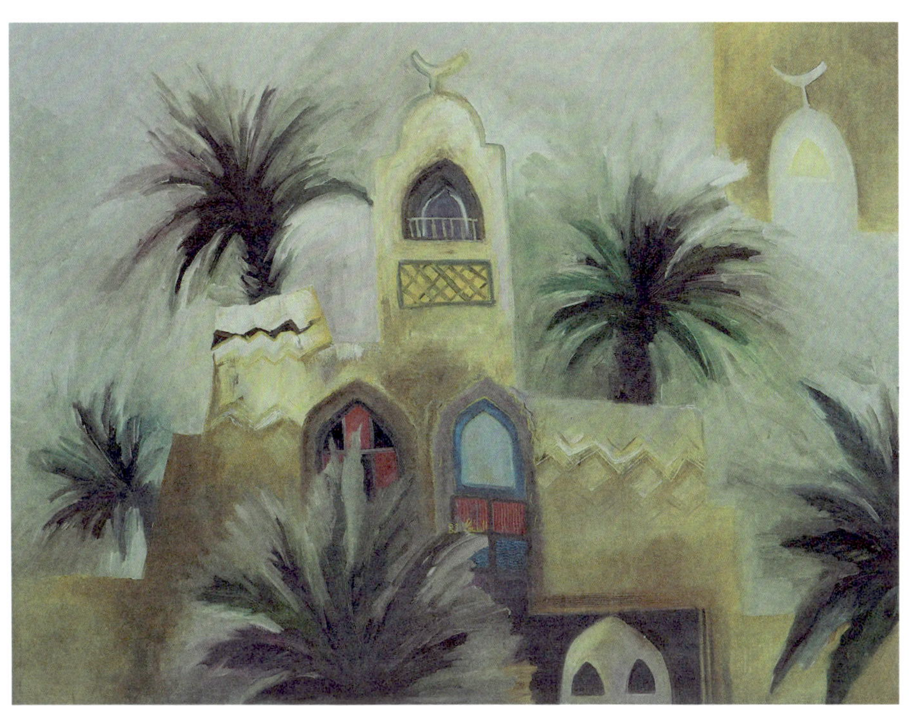

عبـــد الرحمـــن السليمـــــان

(ولد عام 1954م في المملكة العربية السعودية)

التحولات المبكرة، 1980

ألوان زيتية على قماش
56 × 76 سم
بإذن من الفنان

Abdulrahman Alsoliman

(b. 1954, Saudi Arabia)

Early Transitions, 1980

Oil on canvas
56 × 76 cm
Courtesy of the artist

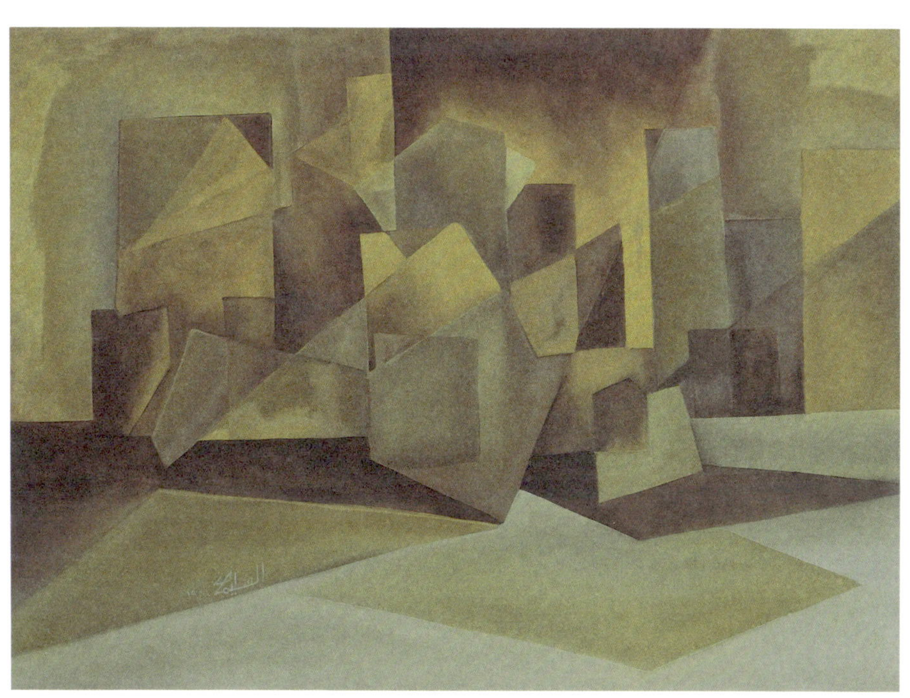

عبــد الســتار الموسى

(ولد عام 1955م في المملكة العربية السعودية)

عبدالستار الموسى فنان سعودي بدأ مسيرته الفنية في مرحلة مبكرة من عمره، دفعه الشغف بالفن للالتحـاق بأكاديمية موسكو للفنـون حيث حصل على درجتـي البكالوريـوس والماجسـتير من قسـم الجرافيك والتكوين عـام 1982م، بعد حصوله على الدرجـات العلمية انتقل إلـى أوكرانيا حيث أنتـج أول أعماله الجدارية.

شـارك خلال مسـيرته الفنيـة فـي العديد من المعـارض الجماعيـة المحليـة والدوليـة، وشـملت: معرض مبـادرة مسـتثمر المسـتقبل Future Investor Initiative فـي الريتـز كارلتـزون فـي الرياض بالمملكة العربية السـعودية عام 2018م، وحافظ جاليـري فـي جـدة بالمملكة العربيـة السعودية عام 2017م، ووزارة الخارجيـة بالمملكة العربيـة السـعودية عـام 2015م، وفي دونيتسك بأوكرانيـا عامـي 1985م و1992م، وماريوبـول بأوكرانيـا عامـي 1985م، 1992م، وفنانـي الاتحـاد السـوفييتي فـي موسـكو بروسـيا عـام 1986م، والفنانين الأوكرانيين في كييف بأوكرانيا في الأعوام 1985م و1987م و1988م، كما أقام معارض فردية فـي القطيـف بالمملكة العربيـة السـعودية عـام 2013م، وأبـو ظبي فـي الإمارات العربيـة المتحدة عام 1992م، وفولفـرات بألمانيا عام 1986م، وفي موسـكو في روسـيا عـام 1981م.

اقتنـت عـدة مؤسسـات عامـة وخاصـة حول العالـم أعماله ومـن أهمها متحف بوشـكن للفنون في روسـيا، وعدة متاحف في أوكرانيا مثل: متحف كييف ومتحف دونيتسـك ومتحف ماريوبول.

عبد السـتار الموسى هو فنـان متخصص في فنـون الطباعة، ونجح في صقـل مهاراته من خلال التعمق في أسـاليب الرسم السـاكن، حيث تعلم هذا الفـن وأتقنه فـي روسـيا؛ وتعكس أعماله المشـاهد الاجتماعيـة المتصلة بالحيـاة اليوميـة مـن خـلال تصوير المناسـبات والطقوس المحليـة في المملكة العربيـة السـعودية، ويظهر فـي أعمـال الموسـى اللونين الأبيض والأسـود ليعكس براعته في التلاعب بالضـوء والظـل باسـتخدام القلم وتقنيـات النحت علـى الكرتون.

"بحـارة 5/5 " 1987م و"بحار 5/4" 1987م همـا جـزء مـن سلسـلة مـن الأعمـال الفنيـة التـي اسـتوحاها الموسـى مـن جـده الـذي امتهـن صيد اللؤلـؤ طـوال حياتـه، ففـي العمل الأول يصور الموسـى رجليـن على قـارب وهما على وشـك رمي شـبكتهما لاصطيـاد اللؤلـؤ، أمـا فـي العمل الثاني فيصور صيَّاداً يهم بإلقاء شبكته على الأرض؛ يعكس كلا العمليـن الأزيـاء التقليدية وتراث صيد الأسـماك.

وتصوِّر لوحة "عرس فـي الرفاع 4/3" 1986م الأعـراف المتبعـة في طلب يـد الفتاة حيث يظهر أبـوان يتناقشـان إمكانيـة تزويـج ابنيهمـا، ويُظهـر العمـل الرجليـن وهمـا يجلسـان علـى الأرض بالزي التقليـدي ويخوضـان في نقـاش عميـق، والبارز في هـذا العمل أن الموسـى أضاف الكثير مـن التفاصيل مثل الفواكـه التي تكون فـي المناسـبات، والنقوش على السـجاد ليضفي عمقـاً وثراءً علـى العمل.

Abdulsattar Almussa

(b. 1955, Saudi Arabia)

Abdulsattar Almussa is a painter who embarked on his artistic journey at an early age. His passion for art led him to study at the Moscow Academy of Fine Arts in Russia, where he obtained both a BA and an MFA in graphics and composition in 1982. After his studies, Almussa moved to Ukraine where he produced his first wall art.

Over the course of his career, Almussa participated in a wide range of exhibitions on both local and international stages. Group exhibitions include *Future Investor Initiative Exhibition*, Ritz Carlton, Riyadh, Saudi Arabia (2018); Hafez Gallery, Saudi Arabia (2017); Ministry of Foreign Affairs, Saudi Arabia (2015); Donetsk, Ukraine (1985, 1992); Mariupol, Ukraine (1985, 1992); *Soviet Union Artists*, Moscow, Russia (1986); and *Ukrainian Artists*, Kiev, Ukraine (1985, 1987, 1988). His solo exhibitions were held in Al-Qatif, Saudi Arabia (2013); Abu Dhabi, the United Arab Emirates (1992); Fulfrate, Germany (1986); and Moscow, Russia (1981).

His works have been collected by institutions and private collectors worldwide. Notably, his artworks can be found in the Pushkin Museum of Fine Arts, Russia; Kiev Museum, Ukraine; the Donetsk Museum, Ukraine; and the Mariupol Museum, Ukraine.

Abdulsattar Almussa honed his skills by exploring techniques in printmaking and still-life drawings during his studies in Russia. Almussa's works primarily revolve around social scenes connected to daily life, depicting customary occasions, and rituals in Saudi Arabia. His black and white graphic works exhibit a play of light and shadow achieved through pen and cardboard carving techniques.

Fishermen 5/5 (1987) and *Fisherman 4/5* (1987) are part of the artist's Fishermen series inspired by Almussa's grandfather's pearl-fishing background. In one scene, he portrays two men on a boat with a net, ready to embark on a pearl-fishing venture, while the other scene captures a man preparing the net on the floor. Both artworks feature traditional clothing, reflecting the heritage of the fishing trade.

In *Wedding in Alriffa' 3/4* (1986), Almussa portrays a customary ritual of a father approaching another man to discuss the possibility of arranging their children's marriage. The artwork depicts the two men sitting on the floor in traditional attire, deep in conversation. Almussa adds details such as fruits, commonly seen in gatherings, and patterns from a traditional carpet, conveying a sense of depth and richness.

Abdulsattar Almussa

(b.1955, Saudi Arabia)

Wedding in Alriffa 3/4, 1986

Relief print
70 × 63 cm
Courtesy of the artist

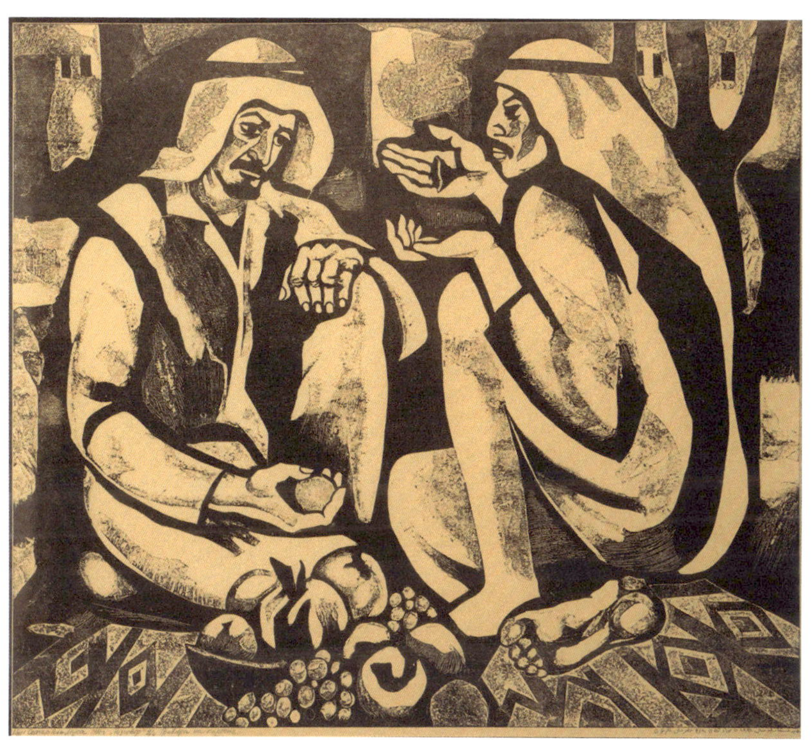

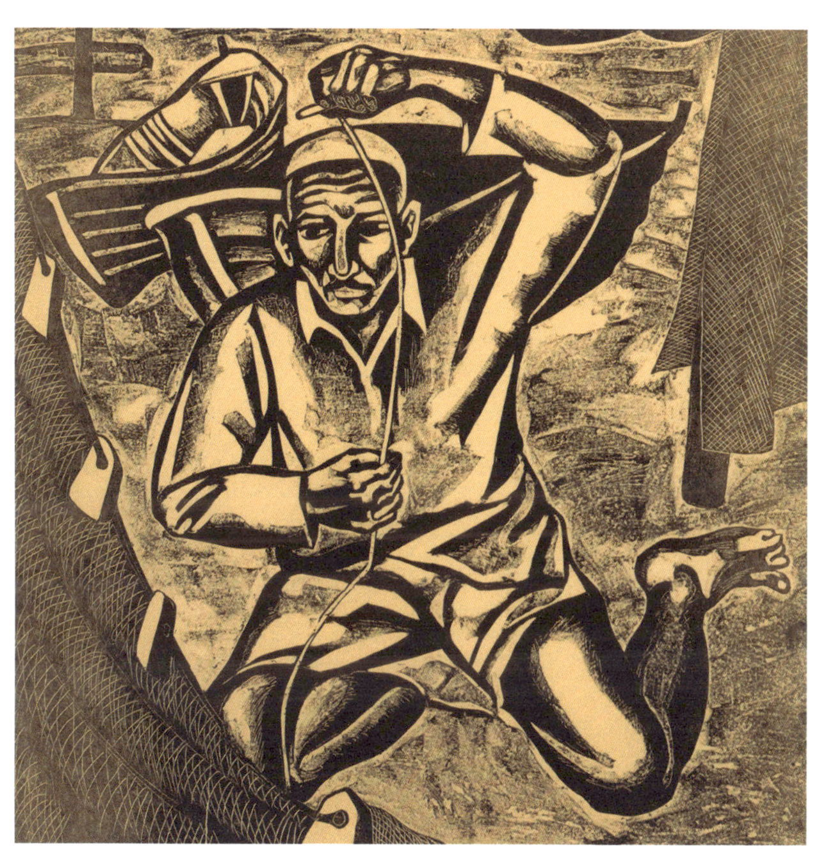

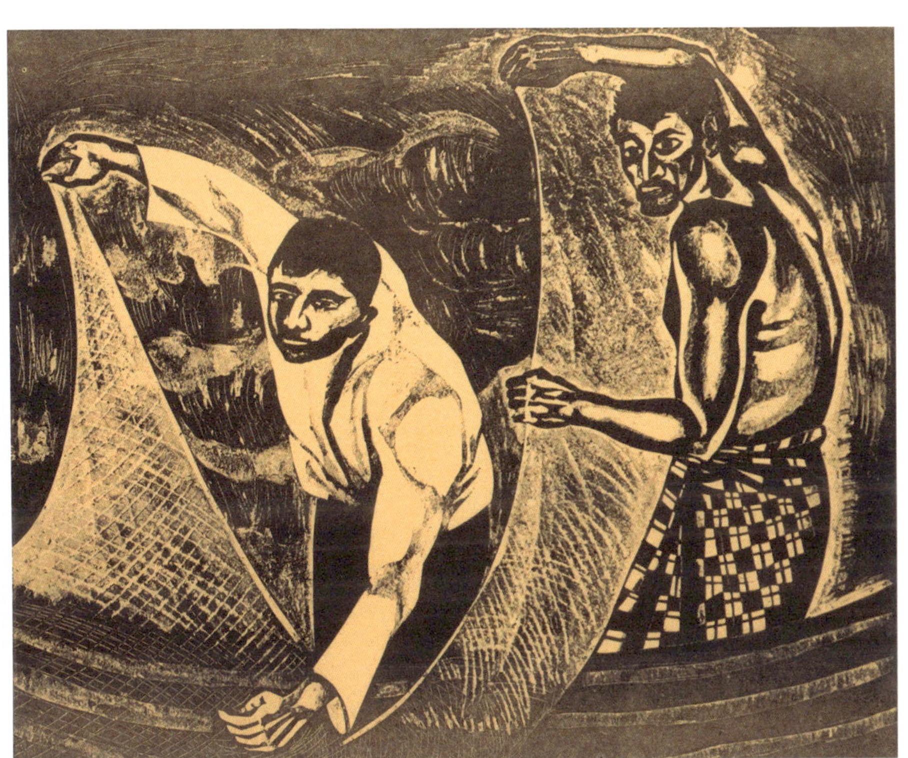

عبــد العزيــز الحمّـــاد

(ولد عام 1946م في المملكة العربية السعودية وتوفي عام 2010م في الولايات المتحدة الأمريكية)

كان للفنان عبد العزيز الحمّاد دورٌ في المشهد الفني السعودي، في عام 1966م، بدأ بالدراسة في معهد التربيــة الفنيـة بالريـاض، وتخـرّج في عـام 1968م ليصبـح معلماً، ومن ثـم حصل على منحة دراسـية مـن وزارة المعـارف (وزارة التعليـم حاليـاً) لإكمـال درجة البكالوريوس في الولايـات المتحدة الأمريكية.

وفـي عـام 1969م عُـدّ مـن أوائـل الفنانيـن السـعوديين الذيـن أقامـوا معـارض فرديـةً فـي المملكة، حيـث أقام معرضاً فرديـاً فـي فنـدق مطـار الظهران، قـدم فيه 35 لوحـة جديدة لاقت استحسـاناً واسـعاً، وشـارك فـي معـارض جماعية مطلع سـبعينيات القرن الماضي مع نخبة من رواد الفـن السـعودي مـن بينهـم: صفيـة بن زقـر وعبد الحليـم رضـوي ومنيـرة موصلـي ومحمـد السـليم.

تتمحور رؤيـة عبد العزيز الحمّـاد الفنية حول تصويـر مجموعة متنوعـة من المناظر فـي المملكة العربيـة السـعودية، وتوضـح أعمالـه غالبـاً الحيـاة الصحراويـة والعامليـن والأحـداث اليوميـة التـي تعكـس مـدى تقديـره وشـغفه بالعناصـر الثقافيـة والبيئيـة لمنطقته.

تصـوّر لوحـة الحمّاد "بدون عنـوان" 1974م خيمة صحراويـة تقليدية محاطة بسـياج من نفس القمـاش لتضفي مزيـداً مـن الخصوصيـة، وتمثـل الخيمـة الصحراويـة أهميـة كبيـرة للكثير مـن البدو فهي بالنسـبة لهم السـكن والمأمن وسط الصحراء؛ يسـتخدم الحمّـاد ألوانـاً دافئـة ودرجـات مختلفة من اللـون البني ليعكس البيئة الصحراويـة والرمال وأشـعة الشـمس والخيمـة، ويدمج داخـل الخيمة خطوطاً باللونين الأحمـر والأزرق.

Abdulaziz Alhammad

(b. 1946, Saudi Arabia – d. 2010,
the United States)

Abdulaziz Alhammad was a painter who played a noteworthy role in the Saudi art scene. In 1966, the artist enrolled in the Institute of Art Education in Riyadh and upon completion of his studies in 1968, he began working as a teacher. Alhammad received a scholarship from the Ministry of Education to pursue a bachelor's degree in the United States.

In 1969, the artist was one of the earliest Saudi artists to hold a solo exhibition in Saudi Arabia. He held a solo exhibition at the Dhahran Airport Hotel, where he presented thirty-five new paintings that received positive reviews. Alhammad participated in group exhibitions in the early seventies alongside pioneering artists Safeya Binzagr, Abdulhalim Radwi, Mounirah Mosley, and Mohammed Alsaleem.

Abdulaziz Alhammad's general practice revolves around depicting various landscapes within Saudi Arabia. Alhammad's artworks often illustrate desert life, workers, and everyday scenarios, showcasing an appreciation for the cultural and environmental aspects of the region.

In his painting *Untitled* (1974), Alhammad portrays a traditional desert tent, surrounded by a fence made of the same fabric as the tent itself, providing an added layer of intimacy. This tent holds great significance as it serves as the home for many Bedouin people in the desert. Alhammad employs warm tones, ranging from various shades of brown, to depict the desert environment, the sand, the radiant sun, and the tent itself. Additionally, he incorporates red and blue stripes to depict the interior of the tent.

عبـــد العزيـــز الحمّــــاد
(ولد عام 1946م في المملكة العربية السـعودية وتوفي عام 2010م في الولايات المتحدة الأمريكية)

بدون عنوان، 1974

ألوان أكريليك على قماش
40 × 60 سم
بإذن من صالة تجريد للفنون

Abdulaziz Alhammad
(b. 1946, Saudi Arabia – d. 2010,
the United States)

Untitled, 1974

Acrylic on canvas
40 × 60 cm
Courtesy of Abstract Art Gallery

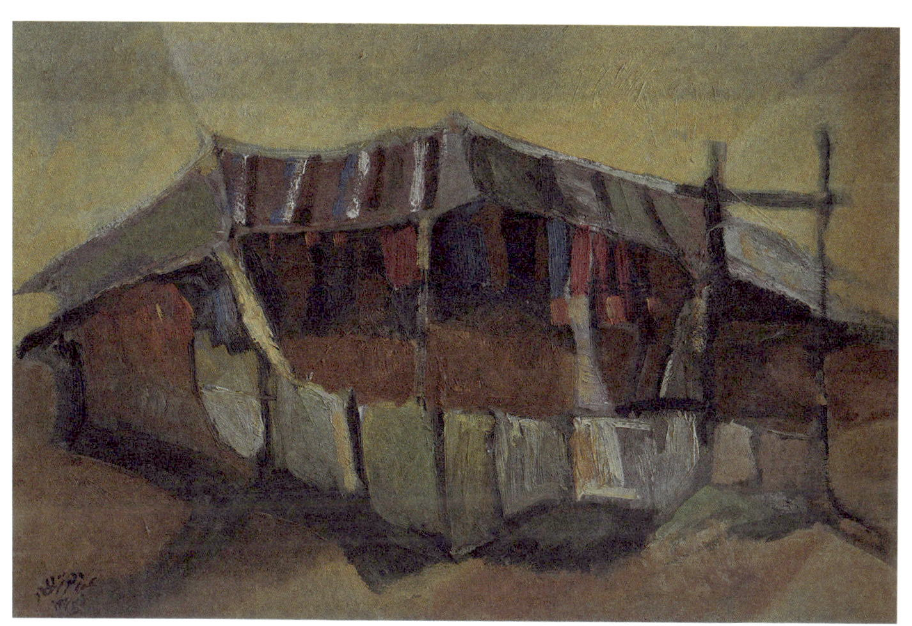

عبــد الله الشــــلتي

(ولد عام 1952م في المملكة العربية السعودية)

يعد عبـد الله الشـلتي فنانـاً تشـكيلياً ومصوراً فوتوغرافيـاً، أكمل تعليمـه العام في أبهـا ثم انتقل إلى الريـاض ليحصل على درجـة الدبلوم في الفنون من معهد التربية الفنية عام 1973م، وبدأ مسـيرته العمليـة في الفن مشـرفاً للتربية الفنية في عسـير.

خلال مسـيرته الفنيـة، عرض أعمالـه في عدة معـارض في السـعودية والجزائر والإمـارات العربية المتحـدة وعمـان ومصر، ومـن ضمنهـا مـا نظمته الرئاسـة العامة لرعاية الشـباب في المملكة العربية السـعودية عامـي 1974م و1975م، والجمعيـة العربيـة السـعودية للثقافـة والفنـون فـي المملكة العربية السعودية عام 1975م، وقرية المفتاحة في المملكة العربية السـعودية عـام 2001م، كما أقام عدة معـارض فرديـة في الريـاض وجدة.

شـارك فـي مسـابقة نظمتهـا الخطـوط السـعودية وحصل على المركز الثالـث وحصل على العديـد مـن الجوائـز المحليـة منهـا: المركـز الأول بجائـزة المفتاحـة والمركـز الأول بجائـزة السـفير بنسـختها الثانيـة والمركـز الثالث في جائزة السـفير بنسـختها الرابعـة، وحصـل علـى المركـز الأول فـي المـزاد العلنـي بمتحـف نصيـف بجـدة فـي عـام 2001م، وكرّمه صاحب السـمو الملكـي الأمير خالد ابـن فيصل آل سـعود كأحـد رواد الفن السـعودي.

يتميـز عبـد اللـه الشـلتي بأنـه فنـان ومصور يحمـل ارتباطـاً عميقاً بمحيطـه، ويستكشـف غالباً بيئته المباشـرة في منطقة عسـير، وعلـى الرغم من صعوبة توفّر كافـة الإمكانـات الفنية هنـاك؛ إلا أن شـغفه الكبيـر بالفن قـاده إلى تقديم أعمال فنية مميزة باسـتخدام المـواد الطبيعيـة المتوفرة مثل زيت السـيارات كبديل للألـوان الزيتية.

تجسّـد لوحة "الميفا" 1985م أسلوب الشلتي الفني المتمثل في ضربات الفرشـاة الحيوية وتصوير

النسـاء وهـن يمارسـن أنشـطة الطبخ المحليـة، ويسـتخدم فـرن التنـور الطينـي لخبـز الميفـا فـي الحقـول الزراعية ليسـلط الضـوء على الـدور المهم الذي تؤديه المرأة في الطبيعة؛ ومن خلال "الميفا"، يمجّـد بذلك العلاقة الوطيدة بين الإنسان والأرض، وتعد هـذه اللوحة تقديـراً للتقاليد بمنطقة عسـير.

Abdullah Alshalti

(b. 1952, Saudi Arabia)

Abdullah Alshalti is a painter and photographer. He completed his primary school education in Abha before moving to Riyadh to obtain a diploma in fine arts from the Institute of Art Education in 1973. Alshalti began his art career as an arts education supervisor in Asir.

Throughout his career, Alshalti exhibited in Saudi Arabia, Algeria, the United Arab Emirates, Oman, and Egypt. His works have been shown in venues organized by the General Presidency of Youth Welfare, Saudi Arabia (1974–1975); the Saudi Arabian Society for Culture and Arts, Saudi Arabia (1975); and Al Muftaha village, Saudi Arabia (2001). The artist has held multiple solo exhibitions in Riyadh and Jeddah.

Alshalti won third place in contests organized by Saudi Airlines and has been recognized with several local prizes, including first place of Al Muftaha Prize, first place in the second Ambassador competition, third place in the fourth Ambassador Competition, and first place in the auction at the Nassif Museum in Jeddah (2001). He was honored as a pioneer of Saudi art by HRH Prince Khalid bin Faisal Al Saud.

Abdullah Alshalti has a deep connection to his surroundings, often exploring his immediate environment and the region of Asir. Despite limited access to art supplies, his passion drove him to create art using natural materials that were at hand, such as car oil as a substitute for oil paints.

The artwork *Almayfa* (1985) exemplifies Alshalti's artistic style through its vivid brushstrokes and depiction of women engaged in local cooking practices, baking a local bread called *almayfa*, using a traditional *tanoor* clay oven. The painting highlights the significance of women within the landscape, donning traditional attire as they work in the fields. Through *Almayfa*, Alshalti pays homage to the art historical tradition that illustrates women in fields while serving as a tribute to the customs of Asir.

الميفا، 1985

ألوان أكريليك على ورق
42 × 30 سم
بإذن من صالة تجريد للفنون

Abdullah Alshalti

(b. 1952, Saudi Arabia)

Almayfa, 1985

Acrylic on paper
42 × 30 cm
Courtesy of Abstract Art Gallery

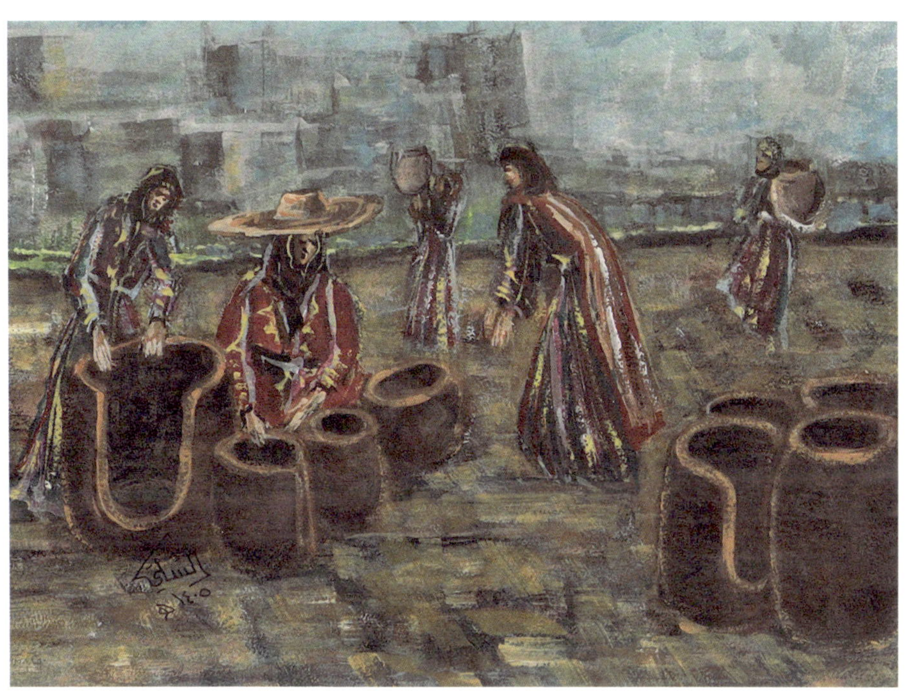

عبـــد الله الشـــيخ

(ولد عام 1936م في العراق وتوفي عام 2019م في المملكة العربية السعودية)

كان عبد الله الشـيخ فناناً تشكيلياً ومصمماً غرافيكياً تخرّج من معهد الفنون فـي بغداد عـام 1959م وحصل عـلى درجة علمية فـي الطباعـة والتصميم مـن كلية التقنية في جنوب شرق إيسكس في المملكـة المتحـدة عـام 1965م، وعمـل كمعلّم للفنـون لمـدة ثلاث سـنوات ثـم كمصمم غرافيك في صناعة الأقمشـة لدى وزارة الصناعة في العراق، وأصبح عند عودته لوطنه الأم رئيس قسم التصميم في الهيئة الملكيـة للجبيل وينبع حيـث تقاعد عام 1999م ليصب جل تركيزه عـلى الفن.

أقام الشـيخ أول معرض فـردي له عام 1981م في الخبر في المملكة العربية السعودية بعد عودته من العراق، وشارك في العديد من المعارض المحلية والدوليـة، ومن ضمن تلك المعـارض ما تم تنظيمه من الرئاسة العامة لرعاية الشباب، والجمعية العربية السعودية للثقافة والفنون إضافة إلى "معرض أرامكو للفنون" في المملكة العربية السعودية عام 2011م، ومعهد العالـم العربـي فـي فرنسا عـام 2002م، وبينالي الشارقة الثالث في الإمارات العربية المتحدة عـام 1997م، و"معـرض الفنانين العـرب" في بكين، بجمهوريـة الصيـن عـام 1996م، وأول بينالـي فـي اللاذقية في سـوريا عـام 1995م، ومعرض "المملكة بيـن الأمس واليوم" وهـو معرض مرتحـل بين عدة دول كالولايـات المتحدة الأمريكية وفرنسا وإنجلترا ومصر بيـن الأعوام 1985م - 1992م.

تـم تكريـم الشـيخ بعـدة جوائـز منهـا: جائـزة السـعفة الفضية في الكويت عام 2003م، والسعفة الذهبيـة فـي سـلطنة عمـان 2001م، والمهرجـان الوطني للتراث والثقافة في المملكة العربية السعودية عام 1999م، وجائزة لجنة التحكيم في بينالي المحبة الأول في اللاذقية في سـوريا عام 1995م، والسعفة الذهبيـة في الإمارات العربية المتحـدة عام 1994م.

اقتنيت أعماله ضمـن العديد من المجموعات الخاصـة والعامـة فـي المملكـة العربية السعودية مثـل: مطار الملـك خالد في الريـاض ومطار الملك فهـد فـي المنطقـة الشـرقية ووزارة الداخليـة فـي المملكة العربية السعودية والأمانة العامة لمجلس التعـاون الخليجي فـي الرياض.

يسـلّط الفنـان عبد الله الشـيخ فـي أعمالـه الضـوء عـلى الموضوعـات الثقافيـة والتاريخيـة والاجتماعيـة والسياسـية للمنطقـة العربيـة، كانـت أعماله الأولى مركزة على اللوحات حيث كان يستلهم أفكاره مـن الفلكلـور والتـراث، وكانت هـذه الأعمال عـادة تدمج عناصر من التراث الشـعبي والقصص التقليدية، ومع تطور أعماله، ركز الشيخ على الخط العربي والأشكال المعمارية الإسلامية، وتتميز أعماله بألوانهـا النابضة بالحياة والتي تقدّم أشـكالاً مجرّدة تتداخـل فيها درجات الألـوان الغامقـة بجرأة.

في لوحته الفنية "عنترة" 1981م، يخلّد الفنان سـيرة الفـارس والشـاعر العربـي الجاهلـي عنترة بن شـداد مسـتخدماً الخط العربي ومقتبسـاً أبياتاً من معلقة عنترة لمحبوبته عبلة، ينقسـم هـذا العمل الفنـي إلى أجـزاء مجـرّدة حيـث تغلب عـلى الجزء العلـوي من اللوحة درجات دافئة من اللون الأحمر يتوسـطها بيت شـعري عن عبلة، يتبعه سهم يأخذ بنظر المشـاهد إلى الجزء الآخر باللون الأزرق والذي تظهر فيه بقية الأبيـات من المعلقة، وتتجلى في اللوحـة كذلك الأنمـاط المسـتوحاة مـن المنـازل التقليدية والمباني التاريخية. أما في أسفل اللوحة، فتبـرز صورة عنترة وهو يرتدي الـزي التقليدي لزمنه وبهـذا العمل الفني، يحتفي آل الشـيخ بثراء الإرث الثقافـي للعالم العربي.

Abdullah Alshaikh

(b. 1936, Iraq – d. 2019, Saudi Arabia)

Abdullah Alshaikh was a painter and a graphic designer. He graduated from the Institute of Fine Arts in Baghdad in 1959 and obtained a printmaking and design degree from South-East Essex Technical College and School of Art, the United Kingdom in 1965. He taught art for three years and then worked as a graphic designer in textiles at the Ministry of Industry in Iraq. Upon returning to Saudi Arabia, he became head of the design department at the Royal Commission Jubail and Yanbu, retiring in 1999 to focus on his art career.

Alshaikh held his first solo exhibition in 1981 in Khobar, Saudi Arabia after his return from Iraq. He participated in many local and international exhibitions, including exhibitions organized by the General Presidency of Youth Welfare and the Saudi Society for Art and Culture, Saudi Arabia, in addition to *Aramco Exhibition of Fine Art*, Saudi Arabia (2011); Institut du Monde Arabe, France (2002); 3rd Sharjah Biennale, United Arab Emirates (1997); *Arab Artists Exhibition in Beijing*, China (1996); 1st Latakia Biennale, Syria (1995); and *Saudi Arabia Yesterday and Today*, traveling exhibition in the United States, France, England, Italy, and Egypt (1985–1992).

Alshaikh has been recognized with several awards including the Silver Palme d'Or Award, Kuwait (2003); the Golden Palme d'Or Award, Muscat (2001); the National Festival Heritage and Culture Award, Saudi Arabia (1999); the Jury Biennale Award of AlMahaba, 1st Biennale in Lattakia, Syria (1995); and the Golden Palme d'Or Award, Sharjah (1994).

Alshaikh's artworks have been acquired by private and public collections in Saudi Arabia including King Khaled Airport, Riyadh; King Fahd Airport, Dhahran; the Ministry of Interior, Saudi Arabia; the Secretariat General of the Gulf Cooperation Council, Riyadh.

Abdullah Alshaikh intertwines themes of cultural, historical, and the socio-political context of the Arab region in his paintings. His early works focused on portraits while drawing inspiration from folklore and heritage. These works often incorporate elements from his local heritage and traditional stories. As his work evolved, he focused on portraying Arabic calligraphy and Islamic architectural forms and symbols. Alshaikh's paintings have vibrant color palettes, presenting abstract compositions of coarse overlapping planes.

In *Antarah* (1981), Alshaikh pays homage to the pre-Islamic Arab knight and poet Antarah bin Shaddad. Within the painting, Alshaikh employs Arabic calligraphy to convey phrases from Antarah's *Mullaqa*, a love poem dedicated to Abla. The composition of the artwork is divided into abstract sections, with the top portion featuring warm tones of deep red, which encompasses a poetic phrase about Abla, following the phrase is an arrow to the blue section, where there may be a continuation of the poem. Alshaikh further incorporates patterns inspired by traditional houses and outlines historical building structures. At the bottom of the painting, the artist presents a portrait of Antarah, adorned in the traditional dress of the era. Through *Antarah*, Alshaikh preserves the rich cultural heritage of the Arab world.

عنترة، 1981

ألوان زيتية على خشب
61 × 92 سم
مجموعة خاصة

Abdullah Alshaikh

(b. 1936, Iraq – d. 2019, Saudi Arabia)

Antarah, 1981

Oil on wood
61 × 92 cm
Private Collection

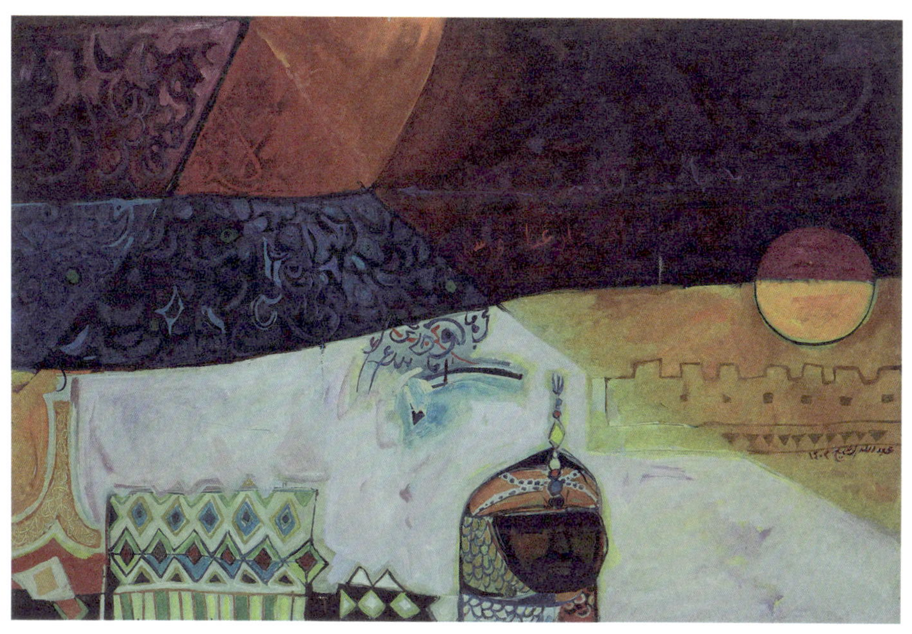

عبــد الله حمّــاس

(ولد عام 1952م في المملكة العربية السعودية)

عبدالله حمّاس فنان تجريدي أنتج أكثر من 3000 لوحة وجدارية خلال مسيرته، بعد تخرجه من معهد التربية الفنية عام 1973م وعلى مدار ثلاثة عقود درّس الفن في الرياض وجدة بينما كان مستمراً في إكمال مسيرته الفنية، أدى حمّاس دوراً هاماً في المشهد الفني في جدة من خلال مشاركته في تأسيس بيت التشكيليين، وقد كان رئيساً له.

في عام 1972م، بدأ بالمشاركة في المعارض التي تقيمها الرئاسة العامة لرعاية الشباب وجمعية الثقافة والفنون، وشارك في عدة معارض فردية وجماعية في المملكة العربية السعودية والكويت ومصر ولبنان والمغرب وتونس والولايات المتحدة الأمريكية والمملكة المتحدة وألمانيا، ومن معارضه الدولية: معرض بنك الرياض في المملكة المتحدة عامي 1985م و1994م، ومعرض مؤسسة العالم الثالث في المملكة المتحدة عام 1981م، ودار الفنون والأدب في لبنان عام 1981م، وفي المجمل أقام 39 معرضاً شخصياً داخل وخارج المملكة.

حاز خلال مسيرته الفنية على أكثر من 180 شهادة تقدير وحصل على عدة جوائز، منها المركز الأول في جائزة الخطوط السعودية عام 1992م والمركز الثاني في معرض الفن السعودي المعاصر عام 1989م. أنشأ الفنان العديدمن الاستديوهات منها الاستديو الخاص، والاستديو الصيفي في أبها وأحدثها في الرياض.

تُعرض أعماله ضمن مجموعات مركز الملك عبد العزيز التاريخي، ووزارة الداخلية، وقصر اليمامة، ومجموعة روشن، بالمملكة العربية السعودية، ويتلقى دعماً من مؤسسة المنصورية.

كان يستمد عبدالله حمّاس إلهامه من الألوان والثقافة والأشكال المعمارية المحيطة به، وتتمحور

معظم أعماله على تصوير منطقة عسير (مسقط رأسه) وإبراز السكان المحليين والعادات والأعراف وأنماط الحياة القروية البسيطة؛ كما تغطي أعماله مجموعة واسعة من الأنماط كالتكعيبية المستوحاة من جورج براك وبابلو بيكاسو والرمزية، ويغلب على أعماله في السبعينيات والثمانينيات الطابع الهندسي والرموز التجريدية والألوان النابضة بالحياة.

وفي عمله "تكوين 1" 1988م، يلتقط لمحةً فريدة من الأحياء القديمة، وتداخلها العشوائي مع ضوء الصباح الخافت؛ وتُقدّم اللوحة تفاعلاً تناغمياً بديعاً بين مختلف العناصر ضمن المشهد الحضري، حيث يمتزج كل عنصر بسلاسة مع الآخر. تصور "تكوين 2" 1988م حنية البيوت القديمة وتداخلها ببعض، ويصور أحجامها المختلفة وبساطتها المتناهية في ألوانها الموحدة؛ استخدم حمّاس اللون الأسود وخففه إلى درجات اللون الأزرق الغامق وجود اللون الأزرق خلف المباني مع مستويات مختلفة للضوء يمثّل تداخلاً دقيقاً بين الضوء والعتمة، ويضفي هذا التفاعل على المباني السوداء تأثيراً يشبه السراب.

Abdullah Hammas

(b. 1952, Saudi Arabia)

Abdullah Hammas is an abstract painter who has created over three thousand artworks and large murals throughout his prolific career. After graduating from the Institute of Art Education in 1973, and over the course of the next three decades, he taught art in Riyadh and Jeddah while simultaneously pursuing his own career as an artist. Hammas played a key role in Jeddah's art scene by co-founding the House of Artists where he was committee president.

In 1972, Hammas began taking part in exhibitions organized by the General Presidency of Youth Welfare and the Saudi Society for Culture and Arts. He has participated in thirty-nine solo and group exhibitions in Saudi Arabia, Kuwait, Egypt, Lebanon, Morocco, Tunisia, the United States, the United Kingdom, and Germany. Selected international exhibitions include *Bank of Riyadh* exhibition, the United Kingdom (1985, 1994); *the Third World Foundation Exhibition*, the United Kingdom (1981); and *Dar Art and Literature Exhibition*, Lebanon (1981).

Throughout his career, Hammas received over 180 certificates of appreciation and won several awards, notably first place in the Saudi Airlines Contest (1992) and second place in the Contemporary Saudi Art Exhibition (1989). He established multiple studios, including his private studio, his summer studio in Abha, and his most recent studio in Riyadh.

His paintings can be found in the collections of the King Abdulaziz Historical Center, Saudi Arabia; the Saudi Ministry of Interior, Saudi Arabia; Al-Yamamah Palace, Saudi Arabia; and the Rochan Collection, Saudi Arabia. Hammas is supported by the Al-Mansouria Foundation.

Abdullah Hammas draws inspiration from the colors, culture, and architecture of his surroundings. He paints his native Asir, portraying the local population, traditional customs, and simple rural lifestyles. His oeuvre encompasses a wide range of styles, including symbolism and cubism, inspired by Georges Braque and Pablo Picasso. His works from the 1970s and 1980s feature geometric shapes, abstract symbols, and blocks of vibrant colors.

In *Composition 1* (1988), Hammas captures a glimpse of old neighborhoods with the dim morning light. The painting presents a harmonious interplay of various elements within the urban landscape, each seamlessly blending into one another. In *Composition 2* (1988), he continues exploring old houses overlapping one another, depicting their different sizes in one predominant color. Hammas utilized black and diluted the color into a blackish-blue hue. The presence of blue behind the buildings, in varying degrees of light, symbolizes the play between light and darkness. This interplay between light and heat on the black buildings creates a mirage-like effect.

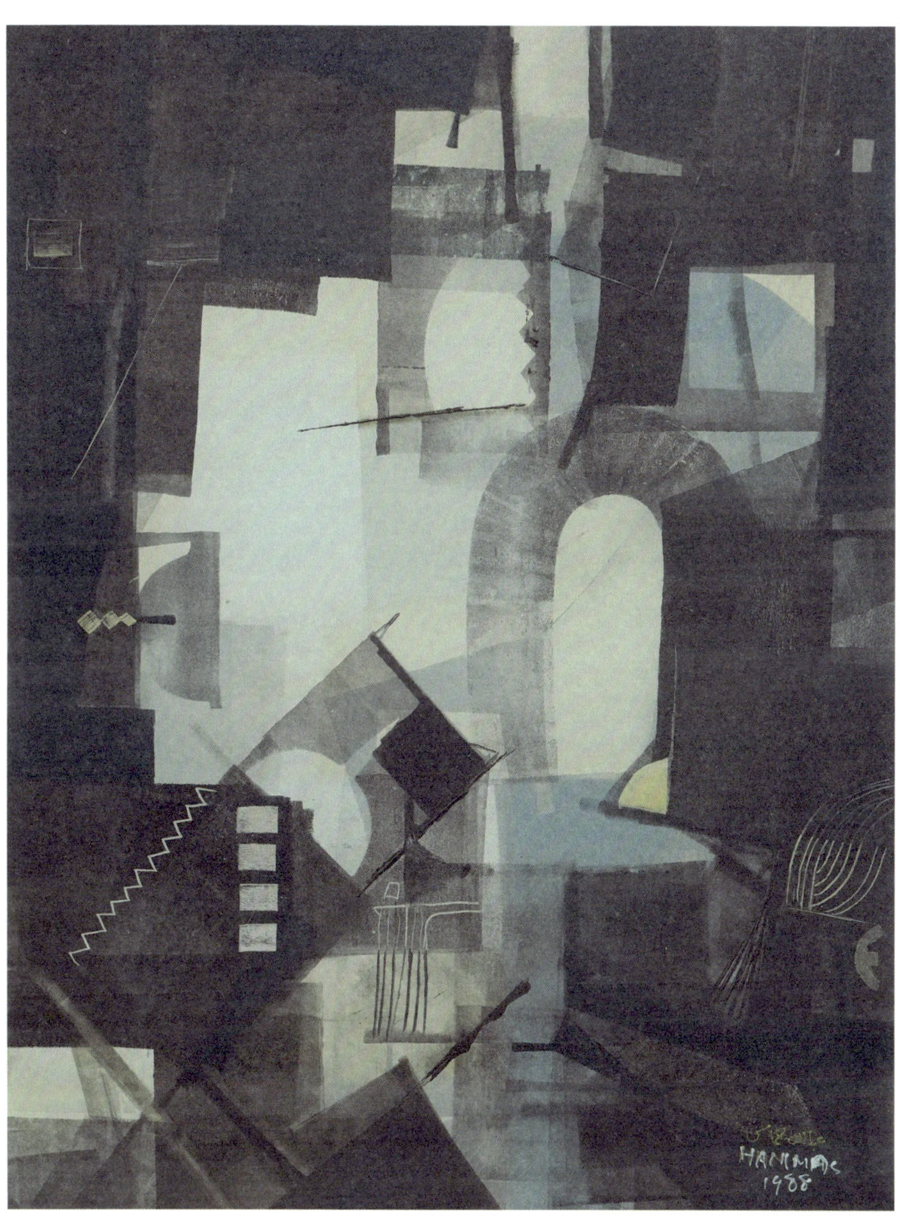

عبـــد الله حمّـــــاس

(ولد عام 1952م في المملكة العربية السعودية)

تكوين *2*، 1988

زيت على ورق

56 × 72 سم

بإذن من الفنان

Abdullah Hammas

(b. 1952, Saudi Arabia)

Composition 2, 1988

Oil on paper
56 × 72 cm
Courtesy of the artist

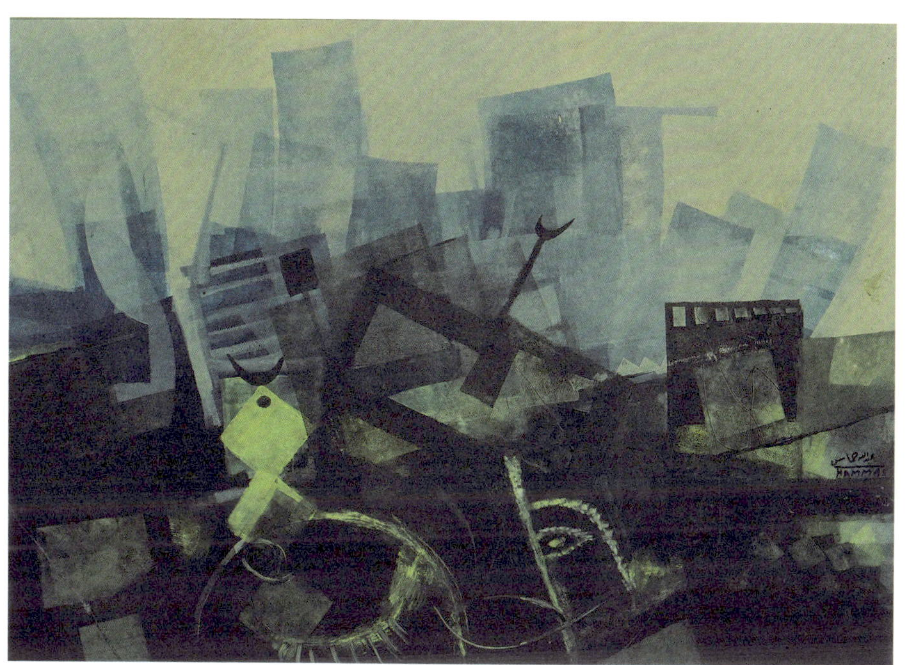

علي الرزيـــزاء

(ولد عام 1944م في المملكة العربية السعودية)

تتميـز أعمـال **علـي الرزيـزاء** بأنها مسـتوحاة مـن الطابع النجدي التقليدي مع آثار دراسته في إيطاليا لتمنـح المشـاهد رؤية فنيـة فريدة؛ عادةً مـا تصوِّر أعماله مشـاهد الحيـاة الاجتماعيـة والثقافيـة في نجد والتفاصيل المعمارية باسـتخدام فن الوسائط المتعـددة لإضفـاء عمق وارتبـاط بالثقافة.

اسـتوحى فكرة "منازل" 1981م من المكونات التقليدية للثقافة النجدية ولاسـيما الإرث المعماري وبالتحديـد المنـازل، وتتجلـى في هـذا العمل رؤية الرزيـزاء الفنيـة فـي اسـتخدام الخطـوط الغامقـة والأشـكال الهندسـية ونقـل الطابع الصحـراوي من خلال رمال الصحراء الممزوجة مـع ألوان الأكريليك والألـوان الزيتية، وتتسـم اللوحـة بالعمق من خلال دمـج خامـات بوسـائط متعـددة لإبـراز المناظـر الطبيعية التي تهدف اللوحة لإظهارها، ويسـتحضر الفنان المناظـر الطبيعية لمنطقة نجد باسـتخدام درجـات اللون الذهبـي والبرونزي.

Ali Alruzaiza

(b. 1944, Saudi Arabia)

Ali Alruzaiza's oeuvre is characterized by a blend of traditional Najd elements with influences from his studies in Italy, resulting in a distinctive artistic vision. His works often depict scenes from Najd's cultural and social settings, emphasizing architectural details and utilizing textured mixed media techniques to create a sense of depth and connection to the culture.

In *Homes* (1981), Alruzaiza depicts scenes of Najd's architectural heritage. The artist unifies the composition through the repetition of bold lines and geometric shapes. The artwork is textured, achieved through desert sand mixed with acrylic and oil paints. This mixed media approach lends the piece a sense of depth, adding a multilayered dimension to the artwork, while depicting the environment it is intended to represent. The natural landscape of Najd is further evoked by the gold and bronze tones in the artwork.

Ali Alruzaiza

(b. 1944, Saudi Arabia)

Homes, 1981

Mixed media on canvas
119.5 × 89 cm
Private Collection

علي الرزيـــــــزاء

(ولد عام 1944م في المملكة العربية السعودية)

منازل، 1981

وسائط مختلفة على قماش
119.5 × 89 سم
مجموعة خاصة

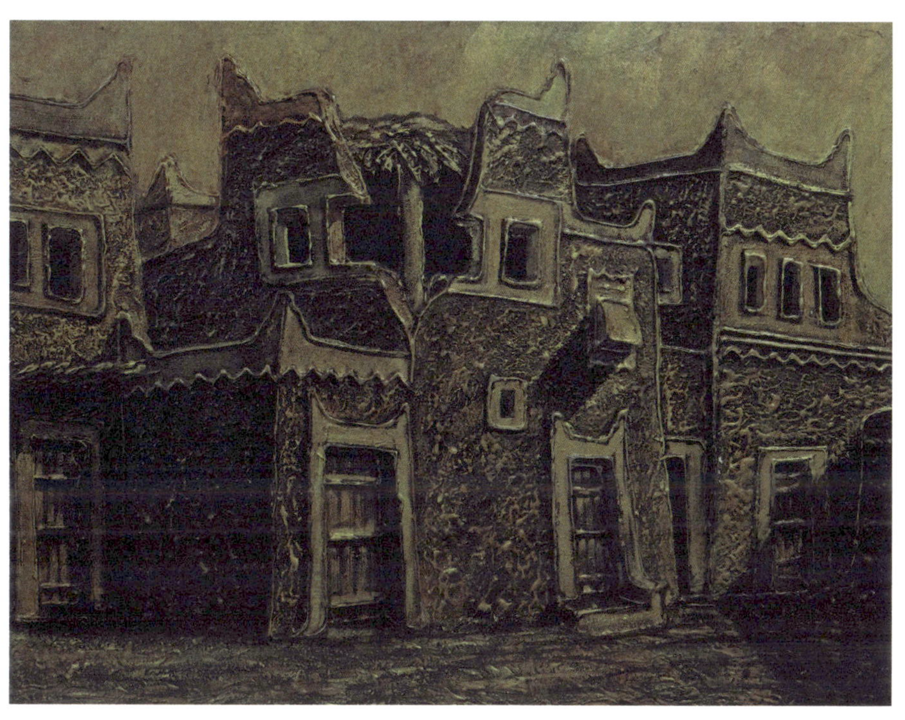

د. فـــؤاد مغربــــل

(ولد عام 1951م في المملكة العربية السعودية)

د.فؤاد مغربل رسـام اشْـتهر بلوحات تهتـم بالتراث والفولكلـور. في عـام 1969م تخـرّج مـن معهـد التربيـة الفنيـة وحصل علـى منحـة للدراسـة في مصـر، وتخـرج بدرجـة البكالوريـوس فـي التربيـة الفنيـة من جامعـة حلـوان بالقاهرة سنـة 1978م، وحصل بعد ذلك على درجة الماجسـتير في التربية الفنيـة في عـام 1984م مـن جامعة نيو مكسـيكو بالولايـات المتحـدة الأمريكيـة، ودرجـة الدكتـوراه في التربيـة الفنيـة مـن جامعة هـال بإنجلتـرا عام 2000م، وقدم مسـاهمات كبيـرة خلال مسـيرته المهنيـة والفنيـة، وهـو عضـو فـي الاتحـاد الدولي للفنـون التشـكيلية منـذ سـنة 1985م، وشـغل منصب رئيس لجنة الفنـون التشـكيلية في جمعية الثقافـة والفنون بالمدينة المنورة مـن 1987م إلى 2005م، ثـم مديـر النشـاطات مـن 2006م إلـى 2007م ومدير فـرع الجمعية فـي 2008م، وكان عضـواً مؤسسـاً لجماعـة فنانـي المدينـة المنـورة التشـكيليين فـي 1980م وعامـلاً فيهـا إلـى الوقـت الحاضـر، كمـا كان عضـواً مؤسسـاً لجماعة أصـدقاء الفن التشـكيلي بـدول الخليج عـام 1985م، وعمل كمشـرف للمعارض والتجميل بهيئة تطوير المدينة المنورة من 2005م إلـى 2008م، وكان عضو هيئة التدريـس بجامعة طيبة منـذ عـام 2008م، وثم أسـتاذاً مشـاركاً (غير متفرغ) في الجامعة من سنة 2015م إلى 2018م، وكان مشرفاً ثقافياً بالملحقية الثقافيـة بإيطاليا مـن 2009م إلى سـنة 2015م.

أقام مغربل 22 معرضاً شـخصياً، وشـارك في أكثر من 100 معرض جماعي داخل وخارج المملكة منـذ عـام 1965م، وتشـمل معارضـه الجماعيـة، "معرض 23" فـي المملكـة العربيـة السـعودية عام 2018م، و"معـرض اليـوم الوطنـي السـعودي" في إيطاليا عـام 2013م، ومعرض الملحقيـة الثقافية السـعودية فـي المملكـة المتحـدة عـام 2000م،

ومعرض السـفارة السـعودية في المملكة المتحدة عام 1997م، ومعرض جاليري روشـان فـي المملكة العربيـة السـعودية عام 1984م، ومعـرض جامعة دنفـر في الولايات المتحدة عـام 1983م، ومعرض جامعـة نيو مكسـيكو فـي الولايـات المتحدة عام 1983م، والمعـرض الكنـدي العالمي فـي كندا عام 1973م وغيرها.

حصل على الجائزة الأولى في المعرض التاسـع للرئاسـة العامة لرعاية الشـباب، كما أصدر أربعة كتب منها كتاب بعنـوان "طيبة في عيون فنان تشـكيلي" عام 1989م، وقد اقتنيت أعماله من قبل مقتني الفن والمؤسسـات الحكومية في المملكة وخارج المملكة.

يتجلـى فـي أعمـال الرسـام د. فـؤاد مغربـل ارتباطـه الوثيـق بـالإرث المعماري لبيئـة المدينـة المنورة حيـث تصور أعماله المركـزة على الفلكلور أزقـة المدينة والملامح الرئيسـية للمنـازل؛ وغالباً ما تتضمـن أعماله توثيقاً للعمال في السـوق الشـعبي والموسـيقيين والطهاة وحفـلات الأعراس، ويعتمد في أسـلوبه علـى الفن شـبه التكعيبي والانطباعي من خـلال تقسـيم العناصـر إلى خطـوط مائلة ويتلاعب بالضوء لعـرض صـور مجـزّأة لإضفـاء تناغـم بيـن الألـوان الزاهية والخـدع البصرية.

مهَّدت أعمال مغربل مـن الثمانينيات الطريق لأعمالـه التكعيبيـة، ففـي "حـي شـعبي" 1982م، يصوّر الحي التقليدي جنوب شـرق المسـجد النبوي فـي المدينـة المنورة والـذي أصبح لاحقـاً جزءاً من سـاحة المسـجد بعد أعمـال التوسـعة، كما يتضمن العمـل عناصر للعمـارة التقليدية وأهمها المشـربية للاحتفاء بتـراث المباني؛ وتتجلى فـي اللّوحة كذلك براعـة مغربـل في دمـج فـن التكعيبية مع السـماء الزرقـاء وجدران المباني بشـكل انسـيابي ومتناغم.

Dr. Fouad Mougharbel

(b. 1951, Saudi Arabia)

Dr. Fouad Mougharbel is an artist known for his paintings depicting heritage and folklore themes. In 1969, he earned a diploma from the Institute of Art Education, Riyadh, and was awarded a scholarship to study art education at Helwan University, Egypt in 1978. He later earned a master's degree in art education in 1984 from New Mexico University in New Mexico, the United States; and a PhD in art education from Hull University in England in 2000. Throughout his career, Mougharbel made significant contributions, he has been a member of the International Federation of Fine Arts since 1985. He was the head of the Fine Arts Committee at the Society of Culture and Arts in Al Madinah from 1987–2005, then the director of activities from 2006–2007, and the branch director in 2008. In 1980, he co-founded the Madinah Artists Group, and still manages the initiative today. He also co-founded the GCC Art Friends Group in 1985. Mougharbel worked as a supervisor of exhibitions and beautification at the Madinah Region Development Authority (2005–2008), a faculty member at Taibah University since 2008, and a part-time associate professor (2015–2018). He was also a cultural supervisor at the Cultural Attaché in Italy from 2009 to 2015.

Mougharbel held twenty-two solo exhibitions and participated in over a hundred group exhibitions both in Saudi Arabia and abroad since 1965. His group participations include *Exhibit 23*, Saudi Arabia (2018); *Saudi National Day Exhibition*, Italy (2013); Saudi Arabian Cultural Mission, the United Kingdom (2000); Saudi Embassy, the United Kingdom (1997); Rochan Gallery, Saudi Arabia (1984); Denver University, the United States (1983); New Mexico University, the United States (1983); and *The World Canadian Expo*, Canada (1973) amongst others.

Recognized for his talent, Mougharbel was awarded the first prize in the Ninth General Exhibition of the General Presidency of Youth Welfare. He also published four books, including *Taiba in the Eyes of a Visual Artist* (1989). His work has been acquired by private collectors and governmental institutions in Saudi Arabia and abroad.

Dr. Fouad Mougharbel is deeply connected to the architectural heritage and environment of Madinah. His paintings of folklore depict the city's alleys and the unique features of the houses. Mougharbel's practice often includes research and documentation of local market workers, musicians, cooks, and wedding celebrations. His artistic style employs a quasi-cubist and impressionistic approach, dividing elements with diagonal lines, playing with light to fragment images, resulting in an interplay of bright color and visual illusions.

His 1980s body of works lays the foundation for his cubist works. In *Old Neighborhood* (1982), Mougharbel paints a traditional neighborhood situated southeast of the Prophet's Mosque in Madinah. The neighborhood eventually became a part of the mosque's square after undergoing expansion. He also incorporates elements of traditional architecture, notably the mashrabiyas, embracing the heritage of the buildings. The subtle incorporation of cubism in the blue sky and walls of the buildings merged seamlessly with the overall composition.

In *New Neighborhood* (1985) Mougharbel depicts a neighborhood from the then-new southern area of the Prophet's Mosque in Madinah. The neighborhood no longer exists due to urban development, making this artwork a record of a bygone era. *New Neighborhood* portrays a sense of depth, punctuated with silhouettes of men strolling down the alley in traditional dress. Mougharbel preserves heritage in his works through the use of traditional aesthetics.

في عمله "حـي جديـد" 1985م، يصـور أحد أحيـاء المنطقـة الجنوبيـة للمسـجد النبـوي فـي المدينـة المنـورة؛ والجديـر بالذكر أن هـذا الحي لم يعـد موجـوداً بسـبب أعمـال التنمية العمرانية ما يجعل هذا العمل الفنِّي تخليداً للحقبة الماضية، أما لوحة حـي جديد فإنها تضفي حسـاً عميقـاً يتخلله ظلال لرجال يمشـون في أزقة الحـي ويرتدون الأزياء التقليديـة؛ ويحرص مغربل على اسـتخدام الأشـكال الجماليـة التقليديـة للحفاظ علـى إرث مدينته.

Dr. Fouad Mougharbel

(b. 1951, Saudi Arabia)

Old Neighborhood, 1982

Oil on canvas
106 × 81 cm
Private Collection

د. فـــــؤاد مـغربـــــــل

(ولد عام 1951م في المملكة العربية السعودية)

حي شعبي، 1982

ألوان زيتية على قماش
106 × 81 سم
مجموعة خاصة

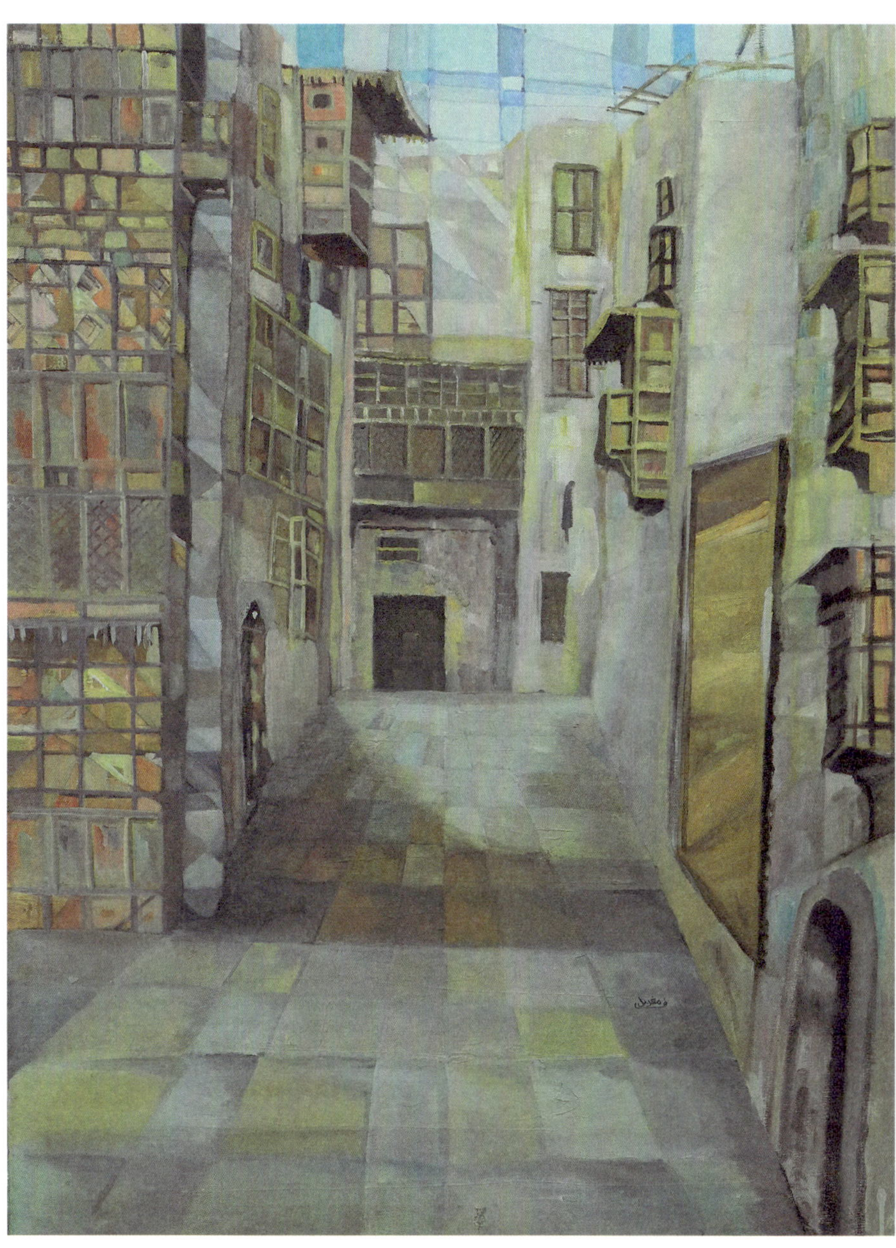

دمشق

Dr. Fouad Mougharbel

(b. 1951, Saudi Arabia)

New Neighborhood, 1985

Oil on canvas
82 × 67 cm
Private Collection

د. فـــــؤاد مـغربـــــــل
(ولد عام 1951م في المملكة العربية السعودية)

حي جديد، 1985

ألوان زيتية على قماش
82 × 67 سم
مجموعة خاصة

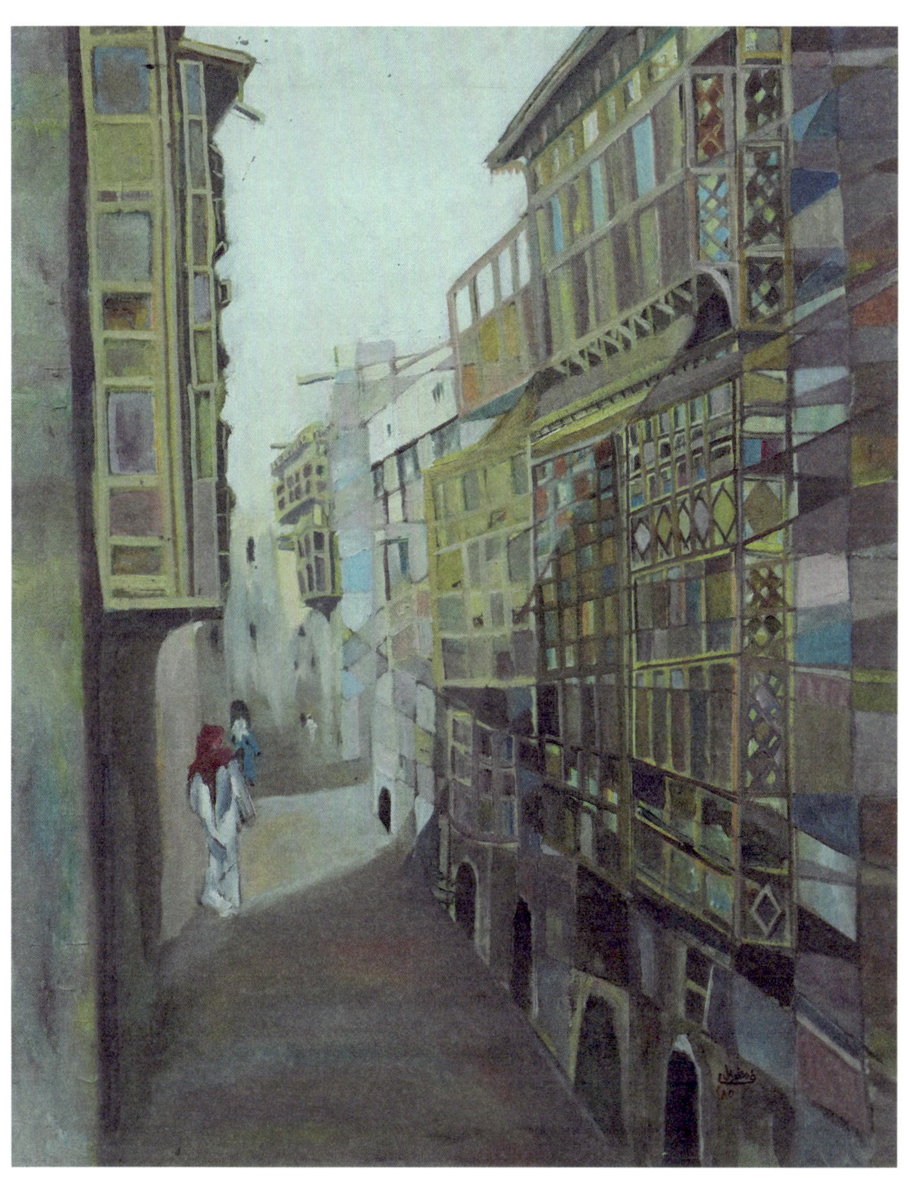

د. محمــد الرصيــص

(ولد عام 1951م في المملكة العربية السعودية)

يعد محمد الرصيص فناناً وكاتباً وناقداً فنياً، وكان من خريجي الدفعة الثانية الحاصلين على دبلوم التربية الفنية من معهد التربية الفنية في الرياض عام 1969م، ثم حصل على بكالوريوس التربية الفنية من جامعة حلوان بمصر عام 1977م، والماجستير في الفنون التشكيلية من جامعة أوهايو الحكومية بالولايات المتحدة الأمريكية عام 1982م، والدكتوراه في مجال المتاحف والتربية الفنية من نفس الجامعة عام 1989م، وعمل محاضراً في جامعة الملك سعود في الرياض بقسم التربية الفنية، ثم أصبح رئيساً للقسم لست سنوات، وبعد تقاعده المبكر من الجامعة تم تكليفه للعمل أميناً للجمعية العربية السعودية للثقافة والفنون عام 2006م لمدة أربع سنوات، ثم رئيساً لمجلس إدارتها لمدة عامين.

شارك خلال مسيرته الفنية في أكثر من خمسين معرضاً محلياً وعالمياً، وعُرضت أعماله في المملكة العربية السعودية، ومصر، والمملكة المتحدة، وتركيا، وإسبانيا، وفرنسا، وتايوان، والولايات المتحدة الأمريكية، وأقام أربعة معارض شخصية ثلاثة في المملكة العربية السعودية في 1972م و1983م و2002م، والمعرض الرابع في الولايات المتحدة الأمريكية في 1982م.

كما يعد كاتباً في الشؤون الفنية وله كثير من المقالات، والأبحاث، والمؤلفات المنشورة منها كتاب "تاريخ الفن التشكيلي في المملكة العربية السعودية" عام 2010م، وقد أصدر كتباً أخرى مثل "الفنون التشكيلية والإنسان، ملخص تاريخي" عام 1992م مع زميله د.صالح الزاير، وكتاب "الفنون التشكيلية في الجنادرية 7 مواد ثقافية توثيقية" عام 1993م، وبحث عن "الفن التشكيلي في الوطن العربي – البدايات والتطورات ورؤية مستقبلية" عام 2002م.

وهناك أكثر من مئة مقال منشور في صحيفة الاقتصادية، ومقالات متفرقة في عدد من الصحف السعودية.

تتمحور أعمال الفنان محمد الرصيص حول موضوعات التراث الوطني، وتدمج لوحاته التجريدية العناصر المعمارية ولاسيما الأبواب والنوافذ، ويصف من خلال فنّه مشاهد من خلفيته، ويدمج عناصر الفن التعبيري والتجريدي والانطباعي، ويركز أسلوبه على المدرسة التكعيبية من خلال الإشارة إلى الأشكال الهندسية للحفاظ على جوهر الموضوع وإضفاء حيوية عليه باستخدام ألوان تنبض بالحياة.

يصوّر الرصيص في لوحته "من العمارة التقليدية" 1981م الطابع المعماري النجدي القديم مستخدماً درجات اللون البني لينقل المشاهد إلى الزمن الماضي وألوان المباني في ذلك الوقت، ويقسّم اللوحة إلى مستويات متداخلة بشكل مبسط، ويدمج في خلفية اللوحة دوائر زرقاء أحادية اللون.

من خلال ألوان دافئة تبعث شعور الحنين، يتشارك "شكل معماري 2" 1982م في روابط فنية مع "عنصر هندسي 5" 1982م، حيث تعكس كلا اللوحتين المنازل القديمة المصنوعة من الطين وتصميماتها المتنوعة. في "عنصر هندسي 5" 1982م، يركز الرصيص على أشكال معمارية معينة من بيوت الطين التقليدية باستخدام فن التناسب والمنظور، وفي حدود هذه العناصر نلاحظ التفريق في درجات الأخضر والأصفر والأزرق؛ الأمر الذي يعطي حيوية للوحة، ويهدف الرصيص من استخدام الألوان الغامقة إلى نقل مشاعر المعاناة محفزاً بذلك فكر المشاهد إلى التأمل في هذا الجمال المعماري المصوّر.

Dr. Mohammed Alresayes

(b. 1951, Saudi Arabia)

Dr. Mohammed Alresayes is a painter, writer, and art critic. Alresayes was one of the first to graduate from the Institute of Art Education in Riyadh in 1969. He then earned a bachelor's degree in art education from Helwan University, Egypt (1977), a master's degree in fine arts and a PhD in art education and museology (1982 and 1989, respectively) from Ohio State University, United States. He was a lecturer at King Saud University's College of Art, in Riyadh in the art education department, then became the department director for six years. In 2006, shortly after his early retirement from the university, he took on the role of secretary for the Saudi Arabian Society for Culture and Arts and held this position for four years. Following this, he served as chairman of the board of directors for the same organization for an additional two years.

Throughout his career, Alresayes participated in over fifty national and international exhibitions. His artworks have been exhibited in Saudi Arabia, Egypt, the United Kingdom, Turkey, Spain, France, Taiwan, and the United States. He has held four solo exhibitions, three in Saudi Arabia (1972, 1983, and 2002); and one in the United States (1982).

Alresayes is an accomplished writer and has published articles and artistic scientific research, and publications including *The History of Plastic Arts in Saudi Arabia* (2010). He has also written several books like *Man and Plastic Arts: A Brief History* (1992) coauthored with Dr. Saleh Alzayer; *Plastic Arts at the Janadriyah 7th Cultural and Documentary Study* (1993); and a research paper on *Fine Art in the Arab World - The History, Developments and Vision for Future* (2002). He has published over a hundred articles in the *Aleqtisadiah* newspaper and in several other Saudi newspapers.

Dr. Mohammed Alresayes's general practice revolves around themes of national heritage. His abstract paintings incorporate architectural elements, particularly doors and windows. He depicts scenes from his personal background, incorporating elements of expressionism, abstraction, and impressionism. Alresayes's style also pays homage to cubism by referring geometric shapes, preserving the general form of the subject, and infusing vibrant colors with vitality.

In *From Traditional Building* (1981), Alresayes paints the traditional Najdi architecture. Employing a brown color palette reminiscent of the original colors of the buildings, the artist divides the composition into planes that slightly overlap, incorporating monochromatic blue circles in the background.

In *Architectural Shape (2)* (1982), Alresayes, focuses on traditional Najdi architectural forms. Through a warm nostalgic palette, this artwork shares thematic connections with *Architectural Element 5* (1982), as both works delve into the intricacies of traditional clay houses and their design. In *Architectural Element 5* (1982), Alresayes zooms in on specific architectural elements from traditional mud houses and plays with proportion, color, and perspective. The outline of the elements is defined by hues of green, yellow, and blue, adding dynamism to the piece. Using dark colors, Alresayes may allude to themes of suffering and misery, providing a thought-provoking contrast to the architectural beauty portrayed.

Dr. Mohammed Alresayes

(b. 1951, Saudi Arabia)

From Traditional Building, 1981

Oil on canvas
61 × 91.5 cm
Courtesy of Hewar Art Gallery

د. محمــــد الرصيـــــــص
(ولد عام 1951م في المملكة العربية السعودية)

من العمارة التقليدية، 1981

ألوان زيتية على قماش
61 × 91.5 سم
بإذن من حوار جاليري

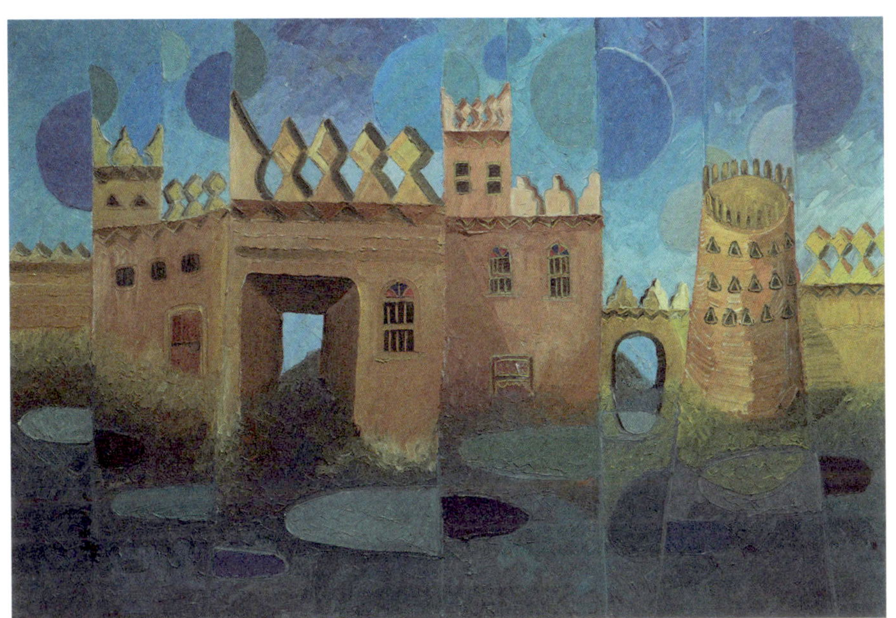

Dr. Mohammed Alresayes

(b. 1951, Saudi Arabia)

Architectural Element 5, 1982

Oil on canvas
117.2 × 87.8 cm
Courtesy of Hewar Art Gallery

د. محمــــد الرصيـــــــص

(ولد عام 1951م في المملكة العربية السعودية)

عنصر هندسي 5، 1982

ألوان زيتية على قماش
117.2 × 87.8 سم
بإذن من حوار جاليري

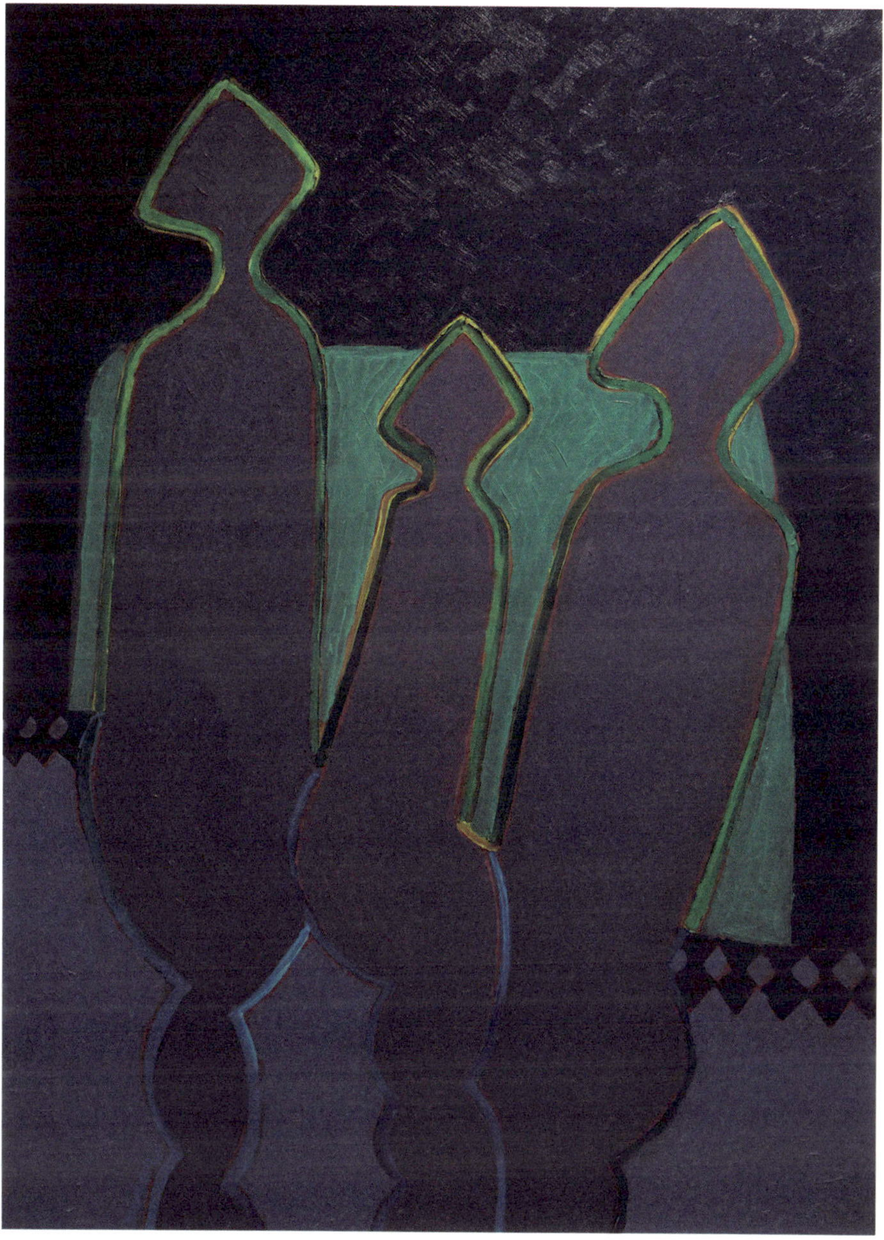

Dr. Mohammed Alresayes

(b. 1951, Saudi Arabia)

Architectural Shape (2), 1982

Oil on canvas
105 × 135 cm
Courtesy of Abstract Art Gallery

د. محمـــد الرصيـــص

(ولد عام 1951م في المملكة العربية السعودية)

شكل معماري (2)، 1982

ألوان زيتية على قماش
105 × 135 سم
بإذن من صالة تجريد للفنون

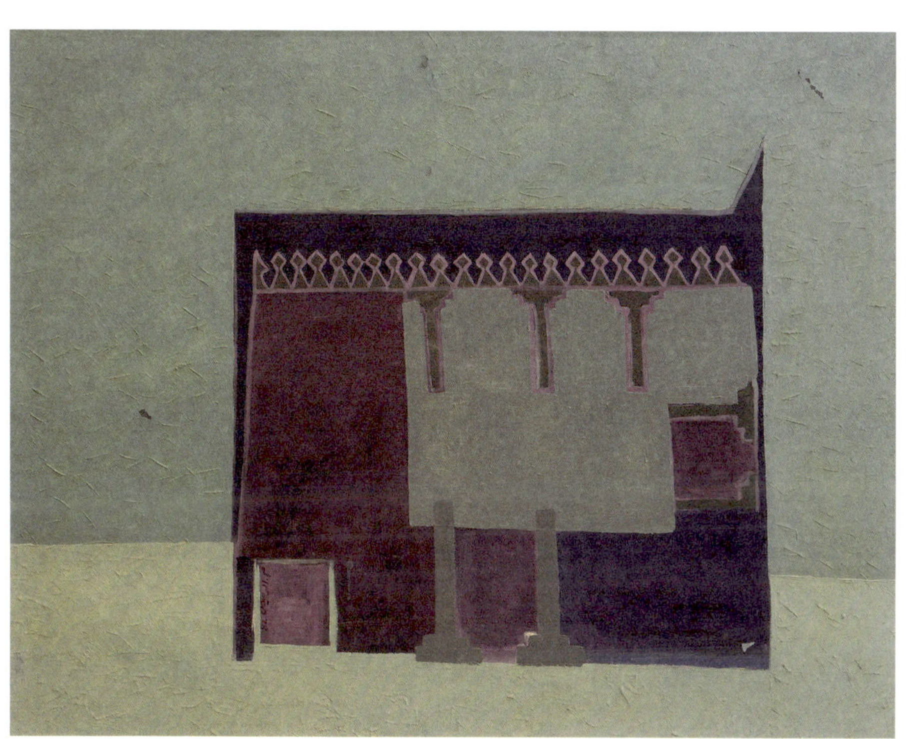

محمد السـليم

(ولد عام 1939م في المملكة العربية السعودية وتوفي عام 1997م في إيطاليا)

بـدأ محمد السـليم مسـيرته المهنية معلمـاً للتربية الفنيـة في مسـقط رأسـه مـرات، في 1957م، كان السليم من الحاصلين على منحة الابتعاث من وزارة الإعلام ليكمل تعليمه فـي أكاديمية Accademia delle Belle Arti فـي فلورنسـا بإيطاليـا، حيـث حصل على درجة الدبلوم في الفن والديكور عام 1973م. وفي عام 1979م، أسس السليم دار الفنون السعودية بالرياض، وهي أول مساحة فنية مستقلة هدفهـا الرئيـس إرشـاد الفنانيـن الصاعديـن وإبـراز المعارض، وتشـمل كذلك اسـتديو تأطير.

بـدأت مشـاركة السـليم في المشـهد الفني السعودي بأربعة معارض أقيمت في المملكة العربية السعودية بين عامي 1967م و1968م. عُرضت أعمال السـليم مؤخـراً في معـارض منهـا معـرض "حداثة خليجية: رواد ومجموعـات فنيـة في شبه الجزيرة العربية" في الإمارات العربية المتحدة عام 2022م، ومعـرض "خوض غمـار حياة ضروس" فـي الإمارات العربيـة المتحدة عام 2018م، ومعـرض "الطليعة" فـي حافظ جاليـري عام 2014م في جـدة بالمملكة العربيـة السعودية. أقام السليم العديد من المعارض الفرديـة فـي المملكة العربيـة السـعودية وإيطاليـا ومصر بحلول عـام 1990م، بلغ عدد المعارض التي أقامها مـا يزيد عن 37 معرضاً شـخصياً.

تعـد أعمـال السـليم جـزءاً مـن مجموعـات فنية لعدة جهات مـن القطاع الخـاص والحكومي والمؤسسـي. في عـام 2018م، قامت ابنـة الفنان الراحـل نجـلاء بإعـادة إحياء إرثـه الفنـي من خلال إعـادة تفعيـل دار الفنون السـعودية.

يتمحور فن محمد السليم بشكل رئيسي حول الصحراء، حيث يستكشف بجرأة أشكالاً جديدة وغير مرئيـة مـن خـلال العمـل بألـوان مختلفـة، وغالبـاً

يسـتخدم ألوانـاً أحادية ويعتمـد أيضاً في عمله على التفاعـل بين الضـوء والظل، ويراقـب تحركات ضوء الشـمس على المناظر الطبيعية الصحراوية، مكرسـاً نفسـه لدراسـة ألوان هذه البيئة وتركيباتها.

وفي لوحته "بدون عنوان" 1968م يستكشف الضـوء والظـل مـن خـلال توزيـع الألوان ويصوّر المسـاحات الصحراويـة الشاسـعة بالخيـام التـي يسـكنها أهل الصحراء، وفـي عمله "بـدون عنوان" 1972م يعكس الصحراء بواحاتها وقدّم منظوراً مختلفـاً بدمجه للألوان المتعددة، وقد قدم الفنان هـذا المنظور الجديد في ممارسـته أثناء دراسـته بإيطاليـا وقـد كانـت التقنيـات المسـتخدمة في هذا العمـل بوابة تجديد فـي ممارسـته الفنية.

الألوان والأشكال التي يسـتخدمها لا تعكس الصحراء بشكل مباشـر، بل بالأحرى تحمل تفسيرات رمزيـة وموضوعيـة، وتدعو المشـاهدين إلـى تفعيل مخيلتهـم؛ صوّر السـليم محيطـه في أعمالـه الأولى بأسـلوب رمـزي يظهر في "بـدون عنوان" 1973م.

ومع تقدمه، طوّر السليم أسلوبه الخاص المعروف باسـم "الآفاقية"، حيث يتميز هذا الأسـلوب بخطوط أفقية وعناصر صحراوية مندمجة بعـض الأحيان مع الخط العربي؛ في لوحة "بدون عنوان" 1977م يستخدم السليم أسلوبه الآفاقي وضربات الفرشاة العريضة لإظهار الامتداد الأفقي للخيم في الصحراء.

يوظف السـليم أسلوبه "الآفاقية" في لوحته "بدون عنوان" 1989م من خلال استخدام الفرشاة العريضة لتصويـر الامتـداد الأفقي للكثبـان الرملية، والذي يجسد إحساسـاً كبيراً بالعمق، وتتفاعل هذه الأعمـال مـع الضـوء والظـلام، مـا يطمس الحـد الفاصل بين الإدراك والغموض، وتقدم لمحـات من واقع يتجاوز الصحراء، يذكرنا بالمدن المبسطة.

Mohammed Alsaleem

(b. 1939, Saudi Arabia – d. 1997, Italy)

Mohammed Alsaleem is a painter who began his career as an art teacher in his hometown of Marat in 1957. Alsaleem received a scholarship from the Ministry of Media to study at the Accademia delle Belle Arti in Florence, Italy, where he earned an arts and décor diploma in 1973. In 1979, he founded the Saudi Arts House in Riyadh, the first independent space dedicated to mentoring young artists and holding exhibitions; it also included a framing studio.

Alsaleem's involvement in the Saudi art scene began with four exhibitions held in Saudi Arabia between 1967 and 1968. More recently, his works have been exhibited in *Khaleeji Modern: Pioneers and Collectives in the Arabian Peninsula*, the United Arab Emirates (2022); *That Feverish Leap into the Fierceness of Life*, the United Arab Emirates (2018); and *Al Taliaa*, Hafez Gallery, Saudi Arabia (2014). He held multiple solo exhibitions in Saudi Arabia, Italy, and Egypt, and by 1990, Alsaleem had hosted over thirty-seven solo exhibitions.

Alsaleem's works are part of several private, government, and institutional collections. In 2018, his daughter Najla Alsaleem revived his legacy through the Saudi Art House Reactivated.

Mohammed Alsaleem's art revolves around the central theme of the desert, where he boldly explored new and unseen forms. Working with various tones and often employing monochromatic colors, the artist relied on the interplay of light and shadow. Alsaleem observed sunlight movement on the desert landscape and dedicated himself to studying the colors and compositions of this environment.

Alsaleem began with a conventional figurative technique. This style is exemplified in *Untitled* (1968), where he explored light and shadow through a monochromatic color scheme, capturing the desert space inhabited by nomads living in tents.

The colors and forms he employed do not directly reflect the desert itself. Instead, they carry symbolic and thematic interpretations. In Alsaleem's early works, he drew inspiration from the luminous effects of divisionism. This influence is particularly evident in his piece *Untitled* (1972), which represents a desert oasis. In this work, he employed expansive areas of color to achieve a vibrant and fresh visual impact. This phase in his artistic journey, which took shape during his training in Italy, marked a crucial turning point in his exploration of pictorial techniques and ultimately laid the foundation for his later works. Alsaleem continued to portray his surroundings in *Untitled* (1973).

As his artistic journey progressed, he developed his signature style, known as *alafakiyah* or "horizonism." This style is characterized by horizontal lines and desert elements often combined with Arabic calligraphy. In *Untitled* (1977), Alsaleem employed his horizonism style through the use of broad brushstrokes to depict the horizontal extension of a desert tent.

In *Untitled* (1989), he used the same style through the use of broad brushstrokes to depict the sand dunes, evoking a profound sense of depth. This work interacts with light and darkness, blurring the boundary between recognition and ambiguity. It offers glimpses of a reality that transcends the desert, reminiscent of stylized cities.

Untitled (1981) embodies the artist's distinctive horizonism style, albeit with a greater emphasis on decorative elements. In contrast, in *Untitled* (1989) he had introduced figurative elements within his signature style, blending his two styles harmoniously. Unlike the more abstract nature of his other paintings, *Untitled* (1989) has more recognizable features, such as a distinct palm tree that evokes the artist's Najd landscape surroundings.

وفي لوحـة "بدون عنـوان" 1981م اسـتخدم السـليم الأسـلوب الآفاقي أيضاً ولكن ركّز بشكل أكبر على عنصر الزخرفة والتزيين، وتجسد "بدون عنوان" 1989م اسـتخدم الواقعيـة مع أسـلوب "الآفاقية" الخـاص بـه، وبالرغـم مـن تركيـزه علـى العناصر التصويرية مقارنـة بلوحاتـه الآفاقيـة الأخرى، يظهر أن الفنـان يمـزج أسـاليبه بشكل متناغـم فـي هذا العمل، وعلى عكـس الطبيعة الأكثر تجريداً للوحاته الأخـرى، إلا أن لوحـة "بـدون عنـوان" 1989م لها ملامـح أكثـر تميـزاً مثل وجـود النخلة بشـكل مميز لتستحضر محيـط الفنان فـي نجد.

محمـــــد الســــليم

(ولد عام 1939م في المملكة العربية السعودية
وتوفي عام 1997م في إيطاليا)

بدون عنوان، 1981

ألوان زيتية على قماش
50 × 80 سم
مجموعة خاصة

Mohammed Alsaleem

(b. 1939, Saudi Arabia – d. 1997, Italy)

Untitled, 1981

Oil on canvas
50 × 80 cm
Private Collection

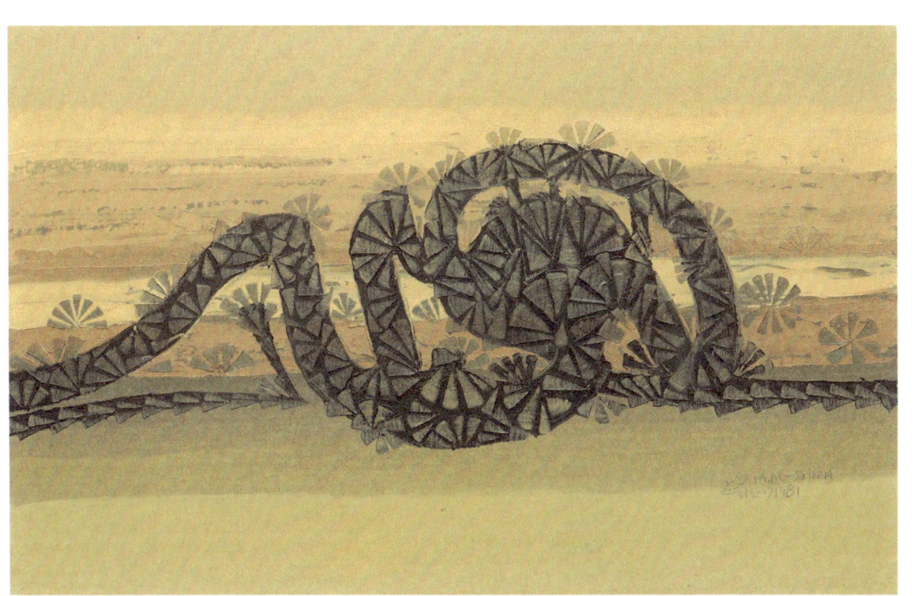

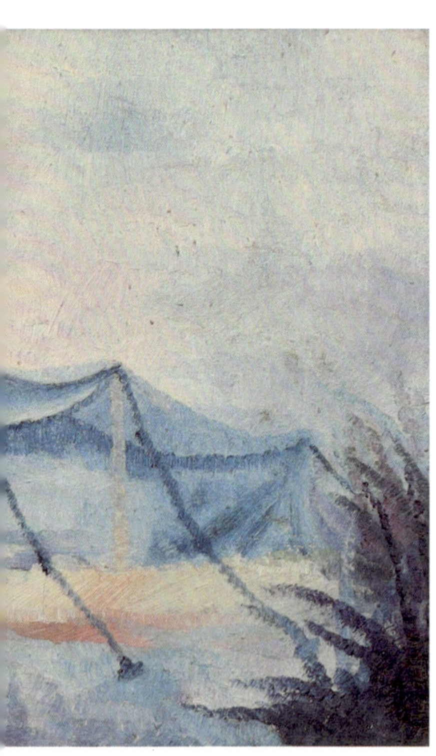

محمـــد الســـــليم

(ولد عام 1939م في المملكة العربية السعودية
وتوفي عام 1997م في إيطاليا)

بدون عنوان، 1968

ألوان زيتية على قماش
35 × 72 سم
مجموعة خاصة

Mohammed Alsaleem

(b. 1939, Saudi Arabia – d. 1997, Italy)

Untitled, 1968

Oil on canvas
35 × 72 cm
Private Collection

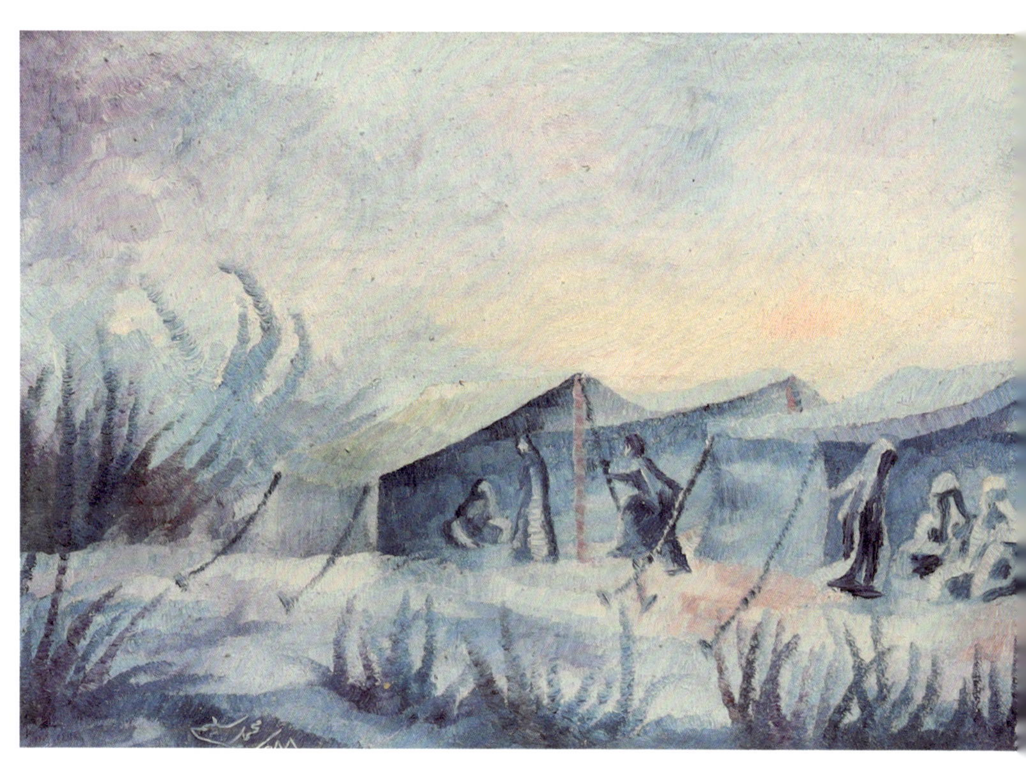

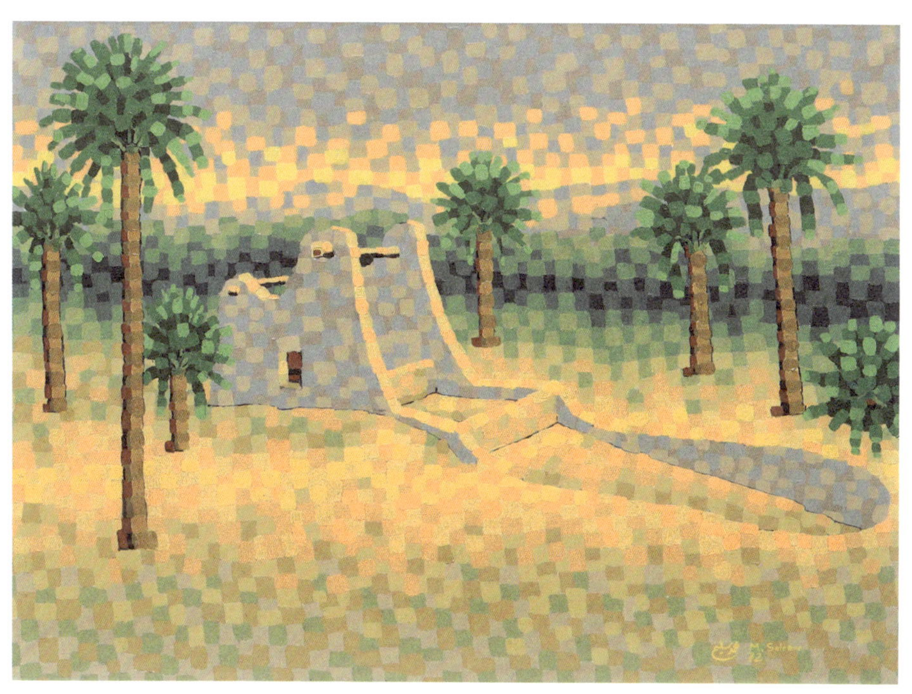

محمـــــد الســـــــليم

(ولد عام 1939م في المملكة العربية السعودية
وتوفي عام 1997م في إيطاليا)

بدون عنوان، 1973

ألوان زيتية على قماش
37.5 × 50.5 سم
بإذن من حوار جاليري

Mohammed Alsaleem

(b. 1939, Saudi Arabia – d. 1997, Italy)

Untitled, 1973

Oil on canvas
50.5 × 37.5 cm
Courtesy of Hewar Art Gallery

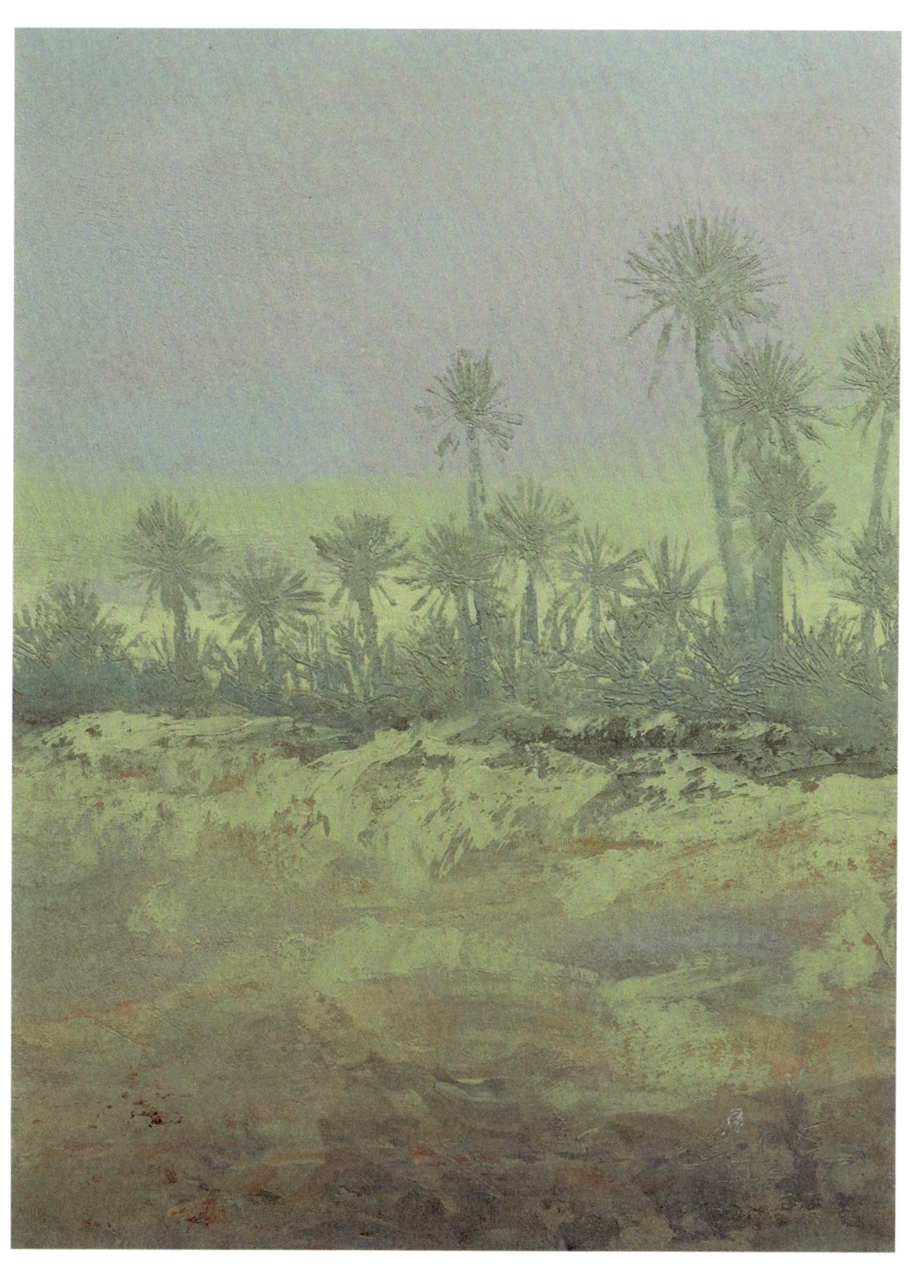

Mohammed Alsaleem

(b. 1939, Saudi Arabia – d. 1997, Italy)

Untitled, 1989

Oil on canvas
105 × 105 cm
Private Collection

محمــــد الســــليم

(ولد عام 1939م في المملكة العربية السعودية
وتوفي عام 1997م في إيطاليا)

بدون عنوان، 1989

ألوان زيتية على قماش
105 × 105 سم
مجموعة خاصة

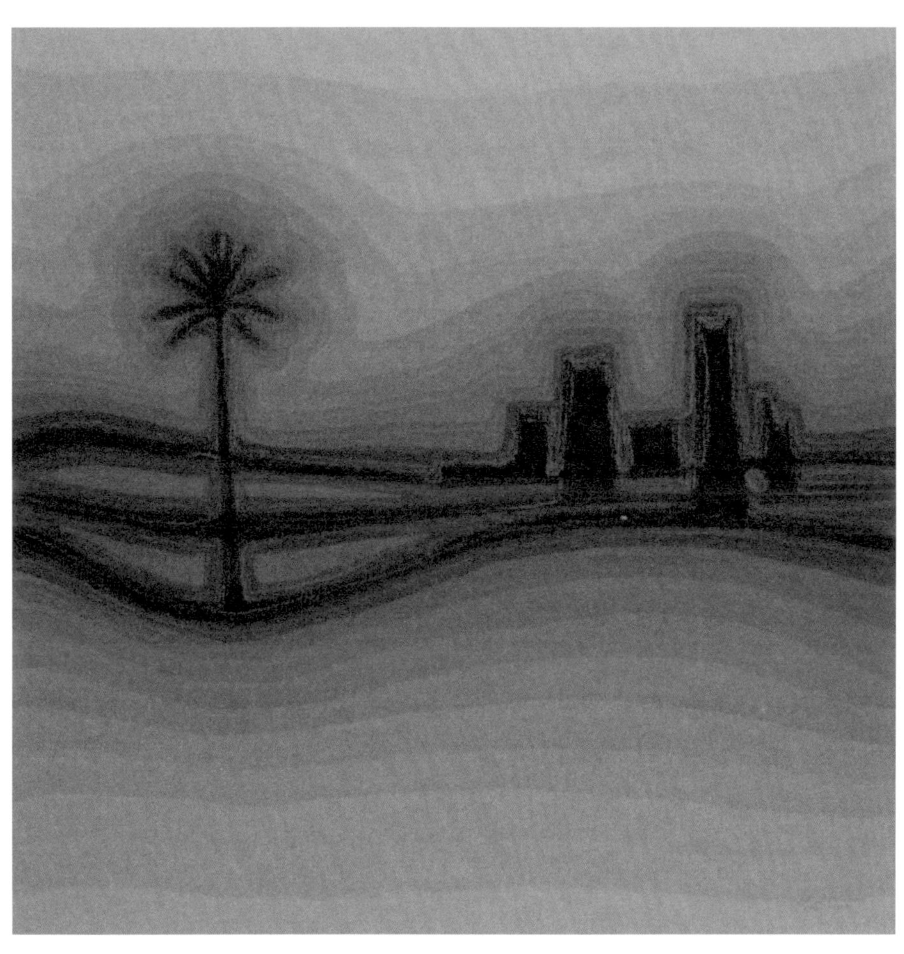

محمـــد الســـليم

(ولد عام 1939م في المملكة العربية السعودية
وتوفي عام 1997م في إيطاليا)

بدون عنوان، 1977

ألوان زيتية على قماش
80 × 80 سم
مجموعة خاصة

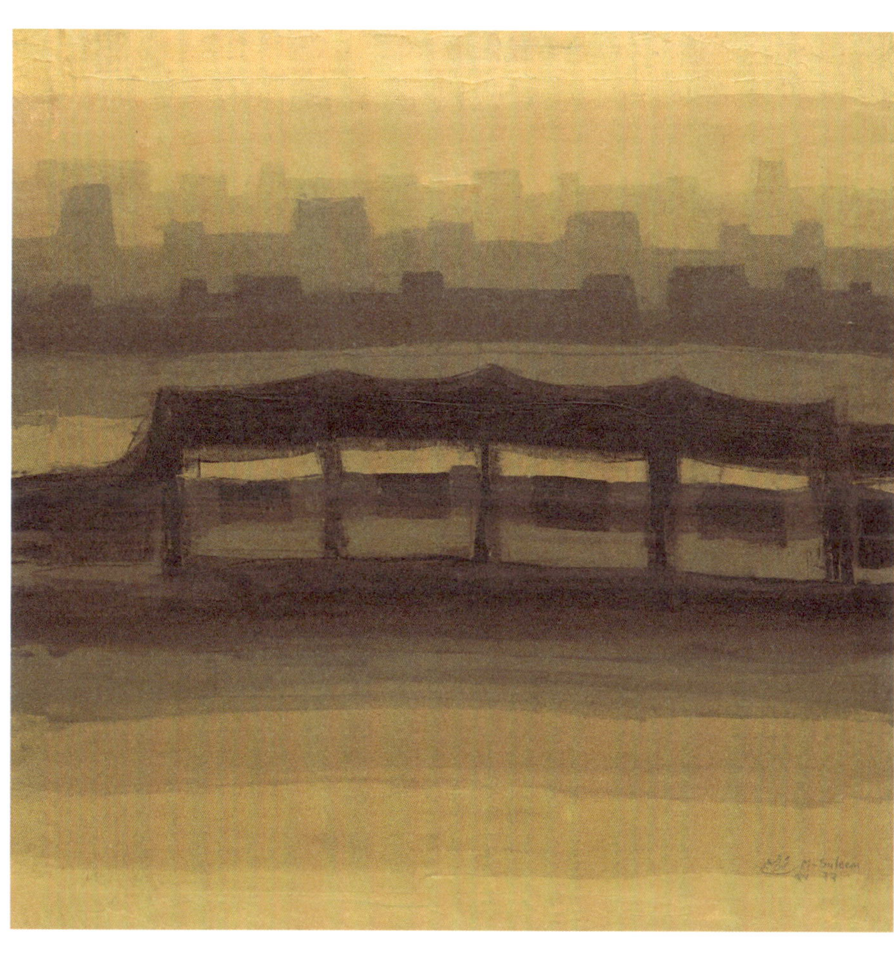

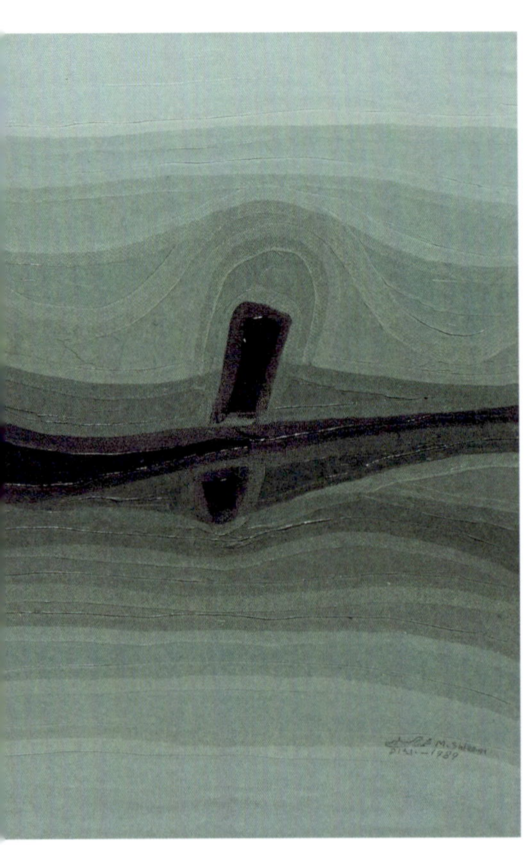

محمـــــد الســـــليم

(ولد عام 1939م في المملكة العربية السعودية
وتوفي عام 1997م في إيطاليا)

بدون عنوان، 1989

ألوان زيتية على قماش
58.7 × 118.8 سم
بإذن من حوار جاليري

Mohammed Alsaleem

(b. 1939, Saudi Arabia – d. 1997, Italy)

Untitled, 1968

Oil on canvas
58.7 × 118.8 cm
Courtesy of Hewar Art Gallery

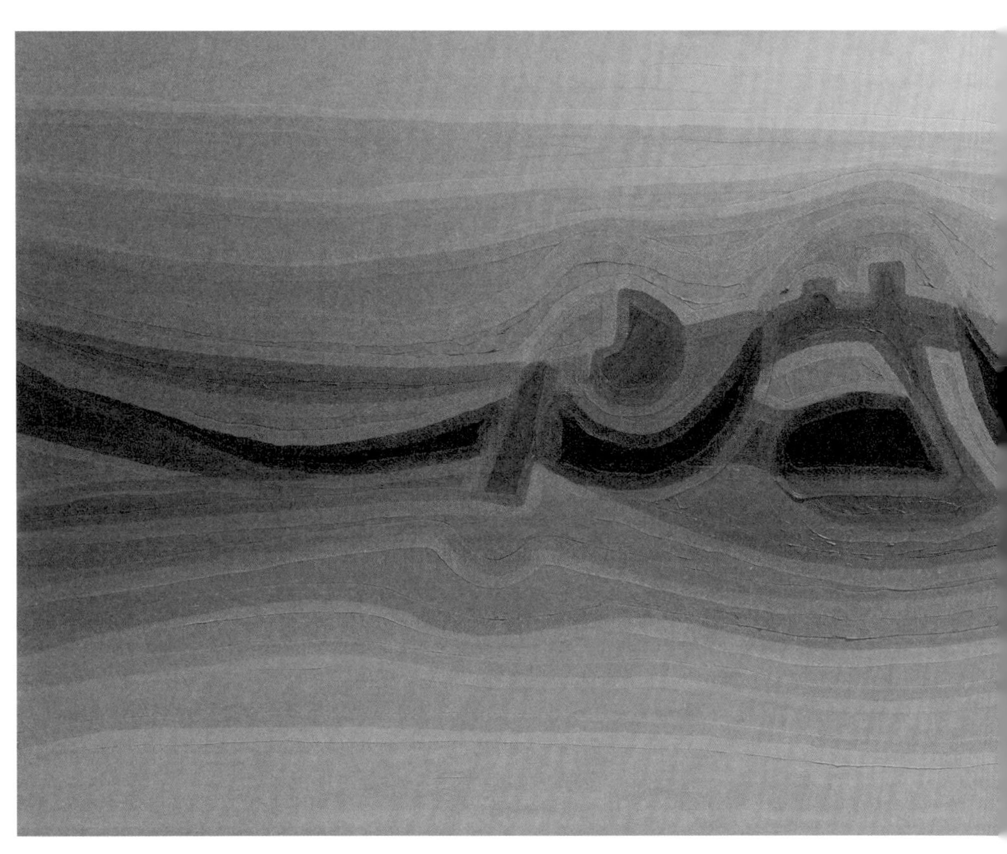

محمـــد المنيـــــف

(ولد عام 1952م في المملكة العربية السعودية)

يعد محمد المنيف فناناً وكاتباً وناقداً فنياً انتقل من مسقط رأسه حوطة سدير إلى العاصمة الرياض عام 1972م ليدرس في معهد التربية الفنية، وباشر فور تخرجه رحلة عملية مدتها 25 عاماً في مجال التعليم وكان في الوقت ذاته كاتباً في مجلة اليمامة ثم عمل محرراً في صفحة تشكيلية في جريدة الجزيرة عام 1976م إلى 2016م قبل أن يكرس كامل وقته للعمل كفنان متفرغ في عام 2020.

عرضت أعماله في عدة معارض عالمية في الإمارات العربية المتحدة، ومصر، والجزائر، وإيطاليا، وفرنسا، وألمانيا، وكندا، والولايات المتحدة الأمريكية؛ كما شارك في معارض جماعية محلية في المملكة العربية السعودية مثل الرئاسة العامة لرعاية الشباب عام 1976م. وأقام تسعة معارض فردية في المملكة العربية السعودية من ضمنها: معرض في حوطة سدير عام 1973م ومعرض في الرياض عام 1974م 1975م و1980م ومعرض في عنيزة عام 1976م.

وحصل على العديد من الجوائز من ضمنها وسام مجلس التعاون للمبدعين في عام 2017م، كما كان نائباً لرئيس الجمعية السعودية للفنون التشكيلية من عام 2012م حتى 2017م ثم رئيساً لمجلس الإدارة.

يستخدم محمد المنيف في أعماله الألوان المائية والزيتية إضافة إلى أنماط وتقنيات مختلفة؛ واستمر خلال الثمانينيات في استكشافاته الفنية التكعيبية، وجرّب الأشكال الهندسية الدقيقة والمدورة، وانصبّ تركيزه الأساسي على تصوير الناس وهم يرتدون الأزياء التقليدية، والمناظر الطبيعية في المملكة العربية السعودية، والبيئة الزراعية المحلية.

تعرض لوحة المنيف "بدون عنوان" 1980م العمارة المحلية من خلال فن التجريد والأشكال الهندسية مع التلاعب بالضوء والظلال واستخدام درجات مختلفة للون البني والألوان الترابية التي تتميز بها البيئة السعودية؛ كما تتجلى في اللوحة براعته في دمج الظلال الناعمة والغامقة واستخدام ضربات الفرشاة الانسيابية والمتكررة لإضفاء وهم بصري لحركة انعكاس الضوء.

Mohammed Almunif

(b. 1952, Saudi Arabia)

Mohammed Almunif is a painter, writer, and art critic who moved to Riyadh from his hometown Hautat Sudair in 1972 to study at the Institute of Art Education. After graduating, he embarked on a twenty-five-year teaching career while simultaneously working as a writer for *Al Yamamah* magazine. In 1976, he was appointed as the editor of the fine arts section of *Al Jazeera* newspaper until 2016, before dedicating himself to being a full-time artist in 2020.

Almunif's artworks have been exhibited in multiple international exhibitions in the United Arab Emirates, Egypt, Algeria, Italy, France, Germany, Canada, and the United States. He was part of local group exhibitions including the General Presidency of Youth Welfare, Saudi Arabia (1976). The artist held nine solo exhibitions in Saudi Arabia including Hautat Sudair (1973), Riyadh (1974, 1975, and 1980), and Unayzah (1976), amongst others.

He has received accolades such as the badge of honor from the Cooperation Council for Creators (2017). He was the vice president of the Saudi Art Association from 2012 until 2017 and then became the chairman of the board.

Mohammed Almunif employs watercolor and oil paint in different styles and techniques. Throughout the 1980s, his artistic exploration continued with cubism elements, where he experimented with soft, rounded, geometric forms. His usual subject of choice depicts local scenes featuring people in traditional clothing, natural Saudi landscapes, and the local agricultural environment.

In *Untitled* (1980), Almunif's surrounding architecture is presented in an abstract manner through geometric shapes and the manipulation of light and shadows. With a palette composed of various shades of browns, the painting exudes the earthy colors characteristic of the Saudi environment. Almunif blends soft and harsh shadows, while employing flowing, repetitive brushstrokes to create the illusion of movement or light reflection.

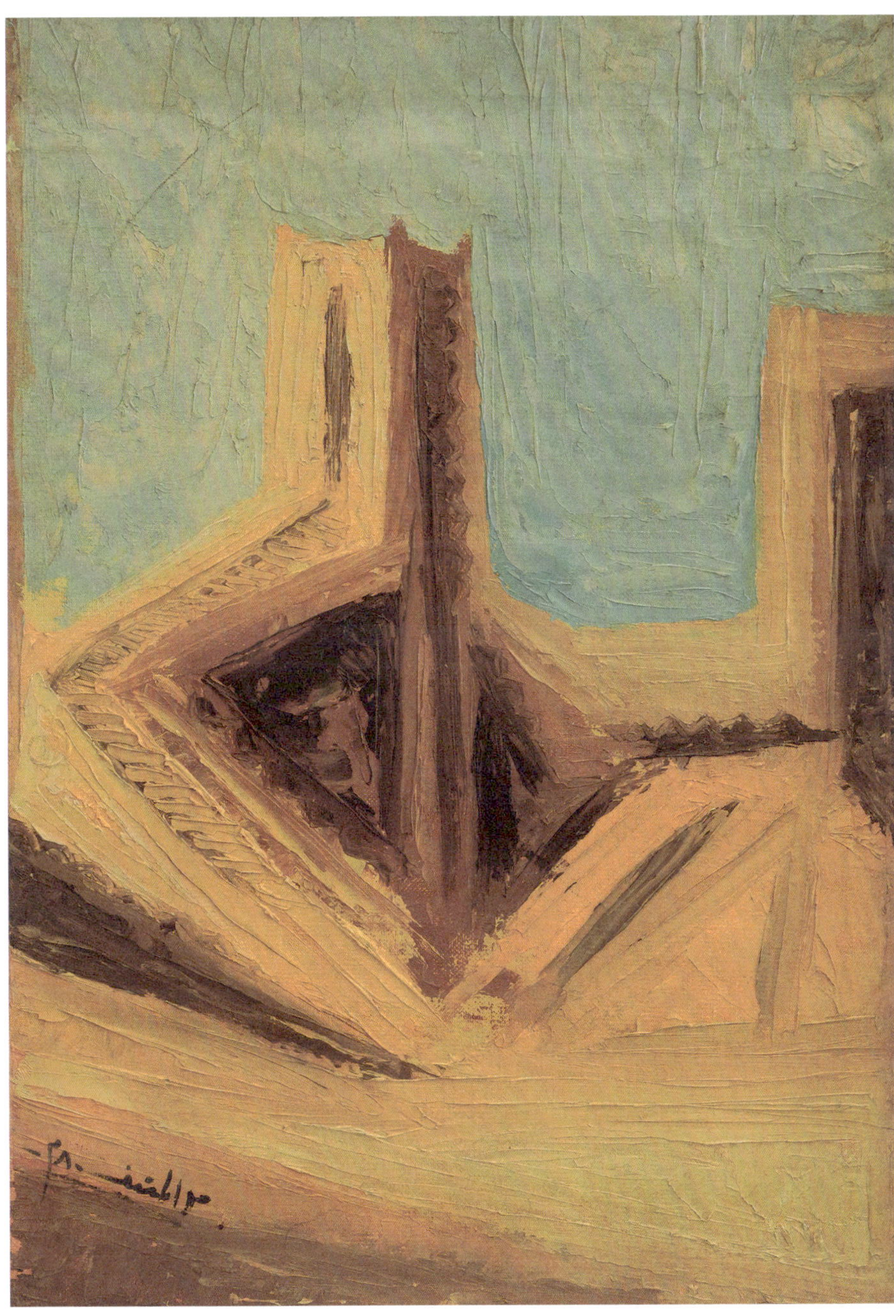

منيرة موصلي

(ولدت عام 1954م في المملكة العربية السعودية وتوفيت عام 2019م في المملكة العربية السعودية)

كانت منيرة موصلي فنانة وسائط مختلطة وكاتبة حاصلة على درجات علمية من كلية الفنون الجميلة بالقاهرة في مصر 1974م ودبلوم في التصميم الجرافيكي من جامعة في كاليفورنيا في الولايات المتحدة الأمريكية، 1979م. عملت في أرامكو لمدة 22 عاماً كمتخصصة في تصميم المنشورات. أقامت الفنانة معارض خاصة عديدة وأولها في جدة عام 1972م، وفي عام 2007م أسست مهرجان الفن في الخُبر؛ أنشأت وأشرفت الفنانة على دورات لتعليم الفنون للأطفال في الدمام.

تعد منيرة موصلي من أوائل النساء اللواتي أقمن معارض فنية في المملكة العربية السعودية في مدرسة دار التربية الحديثة بالمملكة العربية السعودية عام 1968م شاركت الفنانة في معارض جماعية بما في ذلك بينالي القاهرة الثامن في مصر، 2001م، وبينالي الشارقة الرابع في الإمارات العربية المتحدة، 1999م، و"قوى التغيير: فنانون من العالم العربي"، المتحف الوطني للفنون في الولايات المتحدة الأمريكية عام 1994م، والعديد من معارض جماعة أصدقاء الفن التشكيلي الخليجي في الإمارات العربية المتحدة والبحرين وقطر والكويت ومصر وتونس وإسبانيا بين الأعوام 1985م – 1988م، أقامت موصلي العديد من المعارض الفردية بما في ذلك: "على سلالم اللون هناك آثار لخطواتي" في حافظ جاليري في جدة بالمملكة العربية السعودية عام 2016م، "الصبية تضيء ليلتك يا عراق"، في صالة البارح في البحرين عام 2011م، "الواسطي وأنا ومرئيات أخرى"، في لبنان عام 1997م، "يوميات جدارية"، في السفارة الفرنسية في الرياض بالمملكة العربية السعودية عام 1995م.

وحصلت منيرة موصلي على جوائز من الخطوط السعودية عام 1995م والرئاسة العامة لرعاية الشباب عام 1998م، ومؤسسة المنصورية عام 2000م؛ كما كانت عضواً في كل من: جمعية الثقافة والفنون في الدمام والمجلس الدولي للمرأة في الفنون في كاليفورنيا وجمعية الفنون في البحرين وجماعة أصدقاء الفن التشكيلي الخليجي.

واقتنيت أعمالها الفنية في متحف الفن المعاصر بإسبانيا، والأمانة العامة لمجلس التعاون الخليجي والمتحف الوطني الأردني للفنون الجميلة ومؤسسة المنصورية بالمملكة العربية السعودية، ومؤسسة بارجيل للفنون بالإمارات العربية المتحدة.

يتسم الأسلوب الفني لمنيرة موصلي بالجرأة التي تنعكس في استخدامها لمواد مختلفة مثل الورق المصنوع يدوياً والأصباغ الطبيعية والنحاس والنخيل والخشب والبردي لصناعة أعمال نابضة بالحياة تعكس تقاليد المملكة العربية السعودية، ويقودها هذا النهج في التعامل مع المواد إلى استكشاف الوسائط غير التقليدية في ممارستها، وغالباً ما تصور بيئتها ومحيطها، وتربط من خلال ذلك تجاريها الشخصية وملاحظاتها بسياقات اجتماعية وسياسية أوسع.

يمكن أن تستكشف اللوحة المرسومة بألوان زيتية على الخشب، "أرض الجمود" 1970م، القضايا الاجتماعية المرتبطة بالمرأة، مشيرة إلى أدوار الجنسين أو الهوية، وتتكون الألوان الجريئة والمعبرة للوحة بشكل أساسي من الأخضر والأزرق والأبيض ولمسات من اللون البرتقالي لاستحضار المشهد البصري والثقافي الغني للمملكة العربية السعودية، ويُبرز الجزء الأوسط من اللوحة منطقة تشبه البحيرة مصورة باللون الأزرق، فاستخدام هذا اللون يمنح إحساساً بالهدوء، وتوجد في مقدمة اللوحة شخصية تشبه المرأة مغطاة بالكامل بعباءة سوداء، ما يوحي بإحساس بالغموض أو إخفاء الهوية، ويدل وجود القلادة الثمينة على تعبير شخصي على الرغم من المظهر المغطى، تشيّد هذه اللوحة التقاليد التاريخية الفنية المتمثلة في إشراك النساء في المناظر الطبيعية، وتقدم الشخصية على أنها جزء لا يتجزأ من السرد البصري.

Mounirah Mosley

(b. 1954, Saudi Arabia – d. 2019, Saudi Arabia)

Mounirah Mosley was a mixed-media artist and writer who earned degrees from the College of Fine Arts, Cairo, Egypt (1974) and a diploma in graphic design from the United States (1979). She worked at Aramco for twenty-two years as a publication design specialist. Mosley held private exhibitions, the first of which took place in Jeddah in 1972; and in 2007, and established the Art Festival of Alkhobar. The artist developed and led art education courses for children in Dammam.

Mosley is thought to be one of the first women to exhibit in Saudi Arabia in 1968 at Dar Al-Tarbia Al-Hadetha School. The artist participated in group exhibitions including the 8th Cairo Biennale, Egypt (2001); 4th Sharjah Biennale, the United Arab Emirates (1999); *Forces of Change: Artists of the Arab World*, National Gallery of Art, the United States (1994); several of the GCC Art Friends exhibitions in the United Arab Emirates, Bahrain, Qatar, Kuwait, Egypt, Tunisia, and Spain (1985–1988). She held multiple solo exhibitions including *On the Stairs of Color There Are Traces of My Steps*, Hafez Gallery, Saudi Arabia (2016); *Al Sabiya Enlightens Your Night, Iraq*, Albareh Gallery, Bahrain (2011); *Al Wasiti, Myself and Other Visions*, Lebanon (1997); *Mural Banes*, French Embassy in Riyadh, Saudi Arabia (1995).

Mosley earned awards from the Saudi Arabia Airlines (1995); General Presidency of Youth Welfare (1998); and Al-Mansouria Foundation (2000). She was also a member of the Dammam Art and Culture Society; the International Council for Women in the Arts (ICWA) in California; the Bahrain Art Society; and the GCC Art Friends Group.

Her artworks were acquired by the Museum of Contemporary Art, Spain; the Secretariat General of the Gulf Cooperation Council; the National Gallery of Fine Arts, Jordan; the Al-Mansouria Foundation, Saudi Arabia; and the Barjeel Art Foundation, the United Arab Emirates.

Mounirah Mosley's artistic style is bold with daring experimentation. This is reflected in her use of various materials such as handmade paper, natural dyes, copper, palm trees, wood, and papyrus to create vibrant works that reflect on Saudi traditions. This approach to materials leads her to explore unconventional mediums in her practice. She often depicts her environment and surroundings, by doing this, Mosley connects her personal experiences and observations to broader social and political contexts.

The oil on wood painting, *The Land of Solidities* (1970), may suggest a commentary on gender role or identity. The bold, expressive color palette of the painting consists primarily of green, blue, white, and touches of orange to evoke the rich visual and cultural landscape of Saudi Arabia. The middle section of the painting features a lake-like area depicted in blue. This use of color evokes a sense of tranquility and natural surroundings. In the foreground, there is a figure resembling a woman. She is fully covered with a black abaya, which suggests a sense of mystery or anonymity. The presence of the rich necklace indicates personal expression despite the covered appearance. This painting pays homage to the art historical tradition of including women in the landscape, presenting the figure as an integral part of the visual narrative.

Mounirah Mosley

(b. 1954, Saudi Arabia – d. 2019, Saudi Arabia)

The Land of Solidities, 1970

Oil on wood
110 x 80 cm
Collection of Barjeel Art Foundation, Sharjah,
United Arab Emirates

منـــــــيرة موصـــــلي

(ولدت عام 1954م في المملكة العربية السعودية وتوفيت عام 2019م في المملكة العربية السعودية)

أرض الجمود، 1970

ألوان زيتية على خشب
110 × 80 سم
مقتنيات مؤسسة بارجيل للفنون، الشارقة،
الإمارات العربية المتحدة

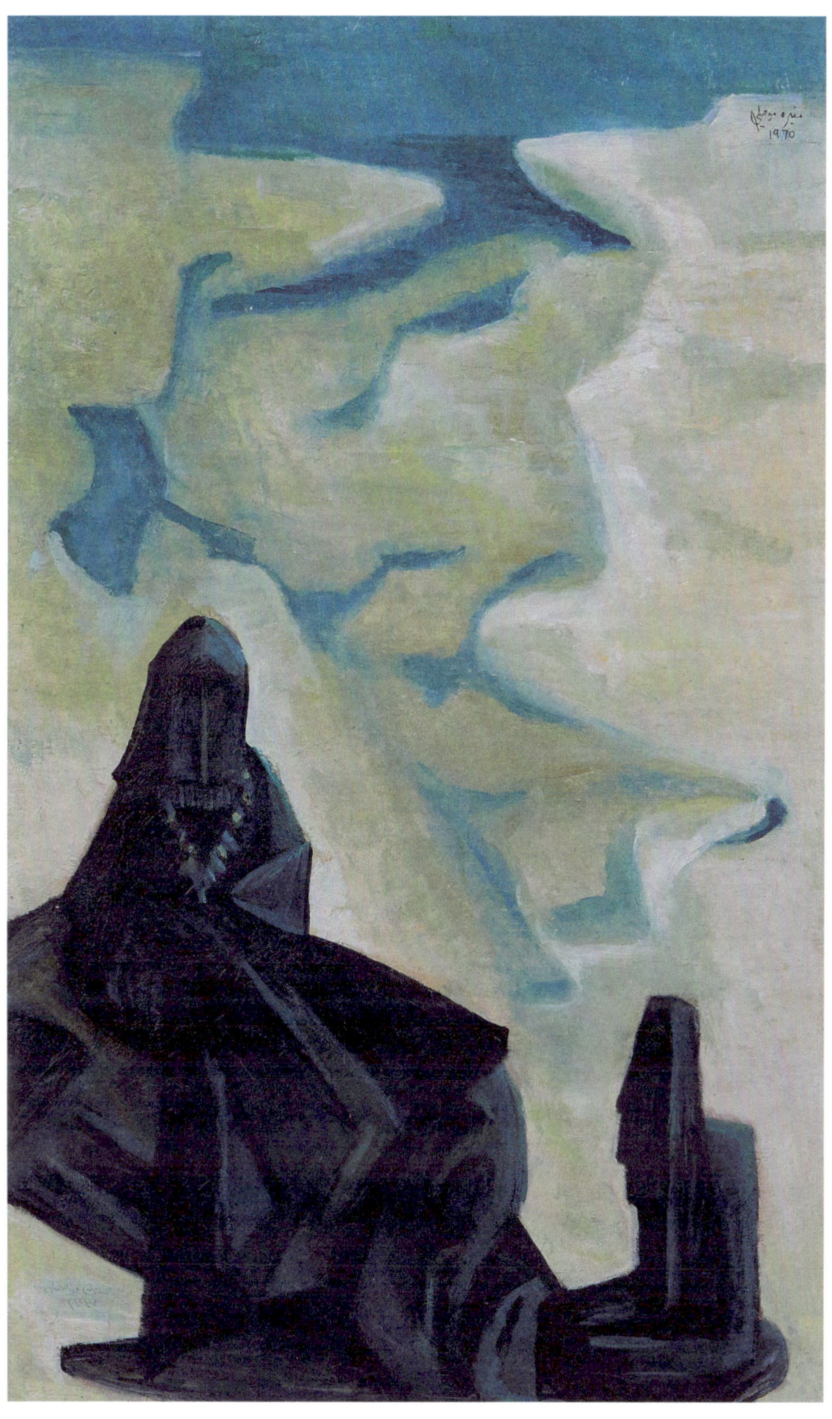

يوسف جـاها

(ولد عام 1954م في المملكة العربية السعودية)

درس يوسف جاها فـي مكة وأكمـل تعليمه العالي في معهـد التربيـة الفنية في الرياض عام 1972م، ثـم حصـل علـى شـهادة البكالوريوس فـي التربية الفنيـة مـن جامعـة أم القـرى بمكة المكرمـة عـام 1983م ودرّس التربيـة الفنيـة فـي المـدارس حتى عام 2008م عندمـا قرّر أن يكرس وقته كاملاً للفن.

شـارك جاهـا فـي عـدة معـارض خارجيـة جماعيـة، منهـا: معـرض Edge of Arabia فـي المملكـة المتحـدة عـام 2008م، بينالـي القاهـرة الدولـي الثامـن في مصر عام 2001م، "معرض الفن العربـي الإسلامي المعاصر" في تركيا عام 1993م، معـرض بينالـي آسـيا للفنـون بنسـخته الرابعة في بنجلاديـش عـام 1989م، "المعـرض السـعودي للفـن والثقافة" في إيطاليا عـام 1984م، "المعرض السـعودي للفنون" في تركيا عام 1984م، "المعرض السـعودي للفنون" في الهنـد عـام 1983م، معـرض Golden Sail Gallery فـي الكويت عـام 1983م. كمـا أقـام جاهـا سـتة معـارض فرديـة فـي المملكة بيـن 1987م و2019م، آخرهـا مشـاركته فـي مونو جاليري في المملكة العربية السعودية عام 2019م.

حصـل جاهـا علـى عـدة جوائـز، منهـا جائـزة تجميل مكة المكرمة في المملكة العربية السـعودية عـام 2010م، وجائـزة الدانة في معـرض 25 فبراير في الكويت عام 1997م، ومسـابقة ملون السعودية فـي المملكـة العربيـة السـعودية عـام 1992م و1997م، وجائـزة السـعفة الذهبيـة فـي المملكـة العربية السـعودية 1989م، وجائـزة المعرض الفني العـام بنسـخته الثالثة عـام 1979م.

اقتنيت أعماله ضمن مجموعات محلية وعالمية، منها المتحف الوطني الأردني للفنون الجميلة، ومطار الملـك فهد الدولـي في المملكـة العربيـة السـعودية، ووزارة الثقافة في المملكة العربية السـعودية.

يـرى يوسـف جاهـا ممارسـته بأكملهـا علـى أنهـا تمثيـل للطبيعـة وارتباطهـا بالـروح البشـرية، حيـث تصور أعماله المبكـرة صوراً واقعيـة ومناظر طبيعيـة وطبيعـة صامتة، ويمثـل جاهـا في لوحاته الأشـخاص باسـتخدام الأشـكال البسـيطة ومجموعة مـن الألوان، وخـلال الفتـرة التي قضاهـا في معهد التربيـة الفنيـة بالرياض، غالباً ما كان يصور الشـوارع والعمارة والناس والمشـهد العـام لمكة، ومع تقدم رحلتـه الفنية، جرب أسـاليت مثـل الحروفية (دمج أشـكال الحروف العربية والخط العربـي) بالإضافة إلـى التعبيريـة؛ تدمـج أعماله جاهـا غالبـاً الطبيعة الخارجيـة والداخليـة للبشـرية، وتخلق اتحـاداً بيـن العناصـر الطبيعيـة (المـاء والنار والهـواء والأرض) وعلـم النفس.

تطـور أسـلوبه في وقت لاحـق إلـى التعبيرية التجريديـة وتشـكل ضربـات الفرشـاة، فـي لوحـة "صيـف الهـدا" 1974م منظـراً طبيعيـاً لمنطقة الهدا في الطائف، يبدأ جاها في هذه اللوحة نهجاً جديداً يرمز إلى بداية تطوره الفني، فيرسـم السماء بضربـات فرشـاة عريضة تمثـل كتـلاً مـن السـحب تضفي جـواً أشـبه بالحلم علـى البيـوت المحلية، والجبـال والأشـجار المتناثـرة، والتي تختلـف عـن تلك الموجودة فـي المناطق الأخرى، وعند سـؤاله عـن هذه اللوحة، عبّر عـن عاطفته العميقة تجاه هـذه المنطقة، وأوضح أنها منطقة تشـكلت فيها الذكريات؛ يُضفي جاهـا علـى لوحاته تقديراً عميقاً للتعايـش بيـن الإنسـان والبيئة.

Yousef Jaha

(b. 1954, Saudi Arabia)

Yousef Jaha studied in Makkah and continued his higher education at the Institute of Art Education in Riyadh (1972). Later, Jaha received a bachelor's degree in art from Umm Al-Qura University, in Makkah (1983) and taught art in schools until 2008; he then decided to dedicate himself to art full-time.

Jaha exhibited extensively in group exhibitions abroad, including *Edge of Arabia*, the United Kingdom (2008); the 8th Cairo International Biennale, Egypt (2001); *The Arab Islamic Contemporary Art Exhibition*, Turkey (1993); *4th Asian Biennale Exhibition*, Bangladesh (1989); *The Art and Culture of Saudi Exhibition*, Italy (1984); *The Saudi Art Exhibition*, Turkey (1984); *The Saudi Art Exhibition*, India (1983); and at the Golden Sail Gallery, Kuwait (1983). Jaha held six solo exhibitions in Saudi Arabia between 1987–2019, the most recent of which was held at Mono Gallery, Saudi Arabia (2019).

Jaha won numerous awards, including the Beautifying Holy Makkah Prize, Saudi Arabia (2010), Al-Danah Award for the 25th February Art Exhibition, Kuwait (1997); Saudia Malwan Art Competition, Saudi Arabia (1992 and 1997); Golden Palm Award, Saudi Arabia (1989); and The Third General Art Exhibition, Saudi Arabia (1979).

His works have been acquired by local and international collections, including the Jordan National Gallery of Fine Arts, Jordan; King Fahd International Airport, Saudi Arabia; and the Ministry of Culture, Saudi Arabia.

Yousef Jaha sees his entire practice as a representation of nature and its connection to the human spirit. His early works depicted realistic portraits, landscapes, and still lives. In his practice, Jaha represents subjects using simple shapes, forms, and a chromatic color palette. During his time at the Institute of Art Education in Riyadh, he often depicted streets, architecture, people, and the general landscape of Makkah. As his artistic journey progressed, he experimented with styles such as hurufiyya (incorporating Arabic letter forms and calligraphy) and expressionism. Often merging the external and internal nature of humanity, Jaha's works create a union between natural elements (water, fire, air, earth) and psychology.

His later style developed into abstract expressionism. Nestled within the brushstrokes of *Alhada Summer* (1974), lies the landscape of the Alhada region in Taif. In this piece, Jaha embarks on a new approach, symbolizing the beginning of his artistic development. The sky is painted with broad brushstrokes representing clumps of clouds casting a dreamlike atmosphere over the local houses, mountains, and scattered trees, distinct from those found in other regions. When asked about this painting, Jaha expressed his deep affection for this area. He explained that it was an area where memories were forged. Jaha imbues his painting with a profound appreciation for the relationship between people and their environment.

يوسـف جـــاها

(ولد عام 1954م في المملكة العربية السعودية)

صيف الهدا، 1974

ألوان زيتية على قماش
120 × 100 سم
بإذن من صالة تجريد للفنون

Yousef Jaha

(b. 1945, Saudi Arabia)

Alhada Summer, 1974

Oil on canvas
100 × 120 cm
Courtesy of Abstract Art Gallery

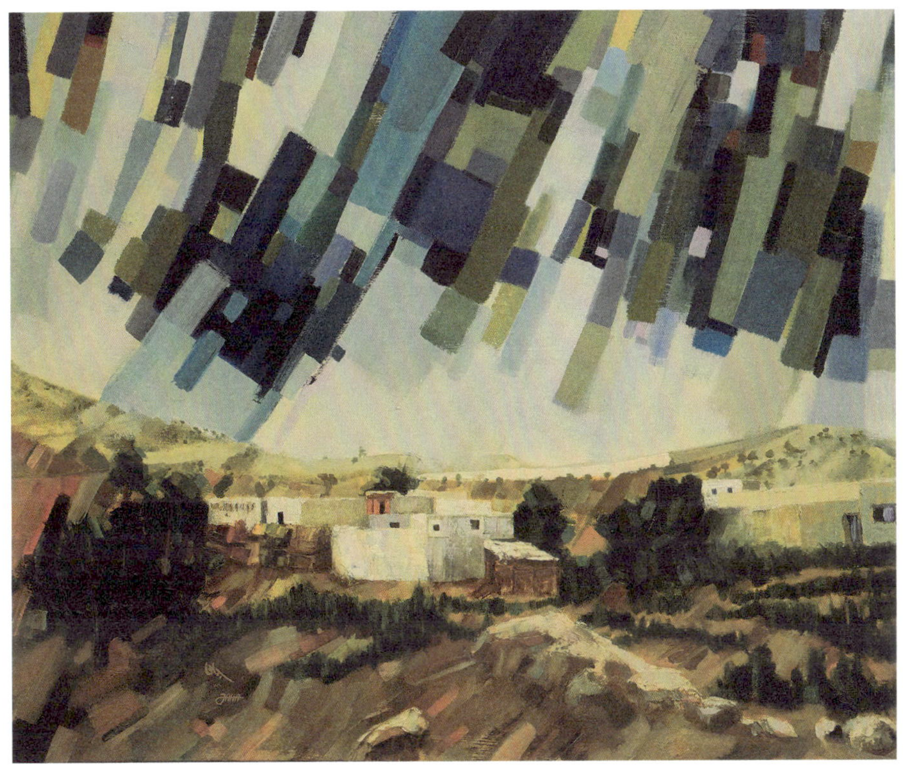

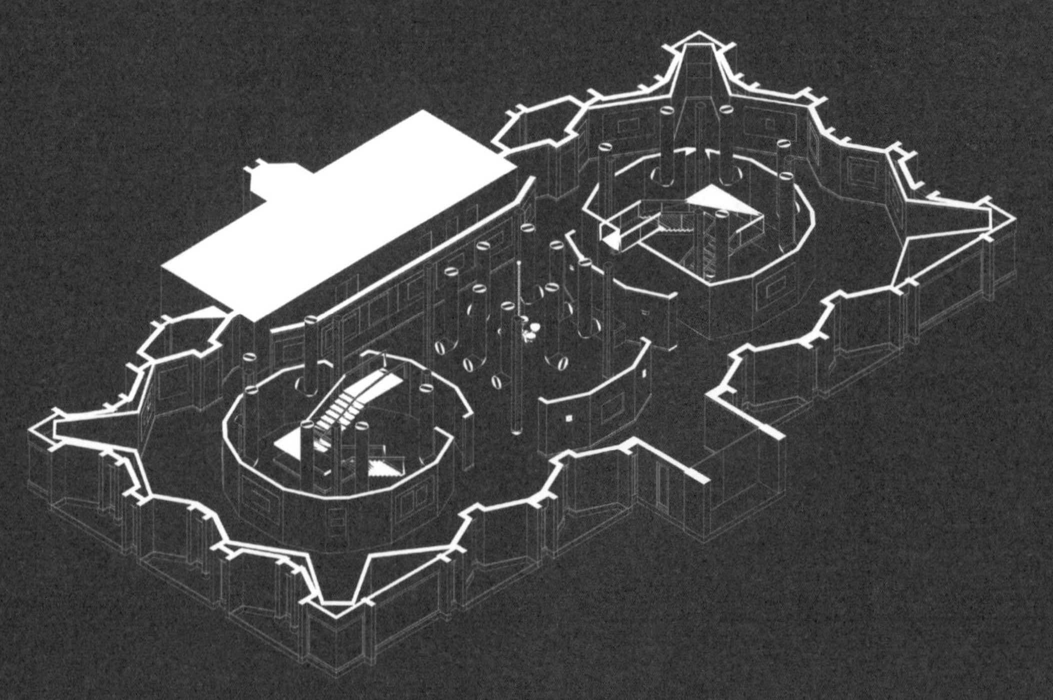

تصميـم المعـرض »من حـولهـم«
Echoing the Land Exhibition Design

بدر زباره
Badr Zabarah

Drawing from the innovative spirit of 1960s–1980s Saudi art, the exhibition design transported visitors back in time through meticulously crafted elements that immersed the senses in the rich cultural milieu from which Saudi art emerged.

For the exhibition design, the goal was to showcase the architectural beauty of the 1980s and emphasize the symmetrical elements of Prince Faisal bin Fahd Arts Hall. Simultaneously, it aimed to recreate the atmosphere of the 1970s and 1980s by incorporating elements evocative of the hall, such as the open spaces, marble flooring, an archiving area, and designated areas for conversations and reading.

The choice to emphasize the symmetrical elements of the building not only showcased its architectural beauty but also reflected the strong and balanced artistic expressions that emerged during the 1980s. The symmetrical design elements created a harmonious backdrop for the exhibited artworks, allowing them to shine and be appreciated in their fullest glory. As the exhibition designer, I selected colors to capture the essence of that particular era while also seeking to incorporate elements of the natural landscape. As a result, I settled on a combination of

استلهامـاً مـن الـروح الابتكاريـة لحقبـة السـتينيات إلى ثمانينيـات القرن الماضي، يأخـذ المعرض زوّاره فـي رحلـة عبـر الزمن إلـى عبـق الماضي مـن خلال تصميـم يتمثـل مـن عناصـر مَصُوغـة بدقـة لتغمر الحـواس فـي البيئـة الثقافيـة الغنية التي نشـأ منها الفن السـعودي.

كان الهدف من تصميـم المعرض إبراز الجمال المعمـاري فـي الثمانينيـات والتأكيـد علـى العناصر المتماثلـة لصالـة الأميـر فيصـل بـن فهـد للفنـون. وفـي نفـس الوقـت، كان يهـدف إلـى إعـادة خلـق أجـواء السـبعينيات والثمانينيـات مـن خـلال دمج عناصر تعبّر عن الصالة، مثل المسـاحات المفتوحة، والأرضيـات الرخاميـة، ومنطقة الأرشـفة، والمناطق المخصصـة للمحادثـات والقراءة.

اختيـار التركيز على العناصـر المتطابقة للمبنى لم يعكس جماله المعماري فحسـب، بل عكس أيضاً التعابيـر الفنيـة المتينة والمتوازنة التي ظهرت خلال الثمانينيـات. خلقـت عناصر التصميم المتناسقة خلفية متناغمة للأعمال الفنية المعروضة، ما سمح لهـا بالتألـق والتقدير بكامـل أوجها ورونقهـا. كوني مصمـم المعرض، اختـرت الألـوان لتجسـيد جوهر تلك الحقبة مع السـعي إلى دمـج عناصر من البيئة الطبيعيـة المحيطة. ونتيجة لذلك، اسـتقررت على مزيج من اللون الأخضر الداكن والأزرق الفاتح، الذي

dark green and light blue, which symbolize the lush greenery, expansive landscape, open sky, and tranquil waters of the time. These colors resonated with the natural ambiance, exuding a modern vintage charm reminiscent of the time.

Additionally, the exhibition space incorporated dedicated areas for gathering, archiving, and reading, reviving the hall's long legacy. These spaces served as gathering points for artists, scholars, and art enthusiasts to engage in intellectual discourse, fostering a sense of community and shared appreciation for Saudi art. Through thoughtful design and attention to historic details, the exhibition transported visitors to the vibrant period that defined the beginnings of Saudi art.

يرمـز إلـى المسـاحات الخضـراء الوافـرة والمناظـر الطبيعيـة الواسـعة والسـماء المفتوحـة والميـاه الهادئـة لتلـك الحقبـة. تتناغـم هـذه الألـوان مـع الأجـواء الطبيعيـة، وتضفـي سـحراً عتيقـاً عصريـاً يذكرنا بذلـك الزمن.

إضافةً إلـى ذلـك، ضمـت مسـاحة المعـرض مناطـق مخصصة للتجمع والأرشـفة والقـراءة، ما أدى إلى إحيـاء التـراث المديد للصالـة. وكانت هذه المسـاحات بمثابـة نقاط تجمـع الفنانيـن والعلماء وعشاق الفن للمشـاركة في الخطاب الفكري، وتعزيز الشـعور بالانتماء للمجتمع والتقدير المشترك للفن السعودي. ومن خلال التصميم المدروس والاهتمام بالتفاصيل التاريخية، ينقل المعرض الزوار إلى الفترة النابضة بالحياة التي حددت بدايات الفن السعودي.

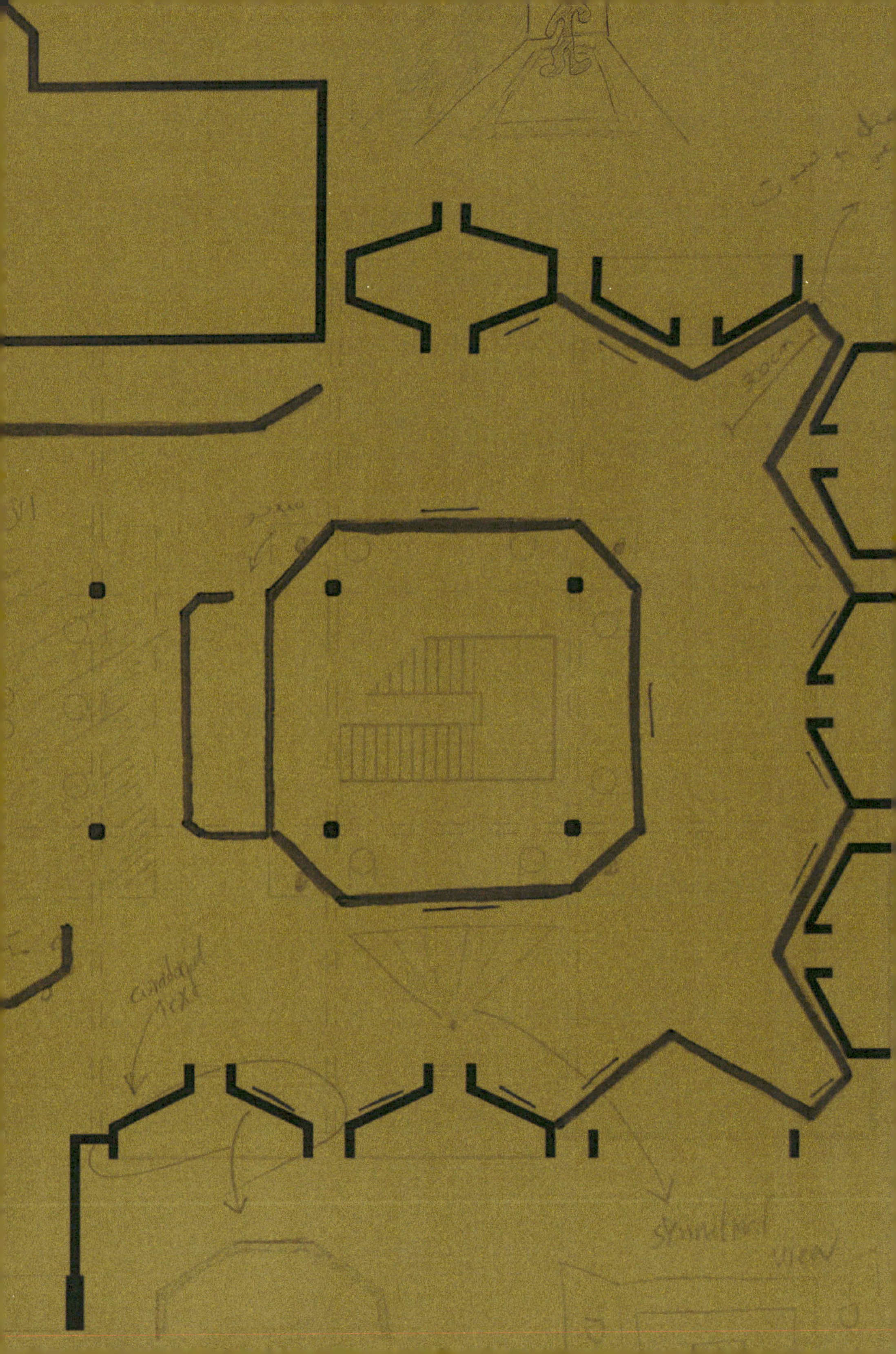
5,0cm

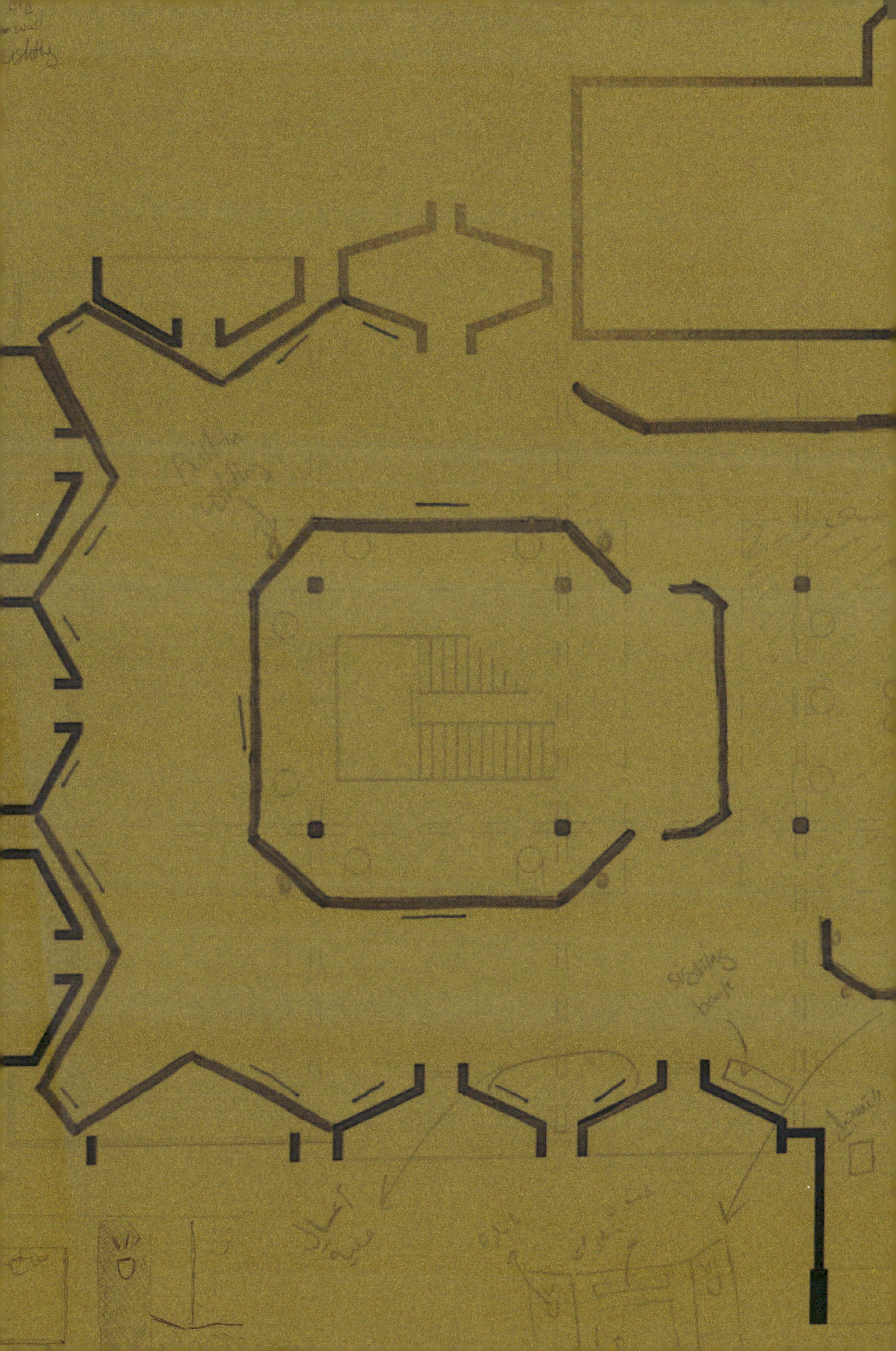
sketching
booth